the simple guide to CHOOSING A DOG

Diane Morgan

T.F.H. Publications, Inc.

For Kathy Kaminski – she asked for it.

I'd like to thank everyone who so generously helped put this book together. John Warner, most of all and always, for his advice and unstinting labor; Stacy Kennedy, my editor at TFH for her guidance and patience; and the scores of owners, breeders, judges, and veterinarians who shared their insights.

Distributed in the UNITED STATES to the Pet Trade by T.F.H. Publications, Inc., 1 TFH Plaza, Neptune City, NJ 07753; on the Internet at www.tfh.com; in CANADA by Rolf C. Hagen Inc., 3225 Sartelon St., Montreal, Quebec H4R 1E8; Pet Trade by H & L Pet Supplies Inc., 27 Kingston Crescent, Kitchener, Ontario N2B 2T6; in ENGLAND by T.F.H. Publications, PO Box 74, Havant PO9 5TT; in AUSTRALIA AND THE SOUTH PACIFIC by T.F.H. (Australia), Pty. Ltd., Box 149, Brookvale 2100 N.S.W., Australia; in NEW ZEALAND by Brooklands Aquarium Ltd., 5 McGiven Drive, New Plymouth, RD1 New Zealand; in SOUTH AFRICA by Rolf C. Hagen S.A. (PTY.) LTD., P.O. Box 201199, Durban North 4016, South Africa; in Japan by T.F.H. Publications. Published by T.F.H. Publications, Inc.

Contents

Shedding &
Professional
Grooming
p. 76-78

Personality Profiles

AKC and Kennel Club Classifications

Interaction
with Children
and Pets

Health Concerns for Every Breed

How to Use this Book

Because this book is designed for a variety of purposes, there are many ways to use it. You can be a traditionalist and turn one page after another until you reach the end–that will give you scope and background and help you come to a better decision. You can rifle through the pages and read the boxes–that will give you some quick insight into which breeds are ones you might want to own and which ones you might want to avoid. If you have a specific dog in mind, you might want to race ahead and look up that special breed.

The breed profiles include some of the more salient and significant characteristics of each breed. This chapter was developed not only from my own experience (while I have owned a lot of breeds, I haven't owned them all), but from independent researchers and in-depth conversations with breeders, judges, and long-time owners. However, remember that no breed is right for everyone (hence the reason for the book), and every breed has its proponents. Each dog is an individual, and with research, you can find the right dog you. Reading this book and doing your homework will help you to make the right decision and build a long and happy relationship with that perfect dog.

Part One

Before You Choose

"Choosing the right dog was always hard for Ted, even more so at parties."

Advice for Dogs
(by Anonymous, a Dog)

This chapter is really for dogs, although I suspect that human beings, nosy as they are, will probably be taking a look at it, so I won't give all our secrets away.

I know that it's usual in this kind of book for the human author to start things off by telling the human reader all about the joys and pains of dog ownership, but, let's face it–by the time some human has bought this book, they've already decided to get a dog.

For a lot of humans, getting a dog is the smartest choice they'll ever make. Studies show that dogs are not only good company and loyal pals, but that they actually help people live longer,

Getting a dog may be the best decision you'll ever make.

To Shed or Not to Shed

One thing that is surprising is the number of folks looking for a non-shedding hypoallergenic dog—they do not exist. All of us shed, with the exception of creatures like the Mexican Hairless. Some of us shed less than others, little enough so that people with mild (and I mean mild) allergies aren't bothered, but a person with severe allergies to dog hair ought to forget about getting a dog until he gets some medical help for the allergy.

These dogs are as shed-free as it gets:

Bedlington Terrier

Poodle

Basenji

Bichon Frise

Puli

Airedale Terrier

Komondor

happier, and healthier lives. Merely petting a dog lowers blood pressure, and studies show that children of dog-owning families relate better to others, have fewer learning disabilities, less aggression, more empathy with other beings, a greater sense of responsibility, and fewer allergies. (Studies at the Medical College of Georgia back up earlier research by showing that exposure to two or more cats or dogs in the house during the first year of life reduces the probability that a child will test positive for skin allergies by 50 percent.)

All this being said, I should tell you that it is still a bad idea for some humans, even the nicest ones, to get a dog at this particular time in their life. It isn't that they picked the wrong dog–the problem is that they decided to get a dog at all.

I have seen humans get a dog because their spouse or kids wanted one, because they saw one in the movies they liked, because they thought a dog was a "status symbol" (whatever that is), or because someone gave them one for Christmas. I have seen people give in to wild impulses when walking past a pet store. I have seen young people get a dog because they wanted some practice in taking care of something before they had a baby–as if we are anything alike. Actually, most of these people would be better with a lower-maintenance pet like a cat, or maybe an aquarium.

The people who did buy this book are not impulse buyers or impulse adopters. They think things through. They care about dogs, and they care a lot. They are open-minded, ready to learn, and haven't locked themselves into a particular breed. They truly want to find the best match.

This is good news for us dogs. We know they are about to make a big decision, a decision that will chart the course of our lives. We need to be in on it. Finding a truly dogworthy human to give your heart to is the most important career move you'll ever make.

In some ways, it's very easy for people to be dogworthy. We don't ask for them to be good-looking (you should see *my* owner), rich, young, brilliant, or even socially acceptable; that's why people like us so much.

Owning a dog can improve the quality of your life.

We dogs are perfectly egalitarian. We are way ahead of people in that regard. We never discriminate on the basis of age, gender, or race. Martin Luther King, Jr. said that people should be judged not by the color of their skin, but by the content of their character—we dogs have been doing that for thousands of years. That doesn't mean we don't have very high standards—we do. We care very much about the really important things and make constant demands on our humans' noblest qualities: compassion, fairness, tolerance, and loyalty. (If only human beings were so wise.)

Therein lies the difficulty. Human beings are much pickier than we are. The least little things, such as chewing up sofas, barking all night, and herding the neighborhood children into a tight little circle, seem to throw them completely off balance. But do we complain when humans stay up all night, run loose in the neighborhood, spill beer on the sofa, or put up Halloween decorations that would terrify a vampire, let alone a little kid? Nope—you never hear a word about it.

Most dogs are happiest when with their favorite people.

Apartment Dogs

Most toy dogs are great for apartments, but some people want a bigger dog without giving up their urban ways. Here are some larger dogs that can manage apartment living. Note: Smaller terriers (with the exception of the Jack Russell) can also handle apartments. Bulldogs, Dachshunds and Bassets are great for apartments, but some can't handle stairs very well.

Keeshond

Basenji

Cocker Spaniel

American Eskimo Dog

Sussex Spaniel

Schipperke

Chinese Shar-pei

Miniature Poodle

The problem with the human-dog relationship is that people usually get to choose the dog, not the other way around. Most of us dogs are stuck with whoever happens to decide we are cute, funny-looking, or a great show prospect. Unfortunately, as we all know, not all humans are worthy of us. Many are, of course: Alexander the Great, Franklin Roosevelt, George Washington, Thomas Jefferson, Winston Churchill, and Gertrude Stein were all dog lovers. But let's face it, some humans, because of poor socialization, inadequate training, or current life circumstances, shouldn't have a dog at all.

I suppose I should say a little more about these life circumstances. Times have changed, and things just aren't the way they used to. In some ways, that's a good thing, in some ways it's not. Back in olden days, the "Mom" usually stayed home, baked cookies, and let the dogs in and out of the house 40 times a day—the good old days. People weren't as apt to have fenced yards back then either, and we dogs trotted around the comparatively empty streets. Now mom is an investment banker or a nuclear physicist. She's gone most of the time. She knows she needs a fenced yard, because it's the law in most places, and even where it's not, she knows it's not safe to let us wander around by ourselves all day. Some people don't even have yards any more—they live in apartments, condominiums, or town houses. There's nothing wrong with this, and lots of us dogs can live perfectly happily in such a set up as long as we get enough exercise. The only problem occurs when humans don't modify their wants to conform to reality. It's just too hard to keep some kinds of dogs in apartments; they aren't suited to it. Some small dogs are too noisy for peaceful apartment living, while some big ones can adjust very well.

Even though there are a lot of resources available for working owners, like doggy day care, some of us just need more.

So, here are my tips on how to evaluate your prospective owner and some questions to ask them (if only you could). The good prospective owner is one who is not rigidly

Big Apartment Dogs

Okay, you like big dogs and live in a studio apartment. The good news is that some of the very largest breeds have low energy requirements, and if you give them a daily long walk are perfectly suited to urban life. Make sure they have enough room to turn around in, though.

Great Dane

Mastiff

Rottweiler

Bullmastiff

Anatolian Shepherd

Doberman Pinscher

Saint Bernard

Chow Chow

Samoyed

Newfoundland

Borzoi

Make sure you have the space, time, and resources to care for all your pets.

attached to a certain breed. Look for someone flexible enough to take your special needs into consideration and sensible enough to choose another breed if your needs and her preferences don't precisely mesh. You'll have to do a little snooping around, of course, but let's start with basics.

What Is a Dog?

This may sound like a trick question, but it isn't. Although most humans can recognize a dog on the street, when it comes to interacting with us, it's amazing how easy it is to get us mixed up with something else, like a human child, a wolf, or a robot. We are none of these things.

Many dogs retain their original characteristics.

Take wolves, for example. It is true we used to be wolves, a long, long, long time ago, but we've moved on. Wolves are wild animals. They prefer to be as far away from people as possible. We dogs are highly domesticated creatures who will die without human care. And while the genetic link with wolves is close enough for interbreeding (ugh), it's just not done, unless forced upon us by humans. Although many of us retain a few wolf-like characteristics, such as pack behavior, roaming, and, in my case, wolfing down my food, there is a deep chasm between them and us.

We're not human children either, although we do have some qualities that remind people of children. (Most of the qualities are retained juvenile characteristics of our ancient wolf days, if you want to know the truth.) We are sweet and dependent. In fact, in many ways, we are more childlike than human kids. We will never grow up, move out, go to college, get married, or even start a paper route. However, we don't think like people, who never seem to be satisfied with things as they are; we just don't have the same goals. Beyond love, food, and a warm place to sleep, we are pretty unambitious. We don't want to be great artists, we don't want to be famous, we don't want to establish a charitable foundation, and we have no need to "self-actualize," since we are already as actual as possible. While we look up to people as our leaders and companions, they aren't our mommies. Our mommies were dogs like us. (Funny the way that worked out.)

We aren't robots either. We are complex, highly advanced animals. We feel pain, anger, love, and jealousy, and, like humans, we are unpredictable. What works with one dog may not work with another; what worked yesterday may be useless today. No matter how well humans think they know us, we can always surprise them. I can't tell you how many times I have heard people say, "Wow, he never did anything like *that* before." This is one of the most entertaining parts of the dog-human relationship–we keep them on their toes.

What Do You Want with a Dog, Anyway?

If you're lucky, your new owner will want you primarily or solely for a pet. Of course, there's nothing wrong with the dog show game, and tracking, hunting, and lure-coursing can be downright fun. (Since I am a Basset Hound, I can't really see the point of chasing a plastic bag around a field, but to each his own.) But after the day at the show or in the woods is over, we really appreciate some cozy down-time with our owners. Even though Harry the Husky doesn't seem to mind the cold, he needs an air-conditioned house in the summer, believe me, and really likes human companionship. Pick an owner who knows that dogs belong in the house except when we are doing great stuff outdoors with them. Keep your eye out for someone who will love you and cherish you, even if you can't cut the mustard in the show ring or don't know a rabbit from a rhinoceros.

Puppies need extra attention and training from their owners.

Is It a Safe Environment?

Does this family have a fenced-in yard? If not, are they committed to taking you on long daily walks? If they have a fence, is it escape proof? Some of us dogs are terrific diggers, climbers, and squeezer-through-ers. It is fun to keep checking to see if somebody left the gate open, but it's much safer when everything is locked up. Electric fences may work for some people with a large properties, but it doesn't keep out nasty neighborhood dogs or teasing kids. A privacy fence makes me feel safest, but any strong, non-climbable fence will work. A few of us dogs promise to stay around the house whether it's fenced or not, but even if we do, we are at risk of being stolen or lost.

Company, Please

These breeds thrive on human or canine company and need companionship more than some other breeds.

Bichon Frise	Fox Terrier (both varieties)
Clumber Spaniel	
Cocker Spaniel (both varieties)	Border Terrier
	Golden Retriever
Japanese Chin	Newfoundland
Old English Sheepdog	Otterhound

Part 1

Some breeds may have health concerns that require special consideration.

Not For the Tropics

Most dogs do not handle heat as well as humans, but these breeds are particularly vulnerable.

Bulldog

French Bulldog

Keeshond

Siberian Husky

Bernese Mountain Dog

Alaskan Malamute

Samoyed

Pekingese

Pomeranian

Pug

Will They Puppy Proof?

If the humans are looking for a puppy, they should be smart enough to know that their house has to be puppy ready: electrical cords taped to the wall; cabinets locked; trash cans secured; and dangerous plants, swallowable objects, and curtain or blind cords put out of the way. They need to realize that puppies explore the world with their mouths, and if they can eat it, chew it, swallow it, or gnaw on it, they will. The same thing goes for backyards and garages. Fertilizers and other chemical lawn treatments can be deadly for dogs, as can unwiped antifreeze spills—not to mention rat poisons and other rodenticides.

Where Do They Live?

Most of us dogs are pretty adaptable, so long as we get our needed exercise. In a city, that's harder to do for sporting dogs, like pointers and setters, and some of the gazehounds, like Whippets, so most of them are better off in a place where they can run and play. And while some dogs are "self-starters" in this regard, others of us need some encouragement to take that run. I know a lot of Beagles and Dachshunds who get disgracefully fat without their daily workout; I know some small "apartment-sized" breeds who make so much noise that their

Home Alone

These breeds can handle being left alone for longer periods than more sociable animals.

Afghan Hound	Irish Water Spaniel
Belgian Sheepdog (all varieties)	Miniature Pinscher
	Pekingese
Canaan Dog	Pomeranian
Chow Chow	Puli
Chihuahua	Briard
Doberman Pinscher	Basenji

Each dog is an individual, and some are more independent than others.

owners risk eviction. On the other hand, I know some big dogs like Saint Bernards that thrive in the city.

A lot of people don't know that the main consideration as to whether a dog can be happy in the city depends more on mental qualities than on physical ones. Calm, low-key, not-easily-stressed dogs can often handle the fast pace, loud noises, and stress of city life better than high-mettled animals (just something to think about).

Are They Really Permitted to Own a Dog?

I know you won't believe this, but some people violate a lease or covenant agreement when they bring home a dog (or another dog). Of course, they eventually get caught, and then guess-who is out of the house. Ask your breeder or rescue organization to get a peek at the lease before you go home with your new owner.

Where Will You Be All Day?

My great-great-great-grandmother told me that once upon a time, there was usually somebody hanging around the house all day to cater to our every whim–not any more. It seems that most owners nowadays go off to work, usually mumbling something about

Children should be taught that caring for a dog is a big responsibility.

"canine upkeep," whatever that is, making it necessary to work an extra shift. A few dogs really cannot tolerate this separation, and nearly all of us enjoy as much human companionship as possible, but we're adaptable, too. We can deal with it, as long as we get plenty of attention and exercise from our owners when they are home. So, taking it for granted that most of us will be left alone for part of the day, the question becomes, exactly where are we going to spend that time and what are supposed to do?

The same great-great-great-grandmother who told me that once upon a time some humans didn't work told me that during that same once upon a time, almost all dogs did! That's progress for you: I can just see myself herding goats, fetching a dead duck out of a mosquito-infested swamp, pulling a sled, or jumping into the freezing ocean to rescue some overboard fisherman–fat chance. However, being dogs of leisure does pose a few problems.

For example, if we are going to be stuck in the house for a long time, who is going to take us out for a morning and afternoon walk and bathroom break? Some of us are pretty good about holding it for a long time, but it's not very comfortable, and those of us who are puppies or have tiny bladders need some relief. Good owners are mindful of this, and remember to ask a neighbor or hire a dog-walking service. Sometimes they install a dog door and let us go in and out as we please, as long as we have a fenced yard in a safe neighborhood. Some owners feel so sorry for us left alone all day that they choose a doggy day care, pet sitter, or dog walker to keep us happy–that works, too.

Who Is Going to Take Care of You?

If the answer is, "the kids," forget it. Of course, the children will volunteer, even beg and bargain for a dog by promising with all their hearts to feed you, walk you, train you, play with you, and snuggle with you at night. Some will actually do some of these things for more than a week; others won't, no matter what they say now. Kids are a lot of fun, but let's face it, they're not as loyal as we are, and they can be pretty forgetful. Watch out for owners who are thinking of getting a dog "for the kids' sake." They should want you for themselves, because chances are they are the ones who will be feeding you and walking you–and they are for darned sure the ones who will be paying your bills.

Check out the "Mom," because she's probably the one who will end up doing most of the work. In fact, according to a recent study by the American Animal Hospital Association, 66 percent of the respondents said that Mom had the primary responsibility for pet care. As for the kids, in fewer than 10 percent of the homes did the children follow through on their promise to care for a dog. If Mom is even slightly uncertain about wanting to take you home, play sick and curl up in the corner.

Kids and dogs can be best friends if they can learn to respect each other.

By the way, if you hear anyone mumbling about "wanting a dog for the kids to grow up with" make it clear (it should be obvious) that the dog will grow up a lot faster than the kid. Kids are better off with older, already grown-up dogs, because they tend to be more tolerant and are through the nipping stage.

And Speaking of Kids....

If there are children, are these the kind of kids with whom you want to spend your life? I know they promised to feed you, walk you, and love you forever, but what if they get bored with you? Kids are great fun for most of us, as long as they are supervised. They can play with a puppy until it drops from exhaustion, because the loyal puppy will continue to try to play as long as it is asked to. The children don't mean to be cruel, they just don't know when to quit and neither does a puppy. That's one reason why it's a pain to be a dog–we have to be loyal. Check to see if the parents are teaching the kids the right way to pick you up and to leave you alone when you are eating or want to sleep. Of course, some of us don't really care for kids. Part of this is a matter of taste, but mostly it's our

All-Around Family Dogs

Basset Hound	Bulldog	Boston Terrier
West Highland White Terrier	Collie	Samoyed
Pug	Shih Tzu	English Setter
American Eskimo Dog	Boxer	Keeshond
Beagle	Bichon Frise	Miniature Schnauzer
Poodle	Newfoundland	Wire Fox Terrier
Golden Retriever	Labrador Retriever	

breeding. Some of us love our *own* kids, but not the neighbors. Parents should find out if we are likely to be kid lovers or not when we grow up.

How Much Time Do They Have?

While some of us are pretty independent and can get along by ourselves, with another dog, or even a cat, for company, it's no fun to be deprived of human companionship day in and day out. And for puppies, being alone for long periods is a real recipe for disaster. Puppies need lots of one-on-one socialization time, so if your prospective owners work full-time, try to steer them toward the shelter or a rescue organization, where they can get a very nice older dog who won't demand so much time and attention. Besides, we older dogs are already housetrained–at least usually.

Are They Adaptable?

Let's face it; we dogs are going to change the lives of our humans. Folks who come to the dog game with rigid expectations are in for a surprise, and so are the folks who want to get a dog just like their old one, then are disappointed because each of is so different. Adjustments will be a lot easier if they come open minded (and open-hearted too).

Finances

Let's talk money–we dogs can be expensive, and that's no joke. We cost more than a lot of people seem to think. Even a "free dog" ends up costing more than you might suppose.

(But you're lucky–at least the people who are considering getting you have already plunked down some cash to buy this book. That alone shows that they are not cheapskates.)

We all know that buying a high-quality, purebred puppy from a responsible breeder will cost hundreds of dollars. A pet store will charge the same price; still a sizeable chunk of change for many people. Even humane society or rescued dogs aren't free. The kind people who saved our lives have to get money from somewhere to continue their good work.

Then, after the purchase or adoption, we dogs eat up the cash. (Sometimes literally. It's not a good idea to for people to leave money lying around. A few pennies can poison us with zinc, and swallowing some greenbacks, while harmless to us, seems to make some owners go red in the face and start yelling.) Big dogs cost more than small ones–there's more of us to feed, for one thing, and boarding kennels and groomers charge more for big dogs. Even veterinarians charge more to spay big dogs than small ones.

Tolerant Dogs

These dogs are good with kids, friendly to strangers, and relaxed in uncertain circumstances. This does not mean that any of these wonderful, stable pets should be subjected to abuse, but it does mean that they are easygoing, tough cookies.

Basset Hound	Scottish Deerhound
Border Terrier	Sealyham Terrier
English Setter	Bloodhound
Flat-Coated Retriever	Bulldog
Mastiff	Newfoundland

Grooming time and expenses should be considered before selecting a breed.

Pampered Pets

These dogs need more-than-average grooming:

- Maltese
- Shih Tzu
- Poodle
- Yorkshire Terrier
- Skye Terrier

Older Children's Playmates

These breeds are not only tolerant, but playful with children. Some are so playful they can knock over a small child, so always supervise.

Boxer	English Springer Spaniel
Beagle	
Siberian Husky	Standard Poodle
Golden Retriever	Bernese Mountain Dog
Labrador Retriever	English Setter
Irish Setter	Samoyed
	Saint Bernard

Regular checkups are an important part of your dog's health care.

And those of us in the "pampered pet" category–Poodles, Shih Tzu, Maltese, and some terriers–really need a professional hairdresser. They wash us, dry us, comb us, brush us, pluck us, shave us, scissor us, clip our nails, clean our ears, perfume us, put a dumb bow on our heads, and there you go–another payment. But we're worth it.

What's for Dinner?

Good food costs money. See if you can find out what they plan to feed you. I like home cooked meals myself, but if you do get an owner who buys commercial foods, don't let him get a brand that is not nutritious or not formulated for your age or medical condition. In the dog food world, at least, there is a close relationship between how much commercial dog food costs and how nutritious it is.

How About Those Checkups?

Now I hate to mention this part, but we should talk about the vet. The veterinarian is our friend. People should choose a vet

Long-Lived Dogs

As a rule, small dogs live longer than large ones, but the average life span of a dog is ten years. These dogs have the longest lifespans:

Manchester Terrier	Miniature Pinscher
Beagle	Papillon
Bichon Frise	Pekingese
Cairn Terrier	Pomeranian
Chihuahua	Scottish Terrier
Dachshund	Schipperke
Italian Greyhound	Shih Tzu
Lhasa Apso	Yorkshire Terrier
Maltese	

Training is an essential aspect of your relationship with your dog.

whose office is relatively close in case of emergency, who has a system ready for after-hours emergencies, and who genuinely loves dogs. It's best if the vet is familiar with the special problems of your breed in particular.

We have to have shots, and we should get our teeth cleaned and get regular health checkups. And what if we eat something awful or get into an accident?

With the right care, we dogs can live well into our teens. Humans can treat and cure illnesses that were death sentences 20 years ago, but it's not cheap. Ultrasounds, echocardiograms, and sophisticated surgery are all expensive, albeit lifesaving, procedures.

A good, really dedicated dog owner will forgo a vacation or cut back on the restaurants to provide for our special needs or medical procedures.

If we could only speak human language, we might say, "What if I come down with an exotic disease, or have an accident that will cost thousands of dollars to fix?" The prospective

Your life will never be the same after you bring a dog into your home.

Calm Trainers Needed

These highly excitable dogs need owners who are patient, relaxed and can keep their cool! They have enough problems with their nerves without having to deal with yours, too.

Doberman Pinscher	English Toy Spaniel
Fox Terrier (both varieties)	Norwegian Elkhounds
	Vizsla
German Shorthaired Pointer	Black and Tan Coonhound
Puli	Weimaraner
Irish Setter	Boxer

owner's answer to that question tells you a lot. Also, if your owner doesn't know about pet health insurance, you should clue him in.

Should I Sit, or What?

Training is one of the most important aspects of our relationship with people. Find out how the owner plans to train you. If she doesn't train you at all, you'll have to train her, and that's always a problem. Stay away from people who yell or hit. There's no excuse to strike a dog; it only makes us fearful or bad-tempered. Also, housetraining is an issue–I mean, humans don't go outside to eliminate, but they expect us to. It's one of those little inconsistencies in life. Owners need to be patient and not resort to weird behavior like screaming, hitting, or rubbing our noses in it. Such owners have been improperly trained themselves and need some reminders about correct housetraining methods.

Try to find out if the owner knows the right training methods and has the right expectations for your breed. Labradors and Goldens just love that obedience stuff, and setters can't get enough of racing around in the fields after some benighted bird. We hounds take easily to trailing rabbits. But what comes easily for some is a real hurdle for

Part 1

The Wet and the Hairy

These breeds are well-known for their slobbering, drooling, and general all-around salivating.

Newfoundland	Basset Hound
Saint Bernard	Gordon Setter
Bloodhound	Irish Setter

These breeds shed more than other breeds.

Alaskan Malamute	Samoyed
Siberian Husky	Great Dane
Norwegian Elkhound	Newfoundland
Belgian Malinois	Pomeranian
Chow Chow	Rough Collie
Akita	Kuvasz
Great Pyrenees	Beagle

There are certain dogs that get along famously with other pets.

others. Owners should know what they can reasonably expect from us. Reading this book may help foster realistic expectations. I have certainly done my part into making my owner more realistic. (She started out thinking a Basset Hound was like a Golden Retriever on short legs. Hah!)

Housekeeping Issues

Find out how house-proud the prospective owners are. If these folks can't stand the sight of dog hair everywhere, they'd better think about getting one of the low-shedding breeds and stay away from us shedders and droolers. And while any dog can be destructive if deprived of sufficient exercise and company, some of us are capable of eating though walls and devouring floors if bored enough.

When you choose the right dog, you gain a friend for life.

The More the Merrier

These breeds not only like you, but they also enjoy your friends, door-to-door salespeople, visiting missionaries, thieves, and especially other dogs.

Foxhound (both varieties)	Siberian Husky
Clumber Spaniel	Beagle
Bichon Frise	Irish Setter
English Cocker Spaniel	Bloodhound
Golden Retriever	Cavalier King Charles Spaniel
Old English Sheepdog	

What About Roommates?

Do they have other dogs or maybe a cat? I subscribe to the "pack" mentality myself: I always like to have another dog or two around for company, but I know a Chow Chow who doesn't like anyone but his owner. Your new owners should think about their current dog, too, and figure out if he'd really like company. Sometimes people get a puppy to keep their old dog company or to cheer him up. This may work, or it may depress the older dog still further. As for cats, I admit to having a sneaking liking for the beasts, but I know some dogs who will chase cats; this seems to be part of their breeding; they just can't help it. They aren't bad dogs, but they face an irresistible temptation. (My own temptations lie in the kitchen department.)

It's funny, but people who already have two cats seem to have better luck with a dog than those with only one. It has something to do with the way cats organize themselves. Apparently, if there's only one of them, they tend to get into a contest with the new dog about who will be boss.

If there is another dog, it usually turns out that dogs of opposite sexes get along better than same-sex pairs. (I guess that's biology for you, a subject I was never very good at, especially since I was neutered.)

The Final Analysis

In the final analysis, getting hooked up with the right person is possible. After all, popular wisdom tells us that human beings are less chained to their genes than dogs are. Humans are a versatile species that can hunt rabbits, do police work, herd sheep, and even do tricks, such as producing dog biscuits on demand. (Firm, consistent training is required, however.) They require less grooming than a Poodle, generally cleaning up with a quick lick to the ears or mouth. With proper accoutrements, they can stand both cold and heat. They are equally suited to town and country, and, as a rule get along well with cats, horses, and children, although not always with each other. Some of them can even be trusted off a leash.

When you get the right human, you are able to form a friendship that lasts, receive love and affection and create a bond that is mutually beneficial for both of you–what could be better than that?

Finding Your Dog

I let the dog write the last chapter because he runs my life. I hope there weren't too many misspellings.

While it's easy to acquire a dog, getting the right dog is a different matter. The hardest part about getting the right dog is knowing what is the right dog for you. Sometimes it's really better to ask yourself, "Am I the right person for this breed?" rather than the other way around. Dogs are our best friends. We all know that. So why is it sometimes so darned hard to forge a relationship that should be–well, as natural as apple pie and ice cream? Because just as with apple pie and ice cream, there's a lot more to a dog than meets the eye. The grim fact is that most people spend more time picking the right

Choosing the best dog for you ensures a long, happy relationship.

Most dogs were originally bred to perform certain jobs for humans.

car than in selecting the right dog, and while the right car will make your life easier, the wrong one won't eat your sofa, bite the kids, or howl all night.

A dog is a many-layered thing. This is obvious to anyone who has looked at a Chihuahua and a St. Bernard, a Papillion and a Great Dane, a Pekingese and a Mastiff. No other animal comes in so many different packages. Yet they all share the same ancestor: the wolf (whether it was one species of wolf or several is a subject of academic debate that doesn't make a whole lot of difference to our current topic, since all species of wolves look and act pretty much alike anyway). Our precious little toy dogs and big, hairy, goofy-looking ones all carry the genetic code for wolf in every cell of their little or big bodies. Many problems we have in dealing with our family pet are due to this inescapable heritage. There is less mitochondrial DNA difference between wolves and dogs than there is between different racial or ethnic groups of human beings. In fact, taxonomists have recently renamed the domestic dog. It is now *Canis lupus familiaris*–the familiar wolf. So it's important to realize that when we are dealing with dogs, we are dealing with modified wolves.

But that's only half the problem. At least 40,000 years ago, when humans domesticated wolves and turned them into dogs, they did so for several reasons, most of which centered directly on food. Sometimes dogs were a food source in themselves, a practice which continues to the present day in many parts of the world. Dogs were enlisted to use their natural heritage to hunt down prey; others were asked to guard food by protecting the livestock or manage food by herding or driving it. Some people recruited dogs to help prepare food by attaching the animal to a butter churn and compelling it to walk around in a circle; some hauled food around on sledges.

Besides the food connection, dogs were called upon to defend the tribe against intruders, both human and beast. As humans became more "civilized," we drafted dogs to attack or threaten other human beings. Dogs fought in wars and helped put down slave rebellions.

As we became even more "advanced," people thought it would be fun to make dogs fight other animals or even each other. Bull-baiting, bear-baiting, and dog-fighting became a cruel form of mass entertainment. Even small lap dogs began their careers with a serious purpose—to destroy small vermin and, in some cases, to draw fleas from unwashed humans onto themselves.

But that was then, this is now. The disparity between what dogs *were* and what dogs *are* has produced an enormous amount of debate in the dog world. Although many breeders honor the idea of retaining the original purpose for which the breed was developed, nearly everyone today wants a dog mainly as a pet. Unfortunately, the qualities that make a dog a good pet are not always found in dogs that maintain their original lifestyles. The noble, beautiful, and elegant sighthound may have a prey drive so sharp it will chase down and devour anything in its path. Scenthounds are gentle and companionable animals, but most of them make following their nose a priority. Their main interest in life is following that nose to the next hill, and they will come home when they are good and ready (that is, if they can remember where home is). Terriers were mostly bred to hunt down and kill rats. Thankfully, most terrier owners fail to have a rat problem. And while we all admire the fierce intelligence of the Border Collie, his passion to round up contrary sheep does not translate well into suburban living. Most seriously, although many people want a dog to give warning of visitors, most of us of us can do without an attack dog, a highly trained, specialized animal more suited to military installations than a private

Bull-Terrier Breeds

A subgroup of terriers has an infusion of Bulldog and Mastiff blood. They are, not surprisingly, called the bull-and-terrier breeds and include the American Staffordshire Terrier, Staffordshire Bull Terrier, Bull Terrier, and others not in the AKC reckoning. These are formidable dogs that combine the power of the Bulldog and Mastiffs with the quickness and feistiness of the terriers. Like terriers, they tend not to like other dogs, but because of their greater power, can be very dangerous if allowed to attack. Although never meant to injure people, it is an undeniabe fact that individuals who are poorly bred or from certain suspect lines can cause serious harm. These dogs are best placed with experienced owners who know how to deal with them.

Scenthounds will always have the urge to follow their noses.

Part 1

Most dogs are happiest when they are able to follow their natural instincts.

Challenging Breeds

These dogs may attempt to wrest control and are only for the most experienced, strong owners. These breeds are all formidable. Some smaller breeds may also attempt to rule the roost, but can be more easily controlled.

American Staffordshire Terrier	Rottweiler
Bull Terrier	Rhodesian Ridgeback
Doberman Pinscher	Kuvasz
Anatolian Shepherd	Giant Schnauzer
Chow Chow	Saint Bernard
	Komondor

home. Untrained "attack dogs" end up hurting innocent people and costing their owners wads of money and sometimes time in jail.

So, we are kind of stuck. We have to contend not only with the wolf in our dogs, but also with the sheepdog without sheep, the retriever without a duck, or the hound without a hunter. What this means is that pet owners have to deal with herding, pulling, roaming, aggressive, even phobic behavior that's appropriate for the breed's original purpose but not appropriate for pet-owner relationships today. To complicate matters, breed clubs often claim that their bench champions represent the working examples of the breed; of course, this is not necessarily true. Conformation Beagles, Siberian Huskies, and setters look little like their working counterparts. They are often different in size, coat, and general "style." They act differently, too. Even American Kennel Club Field Trials, which are designed to be an approximation of real hunting conditions, produce Beagles who are too slow and Gordon Setters who are too fast to be useful to human hunters.

Until people who breed dogs for pet ownership and the show ring (as opposed to the few people who breed dogs for their original function) decide to re-create a dog's temperament, the wary dog owner must pick his way carefully through the breeds, deciding which natural characteristics he can live with. For example, as mentioned earlier, hounds are more interested in following a scent than in following you. (After all, you have no idea where the rabbit went. They do and expect *you* to follow *them*.) Most pet owners would prefer to have a dog that stays reliably at their side. The question becomes, do you want a hound badly enough to make sure he is always safe behind a fence or at the end of a leash? Or let's say you adore Australian Cattle Dogs. How much will it bother you that your pet is likely

Barkiest Barkers

At some point in their development, these breeds were bred to bark to warn of intruders or move livestock. They have retained this instinct, and although they can be trained to quiet down a little, they will always be more vocal—it's their nature.

Dachshund	Finnish Spitz
Shetland Sheepdog	American Eskimo Dog
Beagle	Most terriers
Collie	Newfoundland
Norwegian Elkhound	English Foxhound

to nip the heels of every kid on the block until they are herded into a tight, huddled circle? (This recently happened in my neighborhood. The dog wouldn't let the kids get on the school bus.) Maybe you love the idea of a companionable dog like a Siberian Husky; however, can you live with mounds of dog hair choking your every breath? Are you willing to provide him with all the human and canine friendship he needs? Are you willing to hook him up to a sled and let him run for hours in the bitter cold? (If you're not, don't be surprised when he tears your house apart.) You can, of course, give the dog an equal amount of non-sledding exercise, but Siberians were born to pull sleds. That's what they really like, and nothing quite takes the place of it.

To summarize: For thousands and thousands of years, we human beings have worked at domesticating the dog. This means simply that we have tried to develop an animal that is suited to our needs, and who, in some cases, copies our own neurotic behaviors. To this end, we have created a race of beings, all of whom share at least some of the following attributes:

√ Total dependence upon humans for their care and keeping;

√ Protective instincts that were originally cultivated to save us from attacks by our perceived enemies;

√ Powerful territorial senses to warn of the approach of strangers;

√ Herding instincts to round up livestock;

√ Drafting skills to pull sleds for hundred of miles;

√ Powerful prey drives to attack and kill anything that moves;

√ Powerful senses of smell that lead to independent hunting.

All is not lost, however. You *can* find the right dog for your lifestyle, if you are willing to adjust and do your homework.

Learn everything you can about the breed in which you are interested *before* you go looking at puppies. Read the breed standard, which you can find in the *AKC Complete Dog Book* or on www.akc.org. The breed standard is a picture-in-writing of the ideal dog of that breed. Some breed clubs also produce an "illustrated standard," although this is a risky business that depends on interpretation of the written standard, which is always the final arbiter. You will find no photograph of the perfect dog, for the simple reason that there are no perfect dogs, just approximations of that ever-elusive ideal. I suppose someone has already engineered a computerized perfect dog, but again, that would simply be one person's interpretation of the wonderfully vague breed standard.

Learn how much grooming is required for the breed you want and honestly assess your ability to provide it or have it done for you. For instance, I have always wanted an Afghan Hound, but I have enough trouble combing my own hair, let alone something as silky and long and pretty as that! I must be content to admire the breed from afar. An acquaintance of mine was not so wise. He bought an Afghan when they were at their peak of popularity, but had neither the time nor the inclination to maintain its coat. As a result, the animal became a pathetic mass of tangled hair and sore skin. Thankfully, the

A purebred dog will possess both form and function.

dog was eventually was given away to someone who would care for her properly.

Study the history of the breed. This is a wonderful way to learn its original purpose and what qualities went into making it. Find out what health problems are most common in that breed. This will help you ask screening questions of the breeder.

This sounds as if finding the right dog is hard. It is hard, but not terribly hard, which is often better than having it made too simple. Often, someone just "dumps" a dog on us. Sometimes the abandoned animal turns out to be the "best danged dawg I ever had," but more often, the unfortunate creature, not being the right dog for the household, is neglected or improperly treated. Please don't ever accept a dog that is given or dumped on you, unless you truly want the animal and are willing to care for it.

Here are three extremely bad criteria to use when trying to decide on the right breed.

High-Maintenance Dogs

If you don't like brushing, fussing, and trips to the groomers, the following dogs (and anything similar) may not be for you.

Old English Sheepdog	Maltese
Poodle	Bichon Frise
Briard	Afghan Hound
Collie (the rough-coated variety)	Cocker Spaniel
	Puli
Komondor	

Popularity

This reasoning goes, "Wow, everyone has one of these. They must be the best dogs!" While it's true that popular dogs often have character traits that makes their popularity well-deserved, it is also true that great popularity may lead to the consequent development of poorly bred strains. Besides, just because a dog is popular with others, does not mean it's the best one for you.

Rarity

Some people take the other tack and look for the rarest breed they can find, just to have something "different." The faultiness of this reasoning is obvious. First of all, rare breeds don't stay rare. You may have purchased your Western Colombian Sloth-Hunting Mastiff, confident of being the first on your block to do so, but it won't last. Others will shortly

Top Ten

According to the Veterinary Pet Insurance Claims Statistics, the following ailments are the most common (in all breeds):

Ear infections

Gastritis

Dermatitis

Tumors

Hot spots and pyoderma

Cystitis

Arthritis

Enteritis

Hypothyroidism

Soft tissue trauma

Carefully consider your needs and lifestyle before choosing a breed.

follow, and, pretty soon, you'll just have another trendy dog. Second, there's often a good reason why rare dogs are rare–they are unsuitable pets for some people due to characteristics or unusual physical requirements. In addition, rare breeds have, almost by definition, a smaller gene pool to work with, which may be associated with a higher incidence of hereditary disease.

Nostalgia

Most people start thinking, "Yep, I had a Brittany as a kid on farm. I think I'll get another one. I'm sure he'll be fine in the apartment." Don't kid yourself–the ideal dog of your childhood may not be right for the adult you have become.

Once you do decide the right breed for you, your job is not over. It's important for you to learn everything you can about the finer points of the breed. The more you learn now, the better position you'll be in to pick the right puppy or older dog, and the fewer the surprises waiting in the wings.

The Newspaper

Some people begin their search for a family dog in what seems like the most sensible place–the newspaper classifieds. While you may indeed find a good dog in this way, you're fighting the odds. In the first place, the very best breeders don't advertise in the newspaper, or even in most dog magazines, because they don't need to. They already have a waiting list of knowledgeable buyers.

On the other hand, backyard breeders, puppy millers, and desperate owners, who want to dump their behaviorally challenged dog on the unsuspecting public, go straight to the classifieds. Just remember: Buyer beware. Many of these people use evasive language (and sometimes outright lies) to draw in the unsuspecting public. They use words like "full-blooded" by which one presumes they mean "purebred." However, the term "full-blooded" or "thoroughbred" is not used in dog circles, so it's a guarantee that the seller probably has no idea what he is talking about. Sometimes they offer "papers," but this term is ambiguous. It might mean pedigree, it might mean AKC registration, or it might even mean a dog license or some kind of health certificate.

A favorite term of the backyard breeder is "AKC champion bloodlines." Big deal. A lot of registered dogs have AKC champion bloodlines—if you go back far enough. But these far-off ancestors don't mean much after a couple of generations. If you are considering showing your dog, or even if you want a dog that is a fine physical example of the breed, look for a few champions among nearer relatives, such as the parents and grandparents.

It's hard to resist a group of adorable pups, but try to make an informed decision.

Winning at Westminster

Do you have a passion to take it all at Westminster? Don't get an English Foxhound or a Labrador. If you go by the principle "Do what works," choose a breed whose winning ways have captured the judge's eye and heart for over a century. (Advice in brief is to get some kind of terrier—they have the attitude and solid breeding background that impresses the folks at Westminster.) With history as our guide, here are your Best Bets, starting with the best bet of all—a Wire Fox Terrier, which has claimed the prize nine times:

Wire Fox Terrier	Smooth Fox Terrier	English Setter
Scottish Terrier	Pekingese	Standard Poodle
English Springer Spaniel	Toy Poodle	
Boxer	Miniature Poodle	

In 2003, a terrier took Best in Show again—Kerry Blue!

Visit many breeders and ask lots of questions about the puppies.

In addition, an AKC championship is no guarantee of the health or character of the dog who earns it. I have known dogs with epilepsy, hip dysplasia, and personality defects earn enough points to get their championships. Unfortunately, some breeders care more about ribbons on a wall and bragging about their "gorgeous" dogs than about health and personality. Don't fall for it. "AKC-registered" means nothing in terms of quality, health, or temperament of the dog; it simply means that the breeders have submitted the proper paperwork to the American Kennel Club. Don't make the mistake of thinking that every AKC dog is ready for Westminster. Even casual breeders who have good intentions often simply don't know enough about the perils of genetics and breeding to produce good puppies, especially these days when so many inherited diseases abound. They often fail to perform the proper genetic screening for the parents, thus exacerbating the problems.

Some people are fooled into thinking that "Both parents on premises" is a sign of good breeding. Actually it just means that the breeder had two dogs of opposite sexes. Many good breeders go across the country or have their bitches artificially inseminated; however, you should at least be able to see a picture of the sire.

Some unscrupulous breeders bill their maladjusted, oversized, inappropriately aggressive dogs as "extra": more Rottweiler; more Pit Bull; more Chow Chow; more German Shepherd. Most people have all they can handle with the regular specimens of these breeds, let alone anything "extra." Terms like "Needs adult home" or "Protective" often means the dog is aggressive with kids. It is a bad idea to bring home a dog with behavior problems that you may not be able to handle.

Here's my personal favorite: "Rare color." If a puppy were "rare" in a desirable way, it wouldn't be advertised in the paper. There are no rare colors or patterns in the sense that it makes the dog more valuable. There are however, some "rare" colors that disqualify a dog from the show ring. Parti-colored poodles, "blue bassets," and other anomalies are not desirable, and in some breeds, have genetic problems associated with them. For example, in many breeds, white can signify hearing or eye problems. Check the list of accepted colors for your breed and don't be led astray. The same is true for eye color. With the exception of the Siberian Husky and a very few others, eyes should be brown. Always check the standard before you go looking to find out what is and what is not acceptable.

Checking Out the Dog Shows

Even if you have no intention of ever showing your dog, going to shows and seeing a lot of high-quality dogs up close will give you a good "feel" for what the breed standard looks like in the flesh. The parents of the puppy you choose should be of this quality. If you do see a dog you like, pick a quiet time (usually after the judging) to speak to the exhibitors. Tell them how much you like their dog (they will be flattered), ask if they are planning to breed in the near future, and that you'd like to apply for a puppy. If they are in a hurry, be satisfied with a business card and make arrangements to call or visit their kennel.

Talking of Terriers

By and large, terriers are a homogenous, closely related lot. If you decide on a terrier, take note that you are getting a bigger dog than will be apparent from size alone. Most terriers are feisty, playful, incredibly loyal, and not crazy about other dogs. While many are playful with children, they may not be tolerant of toddlers. To maintain coats in top terrier condition, they need to be stripped (hand-plucked of dead hair), which is tedious and time-consuming. Most owners of pets elect to have their dogs clipped instead, an operation that softens and discolors the trademark terrier coat. True to their heritage, count on a terrier to bark and dig: if a perfect lawn and an eerie silence are your cup of tea, forget about most members of this group.

Most exhibitors will be delighted that you take an interest in the breed and will welcome you to the circle of fanciers. However (and I hate to say it), some dog show exhibitors are just plain rude. I have seen enough of it to be able to state this as a fact. Some may be rude because they just lost, others because they see no reason to be polite to a mere spectator (as if courtesy needs a reason), others just don't know any better. If this happens to you, mumble something about "sorry to have caught you at a bad time" and find someone who will treat you with respect. A good breeder regards every contact he or she has with the public as an opportunity to be an ambassador for his or her breed, and people who don't take on this responsibility with grace are not good breeders in my book.

Part 1

A good breeder will provide the best possible care.

First-Timers

These dogs are great for first-time owners due to their even temperament and trainability:

Golden Retriever

Labrador Retriever

Whippet

Friends and Neighbors

Some people get their pets from a friend, relative, or neighbor. And while this is a good source for an older dog (you probably know everything about the animal already), it may be a poorer place from which to get a puppy, unless that friend, relative, or neighbor is a person who is truly an expert on the breed and proves it by entering competitions like dog shows, field trials, or tracking events. That makes your friend fall into the "breeder class," which we are going to discuss next.

The Responsible Breeder

If you are looking for a puppy, the best way to find one is by contacting a reputable breeder. If you're not planning on showing, explain that you're looking for a "pet-quality" puppy. Pet quality doesn't mean there will be anything wrong with the puppy. It merely means that in the breeder's opinion, the dog will not achieve a championship in the show ring. Eyes that are too light, wrong color nose, or ears hung too high or low are just a few unimportant factors that may limit a dog "show-worthiness" but have no impact on how good a pet the puppy will be. Even stranger, from an outsider's point of view, is that many breeders want their line to have a certain, instantly recognizable "look." That look may involve a particular type of head, coat color, movement, or, in performance dogs, certain special abilities. If the puppy does not measure up to the breeder's particular expectations, it automatically becomes a pet-quality dog, and your golden opportunity.

Whether you're buying for pet or show, a responsible breeder will ask you lots of questions. Some of them may appear personal. Don't be offended; she is merely trying to make sure her dogs are going into the right home. Her questions should make you confident that this is a person who cares about her puppies and who has done a good job of breeding them. Here are some criteria by which to judge a responsible breeder.

Only the best dogs are bred to preserve the quality and health of the puppies.

• A responsible breeder specializes in only one or two breeds. If the person seems to raise dogs of every description, you've stumbled upon a puppy mill. Leave fast. Also, a good breeder does not sell her puppies to a third party, such as pet store or a pet broker.

• A reputable breeder produces well-socialized dogs. This means the dogs seem comfortable with both human beings and their littermates. The personality of the mother dog can tell you a lot, too. I would not trust a breeder who will not let you look at the mother.

• A good breeder will belong to the relevant breed club. Ideally, she would work in your local breed rescue organization as well. If the local breed club has never heard of her, it's usually a bad sign.

• A good breeder has a breeding program–a specific set of goals. Ask the breeder what her breeding goals are. If you get a blank look, you've come to the wrong place–probably a backyard breeder. A responsible breeder is likely to talk your ear off about this, dragging out various pedigrees and old photos.

• A responsible breeder won't sell puppies until they are at least nine weeks old, although she may allow you to put down a deposit earlier. The early weeks of a dog's life are critical for socialization. This is even more essential for slow-maturing breeds. Besides, breeders need the time to evaluate members of the litter for show potential.

If possible, you should try to meet the parents of the puppy.

Sprightly Sports

The sporting dogs (retrievers, setters, pointers, and spaniels) are, by and large, bundles of relentless energy suitable for active families with big yards, time to play, and lots of energy.

• A reputable breeder sells only healthy puppies. This means more than having all their puppy shots. It means the breeder has had the parents evaluated for hereditary problems. She should provide you with the written proof that she has done this and give you the results of any tests. In breeds where hip dysplasia (a debilitating disease affecting many larger breeds, in which the femur does not fit correctly into its socket) is common, ask to see the Orthopedic Foundation for Animals (OFA) results for both parents. The OFA rates hips as excellent, good, fair, borderline, or dysplastic. Puppies cannot be tested for hip dysplasia, because their bone structures have not sufficiently formed to tell how they will develop. Dogs must be two years old before this certification can be given, and it requires an X-ray. Another way to evaluate hips is the PennHIP™, developed by researchers at the University of Pennsylvania, which evaluates hip laxity. These tests are very important, because you can't tell whether or not a dog has hip dysplasia by simply watching it move. This disease is often masked in young dogs and does not manifest itself until later in life. I should mention, however, that breeders of sighthounds may not have this test done because of the sighthound's sensitivity to anesthesia.

Chances of hip dysplasia in the progeny are lowest in puppies whose parents are both rated excellent, although nothing is foolproof. Not only are certain genetic problems clustered in certain breeds, but each line within a breed may have specific health problems as well. A good breeder should volunteer this information. One question to ask a breeder is: At what age did each of your dog's closest relatives die and from what? Questions about hip dysplasia, allergies, and epilepsy are also appropriate. While these diseases are not fatal, they are debilitating and lower the quality of life. Beware of a breeder who claims that none of her dogs have ever had any diseases or a breeder who has never heard of these problems.

For breeds with heritable deafness problems like Dalmatians and English Setters, ask to see the results of the brainstem auditory evoked response (BAER) test that all conscientious breeders should have performed. The Canine Eye Registration Foundation (CERF) has similar tests for breeds that have heritable eye problems.

Your breeder should start your puppy on the road to good health.

• Good breeders charge what their puppies are worth. Get out your wallet, because well-bred dogs are not inexpensive, and some people will pay well over a thousand dollars or more for a show dog. Although you can certainly buy a puppy at a lesser price, the chances are that such "bargain dogs" (or their parents) may not be fully tested for inherited defects like von Willebrand's, a bleeding disorder, or heritable thyroid problems. These tests can get expensive for the breeder. The extra money you pay is well worth it in order to get a healthier dog. If the price the seller is asking is considerably lower than other area breeders, there has to be a reason, and it's probably not a good one. Some good breeders offer pet quality puppies at a lower price than show quality. Others do not, maintaining that while some puppies are pets and some are for show, all are of equal value. (I like this approach myself.)

• A reputable breeder is actively involved in showing her dogs. She is proud of their quality and places them in competition with other quality dogs. Most of the near relatives of your prospective puppy should have an AKC championship or a comparable title in obedience, tracking, herding, retrieving, or field trials. Any AKC titles your dog's ancestors have won will be indicated on the papers. Some national breed clubs also award titles, which will be indicated on official certificates. Showing dogs is important for most breeders, because they want to prove through competition that they are the best. On the other hand, a responsible breeder's primary concern is not showing dogs, but in raising healthy, good-tempered puppies. Of course, she is also interested in producing a handsome representative of the breed. A breeder who raises healthy, good-tempered Basset Hounds that look like Beagles is not a good breeder.

Sincerely Scenthounds

Member of this group, which include Bassets, Beagles, Black and Tan Coonhounds, and Bloodhounds, are almost universally friendly and amiable and often form close bonds with their owners. They are primarily interested in one thing—the scent of their prey. Don't think you can safely allow your scenthound off lead (ever): he will follow his nose until he can't remember where he is anymore, and he won't come home. You'll have to go looking for him. Scenthounds can learn to live amicably with their natural prey (rabbits and such) but need to be supervised closely.

• A quality breeder will give you the dog's registration papers and, for a puppy, the so-called "blue slip." This enables you to apply for full registration. An adult dog will come with a full registration certificate, a white piece of paper with a purple border. (There will be a transfer of ownership form on the back.) You should also get a pedigree with your dog, which goes back three generations. You can apply to the AKC for a longer one if you want, for a fee. The papers should come with the puppy. Don't let the breeder tell you she will send them later. (I fell for this myself years ago when I purchased my first Irish Setter. The papers never came, and while I am reasonably sure my Flannery was an Irish Setter, I never did get the proof of it.)

Puppies should be raised in the breeder's home and meet lots of friendly people.

• A good breeder keeps any puppies for which she cannot find a quality home. She will not get rid of them by giving them away to a rescue organization, shelter, or the kid next door.

• A good breeder provides a written contract, and will agree to take back the puppy if, for any reason, the dog does not work out. This includes an unconditional health contract, agreeing to take back any puppy not found to be healthy by your veterinarian. She will also keep in touch long after the purchase. If you and the breeder live in different legal jurisdictions, the contract should include a special provision called the "forum selection clause" that states that any legal disputes between the parties must be resolved in the state or legal jurisdiction in which the seller resides. (This is advantageous to the seller, of course, but it is the only reasonable way it can be done.)

• A good breeder has her puppies temperament tested by someone certified to do so. The temperament test rates each puppy, among other things, on shyness and aggression. Ask to see the results of the test. Later in this chapter, I provide you with a few things you can do on your own, but a real test by a real expert is also important.

Your puppy should be clean, healthy, and well taken care of.

Unfortunately, not everyone who shows dogs is well-informed or even cares about important health and temperament issues. Some very nice-looking dogs have a shyness or aggression problem that makes them poor choices for a family pet.

• A good breeder will give you references from former customers. Be sure to call them and ask about the health and temperament of the dogs they bought. Also inquire as to whether the breeder was supportive during their adjustment period or if she was helpful if a problem came up. Of course, if a breeder had a problem with a client or dog, you're not likely to be offered that information. It is still a "buyer beware" world.

• Choose a breeder who raises her puppies in her home—not outside in a kennel. A house-raised dog will be better socialized when you bring him home. Living in a home environment from the very beginning will get your future dog accustomed to the sights and sounds of everyday human life—vacuum cleaners, blaring stereos, screaming and running kids. Ideally, this socialization should be accomplished before the puppy is eight weeks old. By 12 weeks, it's much harder—and by the fifth month, it's extremely difficult to "re-program" an unsocialized or undersocialized puppy. Each puppy should receive individual attention from the breeder daily.

• The responsible breeder does pedigree and genetic research before breeding. Some first-time buyers are concerned by what they perceive as incest when they examine the pedigree of their prospective dog. In dog circles, this is called line-breeding. Technically, a line-bred dog is one in which a particular dog's name appears more than once on a three or four-generation pedigree. Line breeding is done to produce more uniformity in the offspring–in other words, to get more predictable and uniform results. However, unless the forebears are of good conformation quality and free of genetic faults, line breeding can be dangerous. And even when the relatives appear perfect, the lessening of the gene pool, which repeated line breeding involves, can be damaging to the breed as whole, even while it benefits your own particular puppy.

• A good breeder keeps her puppies in immaculate surroundings. A filthy kennel area means the breeder does not care about the welfare of her dogs and compromises the health of the puppies and their parents.

• Most importantly, trust your instincts. If the breeder seems evasive, uncommunicative, or noncommittal, or something feels "not quite right," there is probably something wrong.

The well-bred dog comes from well-bred parents.

The Well-Bred Dog

It might be said that a well-bred dog comes from a responsible breeder. And while this rule is true enough for general purposes, there are plenty of exceptions on both sides. I have seen "well-bred" dogs fail in each of these categories, while I have seen puppy mill dogs pass on all counts. Here are the criteria:

• The well-bred dog is a fine physical specimen. He looks good and moves with grace. Further, he meets most of the criteria listed in the breed standard. (This is more important for show dogs than for pets, of course.) His height, weight, coat type and color, and body proportions fall within the parameters of the breed standard. His eyes and nose are the right color. If the dog you are considering doesn't meet all these specifications, take a closer look. Some criteria in the breed standard are a matter of preference. (How many times a tail curls, or how erect the ears are has no bearing on the dog's condition.) I have owned Bassets with long hair, an English Springer Spaniel way over breed standard size, and dogs with other "undesirable" qualities. Other factors, however, may be more critical. It's up to you to educate yourself about your prospective dog's breed standard. If you are planning on showing, the physical aspect of a well-bred dog takes on increased importance, but it should never take precedence over the health and character of the dog.

• The well-bred dog is a healthy dog from healthy parents. He is free from genetic problems that may plague the breed, especially skin disease, hip dysplasia, epilepsy, and cancer. I don't mean to say that such dogs cannot be precious and beloved pets. I do mean these conditions are ones we are trying to eliminate.

• The well-bred dog has a breed-appropriate temperament; a temperament suitable for a pet (which I assume is what you are looking for). To my mind this is the most important criterion of all. A dog with a poor temperament, particularly an aggressive temperament, is a huge liability to you, himself, his breed, and the neighborhood. Finding a good temperament is much more difficult in some breeds than others. This is because temperament is primarily inherited. Most breeds developed for guarding, fighting, and protection are going to have a more aggressive disposition than sporting dogs or hounds. In breeds not bred for protection, there is no excuse whatever for a puppy to show aggressive or antisocial behavior. Such a dog is not well bred, no matter how beautiful it is, how healthy it is, or how glorious a pedigree he carries.

The Application Process

Both breeders and rescues will ask you to fill out an

Terrific Toys

These feisty little dogs need less room than their larger counterparts and are often excellent choices for seniors. They can also be lifted easily in case they need to be carried into a car for a trip to the vet. On the other hand, many toy breeds are hard to house-train, can be excessively noisy, and have a low level of tolerance for children. All are rather fragile and require careful handling.

The breeder will ask you questions about your home and lifestyle.

Part 1

application. Questions may include seemingly nosy ones such as:

• Do you own or rent? If you rent, you may be asked for your landlord's name and phone number. Many times renters get a dog and simply hope the landlord will give and in and change the rules once he sees how cute it is. That doesn't usually happen, however, and the dog ends up back in rescue.

• Is your dwelling a house, apartment, or mobile home? Breeders and rescues need to know how much room you have, and, for some breeds, if they need to climb stairs.

• Do you have a fenced yard? This is always a plus, and, for some breeds, practically a necessity. If you do not have a fenced yard, you'll need to do a lot of walking your pet. The application may ask you details about the fencing type and height.

Enlist your whole family in choosing the right puppy.

• Please list the name and phone number of your veterinarian. Most responsible breeders and rescue organizations will give your vet a call to make sure that you are accustomed to giving your pets standard care or better.

• How many adults live in your home? How many children? What are their ages? Not all dog breeds or lines within breeds are good with young children. Others love to be in a big group of them.

• How much time will your dog need to spend alone every day? Where will he be housed during that time? If indoors for a long period, how will his elimination needs be handled? Most dogs do best with someone home a lot, although certain breeds seem to do pretty well on their own all day. Regardless, someone needs to be responsible for taking the dog out regularly, especially if you are purchasing a puppy and he needs to be housetrained.

• What other pets do you own? How long have you had each one? Some breeds don't do well with other dogs or with cats.

• Why do you want this breed? Breeders and rescues use this question not only to determine your goals but to see if you have realistic expectations about the breed in question.

• Where will the dog sleep at night? Obviously the breeder wants to know if your dog will be safe and happy. While some breeds don't mind an occasional night camping out, most pet dogs should be in the house with you at night.

If you get turned down, ask why. Find out what you can do to qualify or if the breeder thinks another type or breed of dog may suit you better.

Supremely Sighthounds

Sighthounds share the searching, independent spirit of scenthounds; however, they tend to be more aloof with people and a lot more dangerous around small pets, including cats and Chihuahuas.

Picking a Puppy

If possible, take along your whole family as well as a breed-wise friend to help you choose the puppy of your dreams. (The best place to make such a friend is by joining your local breed club.) Let everyone in the family be invested in the final decision, but listen carefully to what your mentor has to say about each puppy. Pay close attention. Buy with your head as well as with your heart. A good breeder will help you choose the right pup for your family. Dominant puppies are for strong, knowledgeable families; very submissive ones are for quiet and gentle people. Very dominant and shy puppies, for opposite reasons, are not best for families with small children. Highly intelligent, curious puppies are for people who are willing to closely supervise them every second.

Look for healthy, active, friendly puppies. You should see how each puppy behaves with his littermates, alone, with you, with his mom, and with the rest of your family. Take your time in assessing this interaction; it's a good way to spot which puppies are likely to turn out to be dominant. One excellent way to assess the adult personality of the puppies is by taking a good look at the mother dog. Don't expect a mom to be brimming with joy at the prospect of large strangers poking around at her puppies, but she shouldn't be aggressive either. Watch the puppy's reactions to his littermates – it's a rule of thumb that his behavior to his littermates will indicate his responses to his humans. If the puppies have any full siblings at the establishment, examine them for temperament as well.

The temperament of each puppy will be different. The one you choose should be suited

The puppy you choose should be alert, active, and curious about you.

to your needs. A dog with "show potential" should be alert and very outgoing. A family pet or even a pup slated for formal obedience work may be more reserved. In general, the behavior that you see in puppyhood will become more pronounced as the puppy grows. For example, submissive puppies turn into more submissive adults; dominant puppies become more dominant adults.

You can also make some observations of the puppy's apparent health. A healthy puppy, whether pet or show quality, will have clear eyes, a bright coat, and a shiny, clean, slightly cool nose. His gums will be a nice healthy pink, not pale or dark red. He should feel solid to the touch; a distended belly may indicate worms. His skin should be pink and elastic with no crusty or red patches, and certainly no fleas or ticks should be visible. No diarrhea should be in evidence; puppy stools should be dark and well formed. The puppy should be able to walk and run without any obvious difficulty.

Ask the breeder if you can briefly test the puppy's temperament yourself. This is best done without the mother dog, littermates, or anyone else present, but some breeders may understandably be reluctant to allow you, a complete stranger, to be alone with the puppy. Still, you can inquire. If the breeder wishes to remain present, you can ask that she step back into the corner while you evaluate your prospective pet.

When you pick the puppy up and cradle him in your arms, he should feel heavier than he looks. That's a sign of health. A good-tempered puppy will also allow you to stroke him all over and look into his eyes, mouth, and ears without too much objection. Dogs who accept such gestures will more likely become easygoing adults. Puppies who stare you confidently in the eye and refuse to look away may one day challenge you for leadership. Any puppy that yelps, growls, runs away, or tries to bite may be physically ill or temperamentally unsuitable to be your pet. (Mouthing, on the other hand, is normal, and the pup's main way of investigating who is touching him.)

SHY GUYS

Many members of these breeds are shy and require consistent, gentle treatment to bring out the best in them.

Chihuahua	Toy Poodle
Shetland Sheepdog	Greyhound
Italian Greyhound	Cavalier King Charles Spaniel
Whippet	
Papillon	Borzoi
Saluki	

Ask the breeder for help when choosing a show-prospect puppy.

Call the puppy to you to see how he responds. Immediate compliance suggests a responsive, obedient adult dog–something most dog owners long for. Remember, however, that there are strong breed differences here. Retrievers are likely to be much more responsive than Chow Chows.

When the puppy is facing the opposite direction, make a noise and note his reaction. If there is none, he may be deaf, a common problem in some breeds. If he runs terrified into the corner, he may be too shy. A puppy that fights or struggles to get away may be more dominant than you can handle, especially as he grows larger. If the puppy refuses to come at all, he just may not like you–or people in general. If you really like a dog that "failed," come back the next day and try the tests again. Of course, one such test means little; try to visit the litter a couple of times before making a decision.

Pet and Show Quality

A show-quality dog is one whose looks and movement would make him a star in the show ring. He may also make an excellent and loving pet. A pet-quality dog is one who has a conformation flaw, often minor, that would make his success in the show ring unlikely. If you don't care about showing, it's often possible to get a really excellent puppy who has a fault that would hurt a show career but not affect his "pet-ability." So-called defects like the

Puppies should spend time with littermates to socialize with other dogs.

Tireless Workers

Dogs in the Herding or Working Group are no-nonsense dogs that thrive with a specific job to do; many of them do best with strong, experienced owners who can take command. They also need a tremendous amount of exercise.

wrong-colored eyes, a mismarked coat, the wrong ear carriage, or a missing tooth does not stop a dog from being an excellent pet.

The truth is that it is often very hard to tell at a young age how the dog will turn out. Many a promising pup has flunked out in the show ring, while occasionally a pet-quality dog unexpectedly "blooms" and turns into a show champion, much to the surprise of his owners. As an owner, your first concern should be getting a healthy dog with a sweet disposition, whose ancestors are of good stock. Of course, he should look nice too, but as I said, you can't tell too much when a puppy is only eight weeks old. At that stage, they're all cute. If you are really interested in buying a show-quality dog, you have to wait until he is at least 9 to 12 weeks old.

Although finding a show-quality pup is always a gamble, you can maximize your chances by taking along a mentor from your local breed club who can help you make a selection. If you don't know where to find the nearest breed club, contact the American Kennel Club for a list of breed clubs; then contact individual clubs for a list of breeders in your state or region. Look for a sturdy, well-balanced puppy with a good front, good angulation, eyes of the correct shape and color, and a correct ear and tail set. These qualities are present even in quite young dogs.

How About Two Puppies?

The advantage of getting two puppies is obvious; they will play together, suffer less anxiety when leaving the litter, and provide you with lots of entertainment. But two puppies are twice the vet bills and twice the training. Interestingly, the question as to whether or not to get two puppies depends somewhat on the breed. Hounds, who are natural pack animals, are a good choice for two puppies, but it's a bad idea with retrievers and some sighthounds, like Pharaoh Hounds; the puppies may bond to each other instead of to you! There's another consideration as well–some day those two cute puppies will become two very old dogs, and you may have the heartbreak of losing both within a short time.

The Right Paperwork
The Bill of Sale

Don't leave the breeder's without a bill of sale. This is the legal proof that you have paid the breeder for your dog. It may be part of the contract or in addition to it, and it may contain some clauses required by state law. Some states, for instance, require that the seller take a dog back and refund your money if the pet becomes ill within 48 hours from the time of purchase.

The Contract

The contract should specify the price of the dog, including a deposit. The contract should state if some of the money will be refunded if you spay or neuter your pet, a proviso sometimes added for a pet-quality dog. The clause should include what proof of neutering or spaying you need to supply, when it should be done, and when the money should be returned to you.

A purebred puppy comes with a lot of paperwork.

The agreement should also designate the primary intended use of the dog, whether it is for pet, show, or performance (like obedience, herding, tracking, or hunting). It may also require the owner to microchip the puppy, although more and more responsible breeders are microchipping their own litters. Microchips can be implanted into the dog to help identify him if he is ever lost or stolen.

Part 1

Most shelters and rescues will screen dogs for health or behavior problems.

The contract should include a health section, with a clause that stipulates you should take the puppy to your veterinarian with 72 hours. If the vet finds the dog to be unsound, the contract should stipulate that the breeder will take the dog back for replacement or full refund. The contract should also state how the breeder will deal with any inherited health problem that might show up.

It also should certify, as a matter of course, that the dog is purebred and eligible for AKC registration. AKC registration is a rather a mystery to some people, but it really shouldn't be. When puppies are born, the breeder registers the whole litter by applying to the AKC. The AKC then sends a "blue slip" for each puppy. At the time of sale, the seller must supply a properly completed AKC registration application. The buyer registers the individual puppy in his name, or the seller may wish to stipulate the registered name. The buyer is responsible for submitting the dog's registration papers by completing the application and sending it in with the required fee. Once a dog is actually registered with the AKC, his name cannot be changed (officially). But don't let that stop you. If your dog's official name is Lord High Muckey Muck, but you want to call him Barney, that's fine.

This application to register the puppy must contain the breeder's signature, as well as the dog's full breeding information, including

• Breed, sex, and color of the dog

• Date of birth

• Registered names (and numbers) of the dog's sire and dam

• Breeder's name

The AKC then sends the buyer a registration certificate. It all sounds very official, and it is, of course. But remember that AKC registration does not guarantee the quality of a puppy. And while the AKC can now do DNA testing to help ensure the true parentage of a puppy, that may not mean much if the parents are unsound or unhealthy to begin with.

Most people care about AKC registration because it lets them participate in AKC activities like obedience, field trials, conformation shows, and agility (although some of the events also have non-AKC sponsors). But you can also get a nice dog from a shelter or a rescue and do many of these activities, especially agility, through other organizations that care nothing about whether your dog has papers or even if he is purebred.

Co-Ownership

While many show breeders like to "co-own" dogs with a show buyer, be aware of what you are getting into. The arrangement may include where a dog will reside, showing responsibilities and expenses, and breeding plan details, including who will pay for what. Arrangements should be made in advance for deciding if the dog will spend time with a handler or trainer, and what happens if the dog is not kept in correct show condition. There are no set rules for co-ownership, but various clauses may require you to (a) show the dog until its championship, which may take a long time and may require you to hire a professional handler; (b) if you have bought a bitch, to pay for some or all of the breeding expenses, while at the same time giving the breeder pick of the litter. This clause may hold good for every litter the bitch whelps. Unless you really know what you are getting into, I would stay away from this option. It can be complicated and people often are disappointed or surprised by the unexpected results of the contract.

Rescue or Shelter: The Other Ethical Option

Another wonderful option is to get your dog from a rescue or a shelter. Unfortunately, not all dogs have the good fortune to be born to a responsible breeder. Some got their start in unscrupulous puppy mills or were born to well-meaning but unknowledgeable backyard breeders. Many of these dogs are sold to people who can't care for them properly, and they end up in the shelter or a dog rescue.

Most counties are required to operate an animal shelter for impoundment of stray dogs and enforcement of cruelty and neglect laws. Some shelters are run as a private humane society that contracts with the county to provide these services; others are operated by the county itself. There are also private shelters that have no contract with any government agency. These are often small and need to rely heavily upon donations and volunteers. Most private shelters do not euthanize healthy, non-aggressive animals, as public shelters are sometimes forced to do for lack of space. Private shelters are not legally required to accept an animal, so they can generally care for the few they have for long periods while waiting for the right adopter to show up. Many shelters use the name SPCA ("Society for the Prevention of Cruelty of Animals") or "Humane Society." The shelter may or may not have connections to the national organization of the same name. (The national ASPCA is centered in New York City, while the Humane Society makes its headquarters in Washington, D.C.) So when you give to one, you are not necessarily helping to fund the other.

A rather recent player in the animal shelter sector is the breed rescue. Although there are all-breed and mixed breed rescues, most rescue groups deal with only one breed, about which the members are experts. Some of these are run by individuals who love the breed, while others are sponsored by local or national breed clubs or rescue networks.

Few breed rescues operate their own kennel or shelter; instead, most use a foster home system. This is a wonderful idea because the foster parents are usually experts on the breed who can carefully evaluate the animal before it is given up for adoption. Some rescues merely operate a referral service, but all can help with problems related to a breed, and

Aggressive Suggestions

No reputable rescue or shelter will adopt out an animal they know to be aggressive. I have found out, however, that in the case of aggression, owners are seldom honest with the shelter. They don't want the dog, but they don't want to have it euthanized either. So they lie to the shelter about its problems, telling the shelter that they have an allergic child, or that they are "moving." Do everything you can to make sure that you have all the history available on the dog before making the commitment to take him home.

It is true that some dogs from shelters may come with "baggage," but a good shelter or rescue will disclose that information and will offer to take back any dog who develops problems while in your care. Some experienced dog owners are willing to work with an animal that has health or behavior problems, although I don't recommend this for a first-time dog owner. Owning a healthy, good-tempered pet can be enough of a challenge for one's first venture into dogdom. After you get your feet wet, you might be up for more of a challenge.

most can arrange to remove a dog from a place where it can no longer be cared for. Finding a responsible dog rescue as a source for your dog is an honorable and kind thing to do. Many of these dogs simply need a loving home and an open heart. You may not get a show-ring champion, but you'll be doing something even better—you'll be saving a dog's life. Responsible and reputable shelters and rescues do temperament testing and health checks on their dogs, too. Many shelters also offer certificates for spay or neuter discount; some alter or sterilize all dogs before they adopt them out. Some shelters even include microchip identification with every animal.

The Key Test

One easy, no-risk way to test for temperament is to drop something small and noisy (like keys) on the floor in front of the dog. If he attacks them, you may be dealing with an aggressive dog, if he cowers and shakes, he may have serious problems with shyness.

You seldom know the history of a shelter animal, so you need to rely heavily upon the care and knowledge of the shelter people. You can also do some of the same tests discussed previously with an older dog. The main problems you want to avoid are aggression and timidity, both of which may be more common with shelter dogs than in the canine population in general.

Don't be afraid to ask questions, especially about the provenance of the animal. Dogs who were turned in by an owner may have been aggressive, had housetraining or behavior problems, or maybe the kids just got bored with the dog.

So, although some dogs may have behavioral or health problems, a good rescue or shelter will evaluate every dog in its care and can give you all the information you'll need to make an informed choice.

Rescue organizations can give you a lot of information about the breed.

Choosing a rescue or shelter dog means saving a life, and getting a companion who will be a faithful (and grateful!) friend. Some people, of course, prefer a puppy, but remember that most rescue dogs are already housetrained, out of the chewing stage, and happy just to tag along on an evening's walk. They are often incredibly loyal, and the perfect choice for many people. As Alisa Garbrick, of Basset Rescue of Old Dominion, writes, "I find that my rescued Bassets that I adopted are so grateful that you took them in and gave them a forever home–even more so than the pups I got from breeders."

The great advantage to breed rescue over shelters is that the people running them are truly experts and can offer a wide choice of dogs all from the same breed. Breed rescues can answer all your questions about the breed, and can advise you as to whether or not one of their charges is right for you. They make sure the dogs under their care have veterinary attention. Most spay or neuter their dogs as soon as they come into the system. They interview each would-be adopter carefully and ask many questions. They want to make sure that this placement will be the dog's last home. The breed rescue I work with does house visits and checks with the adopter's veterinarian.

Rescue dogs are seldom free, however, and for very good reasons. The rescue group I work with spent over $40,000 in vet bills last year; we recoup part of that cost by asking for an adoption fee. Older dogs or dogs with health problems may be a little less expensive. There's another reason as well–a psychological one. We have found that if people are not willing to pay a small fee to adopt a dog in the first place–what will they do if a big vet bill arrives?

Some people wrongly assume that if a dog is in rescue it must have severe behavior problems or be sick. This is simply not true. Many wonderful dogs are dumped because people get tired of them, move away, develop an allergy, get a divorce, or simply can't afford to keep a dog any more. Sometimes owners die. Sometimes the previous owners didn't understand the requirements of the breed in the first place. Some of the more ridiculous things I have heard include:

"I didn't know St. Bernards got so big."

"He doesn't seem to like being home alone 14 hours a day."

"He seems to want a lot of attention."

"I didn't know Akitas could be so hard to handle."

"My Beagle keeps getting lost."

"My Husky is just shedding everywhere, no matter how much I comb him."

"This terrier keeps digging holes in the yard."

The Marvelous Mix

I should say a word about mixed breeds or, as they used to be called, mutts, mongrels, and curs. I happen to like mixed breeds. They are not only a tribute to their parents' ingenuity, but some are blessed with what is called hybrid vigor, which to some degree ensures that they are healthier even than their more carefully bred counterparts. Hybrid vigor, by the way, is term very often misunderstood. It refers to increased productivity and performance in the *first generation* of crossbred animals produced by the mating of dissimilar breeds. The improvement is lost if the hybrids are interbred. Thus it is not necessarily true that mutts are healthier than purebreds. Mixed breed puppies may keep their ultimate size and disposition a secret, but I think they have a unique charm of their own that can never quite be matched by their oh-so-boring-and-uniform pedigreed pals. It is true, however, that since mixed breed dogs draw from a larger gene pool, they are less likely to be cursed with some of the inherited traits that plague purebreds, unless, of course, each parent carries a gene for the condition. This is certainly possible with widespread problems like hip dysplasia and PRA. And a homeless mixed breed adult dog is a unique animal–you'll have the only one like it.

A mixed breed can be a joy to own–and you are saving a life!

The Keys to Canine Contentment (and Yours)

The right dog, carefully chosen, will be your friend for life. He will share your home, shower you with affection, and stand by you in hard times, and you will do the same for him. Choosing the right dog will bring you years of happiness, lots of adventure, and a special love. However, choosing the wrong dog may bring frustration, disappointment, and, in too many cases, a last agonizing trip to the animal shelter. Because you are the selector (at least in most cases), you bear the heavy burden of making the right decision.

The age-old quarrel rages on—nature versus nurture. And while in most fields of inquiry, including that of human development, scientists

Choosing your dog carefully will benefit both dog and owner.

A dog's genetic makeup dictates a portion of his character and temperament.

are coming down more and more in the "nature" camp, the dog world has been rather unaccountably slow to catch on. Of course, there is some truth to the statement: "It's all about training." Experienced handlers can do a lot to control a dog's natural behavior. Still, the hard core of fact is that breeding, more than any other single criterion, determines the temperament of a dog. The more we know about genetics, the more we discover how much it governs our behavior.

Training, while of enormous benefit to every dog, has limited applications. It can't countermand biology. People who run the Iditarod don't use Scottish Terriers. (All right, Doug Suter ran the race a few times with some Standard Poodles on the team, but he didn't win.) People don't ask Chihuahuas to hunt pheasant. Bulldogs make poor agility prospects. Police officers don't choose Beagles as attack dogs. Pekingese make remarkably poor sheepherders. (I am just guessing here. Maybe no one has ever tried training one to herd sheep.) Just as no amount of training can make a Maltese look like a Greater Swiss Mountain Dog, no amount of training can make a Bloodhound act like a Toy Poodle.

There are always exceptions, of course. I have known Chow Chows who doted on strangers. I had a Basset Hound who enjoyed swimming, although she wasn't very good at it. I once met a Bulldog who excelled at obedience work. I have seen Labradors that couldn't stand kids. A friend of mine had a Beagle who never looked at a rabbit and preferred hanging around her owner every second. I even heard of a Siberian Husky who was afraid of the snow. But these are exceptions. As a rule, dogs follow the dictates of their heritage. That's why we have dog breeds in the first place. People recognized quite early on that desirable physical characteristics and appropriate temperament could be passed on, fairly reliably, from one generation to the next.

Different needs and varying human preferences shaped the way breeds developed. Some breeds were bred to do one thing superbly well. Others were charged with a multitude of

Tough Guys

While members of these breeds can provide reliable protection, they must be properly trained:

Akita	Chesapeake Bay Retriever
Giant Schnauzer	Doberman Pinscher
German Shepherd	Standard Schnauzer
Anatolian Shepherd	Bouvier Des Flandres
Rottweiler	Bullmastiff
Briard	
Kuvasz	

tasks. The Germans, in particular, seemed obsessed with developing a single dog that could find, tackle, and kill any living creature, and herd livestock and guard houses in its spare time. They were never completely successful, but the multitude of German breeds today attests to their earnestness in trying.

Unless you like a challenge that puts you and your dog at risk of permanent unhappiness, it is always best to play it safe and select a dog whose breeding makes it likely he will be what you want him to be. People who attempt to train dogs away from their heritage are fighting a tough uphill battle, swimming against the tide, shouting against the wind, or whatever other metaphor you prefer. Let's put it this way: It's hard, and, in some cases, impossible.

However, none of this means that there is a specific "gene," or even a group of genes, that makes a dog have an aggressive or unstable temperament, any more than there is a specific gene or group of genes

Good temperament is usually passed down through generations.

that makes a dog a good herding dog. Genes don't code for behaviors–all a gene does is to code for amino acid sequences in protein molecules. So what's the connection? Genes modify the basic elements of behavior and control relative threshold for stimulus and intensity. For example, it has been shown that dogs that guard livestock have lower levels of dopamine (a neurotransmitter) than dogs that herd livestock. Things like this make a difference. It is important for guarding dogs to be less stimulated by the movements of sheep than herding dogs.

Shyness and aggression are also qualities that have been shown by researchers to be predominantly genetically controlled irrespective of socialization. This doesn't mean that the genetics for aggression are locked into a breed. For example, breeders have been very successful in softening the temperaments of Dobermans, while keeping more valued characteristics, by continually breeding less aggressive individuals. There is no inherent reason why this cannot be done with any breed that has a bad reputation. But it is something that can only be accomplished by careful breeding. Training is not enough.

A study published in the Journal of the American Veterinary Medical Association in 1985 found that most of the variation between breeds can be accounted for by one of three elements: reactivity, aggression, and trainability. These elements, in various proportions, account for most of the diverse behavior that we see among the various dog breeds today.

A dog's behavior is determined by training and breeding.

Every dog is an individual and can defy breed "generalities." What I list in my dog profiles are tendencies, not certainties. There are lethargic Dalmatians and over-excitable Bulldogs. There are aggressive Labradors and pussy-cat Komondorok. In this book we can only generalize, keeping in mind the attendant and necessary evils thereof.

Obviously I did not rely solely upon my own experience is developing these profiles. I have owned dogs all my life, mostly hounds and sporting breeds, with a few toy dogs as well. However, no one person is learned enough to qualify as expert on all breeds. So I have had to rely a good deal on the opinions of people I respect. Of course, my consultants may also be biased. It is an incontrovertible fact that the people who know the most about each individual breed are breeders. But breeders may also be prejudiced not only in favor of their breed over others, but also in favor of certain characteristics they try to produce in their breed. This can account for varying descriptions of character. This is one reason why I did not rely upon breeders only as consultants, but also surveyed experienced pet owners, including people who have no particular attachment to any one breed. They proved to have the most interesting opinions of all. To get an insider's view of the possible problems with a particular breed, examine the breed standard and read between the lines. If the standard says that the breed should never be timid, for example, you can bet that excessive timidity is a problem the breeders are trying to correct.

Have a Nice Day!
Some dogs are friendlier to people than others; for example, the English Setter, Golden Retriever, Irish Setter, and Beagle never met a person they didn't like.

Character traits, for example, were assembled from both my own knowledge and with the suggestions of long-time breeders and owners, many of whom quailed at the thought of saying something "negative" about their beloved breed, but who bravely did so anyway. No breed is perfect, and no breed is perfect for every family. Skillful training and individual genetic quirks can make important differences in how each dog may react. That being said, I'm going to talk a little bit about some important considerations you need to make in choosing your dog.

Although breeds can share characteristics, each dog is an individual.

Character

To my mind, nothing is more important than the character of the dog you choose, and, remember, character is mostly inherited and thus closely related to breeding. Training can modify, but not alter, the basic character of any dog. Of course, not every person wants the same character in his

Water Dogs

If you live near the water, treat yourself to a breed that can take full advantage of the opportunity to swim, such as:

Curly-Coated Retriever	American Water Spaniel
Labrador Retriever	Portuguese Water Dog
Chesapeake Bay Retriever	Flat-Coated Retriever
Newfoundland	Golden Retriever
Irish Water Spaniel	Poodle

or her pet. Some people prefer a adoring lapdog, others an independent partner in play.

Character is bred into dogs in the same way that instinctive ability is. In fact, ability is largely a function of character, rather than any special combination of muscles. Gordon Setters have the physical ability to herd sheep–they're just not interested. The character traits associated with herding ability remain with the herding dog whether there are any sheep around or not.

Some breeds seem to possess a sense of humor and are eager to please.

Make Me Laugh

The following breeds seem to have a sense of humor.

Basset Hound

Chinese Crested   Pug

Bulldog   Old English Sheepdog

                                    Spinone Italiano

For an interesting sidelight on the possible defects of your breed's character, read the breed standard. If the standard says something like, "Should never be shy," it means that shyness is a problem in the breed. The German Shepherd standard informs us that dogs that bite the judge will be disqualified from the show ring. Actually, any dog of any breed that bites the judge is disqualified, but when a standard goes out of its way to mention the possibility, one has to wonder.

I should also state the obvious: Dogs are individuals, and while a certain character trait may be true of the breed as a whole, it may not apply to a particular dog. With this caveat clearly in mind, it is safe and prudent to generalize about breeds. It would not serve you well to merely remark that every dog is different, and that you are basically on your own trying to find a dog whose temperament you can manage.

I have left off "intelligent" under character. All dogs are about as smart as they want to be, and intelligence means difference things under different circumstances. While a Bloodhound is unlikely to be an Obedience Trial Champion, he is hard to beat at tracking. Besides, aficionados of each breed always claim that their breed is brilliant.

Sometimes you will note apparently opposite characteristics being assigned to the same breed. There are two possible reasons. One reason may be that there is a wider than usual divergence among individual members of the breed; some, for example, being very serious, others carefree, so I might use both adjectives. In other cases, I received enough contradictory descriptions from my consultants that I decided to play it safe and put down both characteristics.

One problem in trying to ascertain a dog's character is trying to find out exactly what that character is. There are not only differences between individual dogs, which we expect, and disputes among experts, which we also expect, but there are frequently internal contradictions within sources. In researching this book, I have come upon this

The original purpose of your dog plays a big part in his personality.

Part 1

phenomenon over and over. In one obviously hypothetical example, the writer asserts that the Northern Flatland Retrieving Moosedog is just jim-dandy with kids; ten pages later, he solemnly warns you against owning one if you have any children under 12 because the Northern Flatland Retrieving Moosedog is unreliable, irritable, aggressive, and very large.

Origin

This refers to the area or region where it is commonly believed the breed originated. Sometimes this is nothing more than a guess, because we simply aren't sure where a breed got its start. For very old breeds, the problem is more complex, because ancient people used different standards to determine what a breed was. For them, a breed was a particular group of dogs that were accomplished at an assigned task. Various members of a herding "breed" might look quite different, something that we still see to some extent in working Border Collies, who often bear scant resemblance to their show counterparts–or even to each other.

Size should be a consideration when choosing a dog.

Original Purpose

While we are pretty sure of the primary function of many breeds, we do well to remember that many of them had more than one purpose.

Physical Attributes

The physical appearance of a dog is the first thing we see, and, for many people, it's a determining factor. It shouldn't be–at least it shouldn't be a determining factor in favor of a dog, although it could conceivably be the single most important criterion in deciding against a certain breed. Even the dog that looks just right may be all wrong for you. Also, some breeds are regularly shown in this country with docked tails and/or cropped ears, of which I have noted many.

Size

I give the minimum and maximum average height at the withers for each breed, as well as minimum and maximum acceptable weight. My listing does not always correspond to the breed standard, since in some breeds, animals

74

Jogging Partners

These dogs are great company on a jog can physically handle the effort, if conditioned slowly and properly. Mind the weather though; dogs, like people, have problems handling the heat or cold.

Dalmatian	Standard Schnauzer
Irish Setter	Doberman Pinscher
Portuguese Water Dog	Greyhound
Siberian Husky (but not in the heat, please. Anything above 40 degrees is the heat.)	Saluki
	Whippet
Airedale Terrier	Border Collie (but this brainy breed needs so much more)

routinely run larger or smaller than this standard. In many breeds, it is very common for show dogs to be larger than field dogs and for pets to be bigger than either.

In most breeds (but not all), males are larger than females. In a few cases, the difference is considerable. (This is called sexual dimorphism and is characteristic of human beings as well.) If you are buying a puppy and size is critical, ask the breeder if the males are likely to be much larger or heavier than the females.

While most people have a prejudice in favor of a certain-sized dog, we shouldn't let our biases be the sole determinant. For example, many big dogs are not right for small apartments, older people, timid, easily intimated people, or couples with toddlers. Toy breeds carry their own risk factors; many are easily knocked over or dropped by rambunctious youngsters, and a frail elderly person could get hurt tripping over a Basset Hound. There are many exceptions, of course, but common sense tells us to choose a dog of the right size for our needs and ability to handle safely.

In this section I have also noted cases where dogs are notorious barkers or diggers. While some people want their dogs to warn of visitors, the dogs I have listed as barkers may bark to the point of annoyance. Digging is also usually frowned upon, but many breeds such as

The standard of the breed will tell you the correct coat and color of your dog.

terriers and Siberian Huskies dig by nature. (Most dogs dig just for the fun of it, but others do use it as an escape tool). If dogs would only bark when they were digging, of course, owners would be alerted to their nefarious activity, and go out to stop it, Sadly, most dogs, even barky ones, are ominously quiet when they dig.

Color

Under this heading, I have included all the acceptable colors of each breed. If a breeder tries to sell you a different color from one listed, that color is non-standard and probably not acceptable. If any particular color is preferred, I have so stated. For example, Scottish Terriers come in several colors, although we usually think of them as black. There are, of course, some unconfessed preferences. For example, many show judges prefer a red Chow Chow to a black one, merely because they can see its features more clearly. Other judges have personal preferences. Dappled Dachshunds, for example, were rarely seen because judges did not prefer them. Now they're showing up in the ring again. A lot of show judges seem to like a lemon-and-white or red-and-white Beagle over an equally nice tricolor. You just have to decide what is important to you.

Coat Type and Grooming

Some people actually enjoy grooming dogs, while other people (like me) would rather be doing something else. Don't select a breed whose grooming requirements are more than you can realistically handle. Some breeds, like terriers, Cocker Spaniels, and Poodles, require regular professional trims to look their best, while others, like Weimaraners and Pointers, are basically wash-and-wear dogs. Of course, if you are planning on showing a dog, the grooming commitment rises exponentially. This is especially true with some breeds whose elaborate coats require hours of professional skill. For example, a show terrier's coat needs to plucked or stripped in a time-consuming process; pet terriers can simply be clipped. Show Yorkies, Old English Sheepdogs, and Maltese have incredibly long and spectacular coats; your lucky pet, however, can get away with a quick trim.

In addition, some dogs, notably many hounds and some water dogs, have an oily skin than may lead to unpleasant doggy odor. Again, it all depends on what's important to you. And while you may think the perfect answer is the hairless variety of Chinese Crested, be advised that this breed needs to be generously lathered with suntan lotion before it goes out in the sun. And as you might expect, many longhaired breeds suffer in the heat, and very shorthaired dogs (even big ones like Doberman Pinschers) can't handle the cold.

Certain breeds require extensive grooming, especially for the show ring.

Professional Grooming

Obviously it doesn't hurt to have any dog professionally groomed, especially if he rolls in something horrible. It's also true that no dog really *needs* to be professionally groomed, especially if you yourself are handy with the clippers. For general purposes, however, and assuming that you're like me (not knowing left-handed scissors from right-handed ones), I list those breeds that are commonly taken to the groomers for shaping and trimming.

Shedding

Don't get easy grooming mixed up with allergy potential. People allergic to dog hair often find that terriers and Poodles shed very little, while a Dalmatian or Siberian Husky seems to float in an eternal aura of loose hair. What is shed most often is the undercoat, and dogs with little or no undercoat tend to shed less than dogs with a lot of undercoat. White dogs seem to shed more than dark ones; northern breeds with heavy double coats are supposed to shed only twice a year, but because they no longer live in arctic conditions, they may shed at any time or all the time. Dogs with longer hair, like setters or Afghans, have a longer shed cycle than shorter-haired dogs, so they actually shed less. While I have listed the shedding potential of each breed, it's

> ### Salon Style
>
> If you are considering showing your dog, be sure to speak to a handler about the proper haircut. Most pet groomers aren't qualified to groom or trim a show coat, which requires an exact knowledge of the breed standard and the consequent ability to minimize flaws and enhance strong points.

Part 1

A regular grooming routine helps ensure the health of your dog.

Dogs Without the Doggy Smell

You know that doggy smell—the one that precedes some breeds before the enter the room. These dogs are relatively odor-free:

Whippet	Standard Schnauzer
Italian Greyhound	Finnish Spitz
Siberian Husky	Dachshund
Poodle	Pharaoh Hound
Saluki	

important to remember that shedding is variable within breeds, at least to some degree. Regular grooming and proper nutrition keeps shedding down to its natural minimum.

Health Concerns

Each breed has specific health issues. Many of these diseases are heritable and have developed, almost of necessity, with the rise of specific breeds. Only wild, randomly bred animals are mostly free of dangerous genetic diseases. Responsible breeders are doing their best to eliminate serious genetic problems in their breed, but because many are working with a small gene pool to begin with (a problem than can be exacerbated with so-called line breeding or inbreeding), it is hard to eradicate all problems. You can do your part by finding out what diseases are in the breed and line you are looking at. Luckily for adopters (as opposed to puppy buyers), many genetic problems show up in very young dogs, and they are not bred. In this section, I have listed the most common health ailments, some by their abbreviations, which can be found in the glossary in the back of this book.

Certain orthopedic problems, like hip and elbow dysplasia, threaten many larger breeds, while toy breeds have a predilection for patellar luxation (loose kneecaps). Eye problems, allergies and skin diseases, and von Willebrand's disease (a bleeding disorder) can be inherited and affect many breeds. Short-snouted or pug-faced dogs are prone to breathing difficulties and respiratory ailments, some of which are so bad that airlines won't permit them to fly. (They snore, too.) Many sighthounds, like Greyhounds and Salukis, are sensitive to anesthesia. As a rule, the heaviest and largest breeds tend to live shorter lives than their smaller cousins. In this section, I list some problems that may affect your breed more commonly. However, most of these problems are fairly rare.

Before being bred, the hips or elbows of breeds vulnerable to dysplasia should be x-rayed and the radiographs examined by OFA or PennHip™. OFA makes preliminary readings before the dog reaches two years of age and permanent readings after two years of age. PennHip™, which some veterinarians consider more practical, takes three separate radiographs to check hip joint flexibility.

Eye tests are performed by veterinary ophthalmologists and sent to the Canine Eye Registration Foundation (CERF) for certification. Eye tests must be repeated annually; however, hip x-rays must only be done once unless the breeder chooses to do a preliminary check on a young dog. Tests for many bleeding disorders, including von Willebrand's, can also be performed, and affected animals eliminated from the breeding stock.

However, don't let this litany of potential health problems frighten you. Your dog probably will not get any of the diseases listed. The list simply means that these diseases are more common in that breed than in others. In cases where there is genetic predisposition, your dog or its parents should be screened if possible.

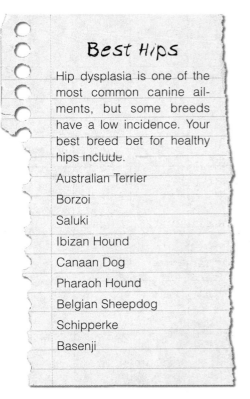

Best Hips

Hip dysplasia is one of the most common canine ailments, but some breeds have a low incidence. Your best breed bet for healthy hips include.

Australian Terrier

Borzoi

Saluki

Ibizan Hound

Canaan Dog

Pharaoh Hound

Belgian Sheepdog

Schipperke

Basenji

Make sure your dog and his parents have been certified as healthy.

Allergy Prone

While any dog can become allergic, the following breeds appear to be more susceptible. Allergic dogs tend to skin problems. They will scratch, rather than sniffle or sneeze.

Labrador Retriever	Lhasa Apso
Bichon Frise	Miniature Schnauzer
Dalmatian	Rottweiler
Golden Retriever	Poodle
Collie (food allergies)	Pug
Chinese Shar-Pei	Shih Tzu
Boxer	West Highland White Terrier
German Shepherd Dog	Skye Terrier
Irish Setter	Boston Terrier
Cocker Spaniel	Scottish Terrier

Exercise

Before you choose a dog, realistically assess how much time you can give to your dog's exercise needs. Any dog who does not get sufficient exercise is likely to develop behavior problems. Energy level can be linked directly to metabolism, which is partly a function of breed. Diet also plays a role, as does climate. The size of the dog is only indirectly linked to exercise needs. Many small dogs need proportionally much more exercise than larger ones, but the toy breeds can usually satisfy their requirements by tearing around your apartment. Some very large breeds, like Saint Bernards and Great Danes, actually do not require nearly as much exercise as you might think. They can even be kept in an apartment, as long as they get a good walk twice a day. On the other hand, setters and pointers need acres of free-range exercise to be kept at their happiest; if given enough room, most of them will self-exercise. Sighthounds, like Deerhounds, Rhodesian Ridgebacks, and Greyhounds, although they need a lot of exercise to keep trim, need stimulus to get it. They won't just take off on their own around the field. This is true of many other individual dogs as well. Just because you have a fenced-in yard does not mean automatically that your dog will use it to exercise. Many apartment dogs that are walked daily get much more exercise than a perpetually fenced suburban dog.

Housing

Here I indicate whether or not a dog is suited to live an urban lifestyle. Nearly all dogs are fine for the country or suburban home, as long as they are not left outside at night. As a rule, of course, small dogs are better suited to apartments than are large ones. But this is a rule with many exceptions. Certain large dogs are phlegmatic and unflappable enough to thrive in the city, while some small dogs are too energetic or noisy to be ideal urban pets.

Interaction with Others

The first part of the category notes how well the average member of the breed behaves with children. (I am referring to the family's children here. Other children can be classed as strangers.) A dog that is "good with children" means that he is not likely to challenge them for dominance, and that the breed tends to be tolerant. Of course, there are limits to tolerance, and the most even tempered of dogs can be provoked. Not all breeds that are good with kids are playful or make good companion dogs in the sense that they will play fetch for hours or are safe off a leash. Those qualities are listed elsewhere.

On the other hand, just because I have a breed listed as "not good with children," it doesn't mean your family can't own such a dog. It means you have to be careful and be fully committed to socializing your child and your dog. Be prepared to work hard and keep an eye on child-dog interactions until you know for certain they are firm friends. It also means you have a well-disciplined, kind-hearted child who can follow your directions about interacting with the dog.

Highs and Lows

Every breed has certain energy levels and needs; for example, the Dalmatian, Border Collie, Jack Russell Terrier, and Irish Setter would be considered very high energy, while the Basset Hound, Clumber Spaniel, Whippet, and Bulldog win the awards for Best Couch Potatoes.

Exercise is essential to your dog's physical and mental well-being.

A NYlabone® Fold Away Pet Carrier allows your dog to retreat and relax.

King of the Lap

These dogs are happiest inside with their owners, snuggling. They have also been voted Most Likely to Be Seen in a Pocketbook on a City Bus:

Pomeranian

Japanese Chin

English Toy Spaniel

Maltese

Yorkshire Terrier

Cavalier King Charles Spaniel

Chihuahua

Interaction with "strangers" is a little different. A stranger is not necessarily a serial killer skulking around the bushes outside your house. A stranger is someone your dog does not know, even if you do. The category includes strange children, so be careful if yours is a breed that doesn't cotton to strangers.

Trainability

Trainability has very little to do with intelligence, although the two are often confused. People tend to think that the smartest dogs are the ones that do what we want. These breeds include retrievers and herding dogs that were brought up to follow specific directions and to work closely with humans. However, some dogs were bred to be leaders. They expect you to follow them, not the other way around. In consequence, these independent, highly intelligent animals are sometimes labeled "dumb" because they obey their own instincts rather than your orders. This doesn't mean these breeds can't be trained; however, it often requires more patience and different methods. I have also occasionally indicated in this section whether members of this breed should be trusted off-lead.

Activities

This category contains some important structured activities you might wish to participate in with your dog. Activities include both dog sports and dogs at work. Dogs sports include

Old Friends

Seniors are better off with smaller dogs that they can carry to the vet if necessary and that are easier to handle. These breeds include:

Dachshund	Miniature Poodle
Bichon Frise	Bulldog
Toy Poodle	Miniature Pinscher
Pug	Miniature Schnauzer
Cairn Terrier	Papillon
Maltese	Boston Terrier
Cavalier King Charles Spaniel	Brussels Griffon
	Shih Tzu
Chihuahua	Yorkshire Terrier

Some breeds get along great with kids and are happy to see visitors.

agility, canine freestyle, carting, coonhound events, earthdog trials, flyball, flying disc events, foxhound events, herding, lure coursing, obedience trials, pointer tests and trials, rabbit hound events, retriever tests and trials, Schutzhund competition, sled dog racing, tracking, and weight pulling, all of which are defined in the glossary at the back of this book. A working dog's activities include acting as assistance dogs, guide dogs, guard dogs, herders and livestock protection dogs, military and police dogs, bomb, drug, and accelerant sniffers, search and rescue dogs, sled dogs, and therapy dogs.

One favorite canine-human occupation of mine is therapy work. Your dog doesn't have to be purebred to participate or have any particular talents beyond controllability, calmness, and quiet friendliness. Most nursing homes, hospitals, and rehabilitation places will welcome your visits, although some require certification from a recognized program like Therapy Dogs International or the Delta Society. Certification programs vary, but many require that your dog complete a full obedience course and a health screen, and be of a certain age (usually one year) and well-groomed and clean. To find out what programs may be available in your area, contact a local nursing home or hospital.

Most dogs have certain activities in which they naturally excel.

Obedience Champions

While all breeds can participate in AKC obedience, take a closer look at the following if you want to become a serious competitor:

Belgian Sheepdog (all varieties)	Doberman Pinscher
	German Shepherd Dog
Collie	Golden Retriever
Bichon Frise	Labrador Retriever
Poodle (all varieties)	English Springer Spaniel
Welsh Corgi (both varieties)	Bernese Mountain Dog
Border Collie	West Highland White Terrier

Many breeds are smart enough for obedience, but just don't seem to enjoy it. Some get bored by the mindless repetition; others are just too stubborn to find obedience a thrill. That doesn't mean you can't take your Bulldog to obedience trials if you want; in fact, you should. Those events need more fun injected into them, and your charming Bulldog pitted against those humorless Labradors, Golden Retrievers, and Border Collies would be a welcome change. The AKC and various breed clubs can offer more information about many of these programs.

All dogs, whether they "do" anything or not, of course, can be great companions. If you're like me, you may want nothing more from your pet than to be a walking companion, good listener, snugglebug, and source of joy. Other people want more. For each breed I've listed, I have included some activities for which the breed is famous.

Getting involved with these events is fun for your dogs and fun for the family. It's a wonderful opportunity for everyone to work together in healthy competition, and gives your dog a great mix of pampering and good training. Many of these events are noncompetitive, in the sense that they are "pass-fail" and so everyone can "win." Some of these same events also award a high point achievement award to the best of the winners,

Most Agile

The Border Collie and the Australian Shepherd are two breeds that excel in agility competitions.

No matter what your dog does, he will be a great companion.

so in a sense the same event is both competitive and non-competitive–the best of both worlds. Before trying any event though, follow these simple guidelines:

√ Research the activity. Discover if you have the time, money, energy, or even a real interest in it.

√ Get your dog a thorough veterinary checkup. You not only don't want to work a sick dog, but you want to know what your dog's general health is before you embark on an canine event. If it's an activity that requires you to run around as well, you might want to get a checkup yourself.

√ Start easy. Even if your dog gets a clean bill of health, go slow, just as a human athlete would. Conditioning is important to avoid injuries.

√ Take it easy. Don't stress your dog beyond his natural limits.

√ If your dog will be doing endurance work, beef up his fat and protein intake.

√ Quit when you've had enough. Quit for the day when you're tired. And quit for good if you're sick and tired. Remember canine events should be fun!

Part Two
Choosing Your
Dog

"You know, I've always wanted a dog, but up until a few weeks ago
I've just been more of a platypus person."

Breed Profiles

The following is a list and brief profile of AKC-recognized breeds, including important traits such as character, exercise needs, trainability, etc. By following the AKC's list of breeds, I made it easy on myself. It's not even certain what a "breed" actually is. My Webster's Ninth New Collegiate Dictionary states that a breed is "a group of animals or plants presumably (now that's an interesting qualifier) related by descent from common ancestors and visibly similar in most characteristics." Going by this definition, one could get into an argument as to whether the various sorts of Sheepdogs, Corgis, Fox Terriers, Dachshunds, Poodles, and Schnauzers should be grouped together or separated.

Each breed of dog is grouped according to backgrounds and abilities.

Breeds were carefully developed throughout the years.

A purebred dog should look similar to his ancestors.

The redoubtable *Oxford English Dictionary* declares that a breed comprises "a line of descendants perpetuating particular hereditary qualities," but doesn't say which ones. Webster's Desk Dictionary of the English Language tries to be more helpful by defining a breed as "a homogeneous grouping of animals within a species, developed by humans." I like the "developed by humans" part, because it gets us closer to understanding that dog breeds relate to certain human-designed functions.

It takes many, many years to produce a new "breed." You know that the goal is achieved when the puppies look exactly like the parents generation after generation. Crossing two purebred dogs of different breed produces a cross, not a new purebred. If you bred two members of the same cross, the puppies might look like anything and might not even resemble each other.

Because of the complexities in trying to decide what is and is not a breed, it is perfectly understandable that different kennel clubs in different countries have come to their own decisions. I have chosen to use the AKC designations, not necessarily because they are the best or most accurate, but because they are the most familiar. I should note that new breeds are entering the AKC lists at almost lightning speed. Prospective AKC breeds are first listed under the Miscellaneous Group and then filter their way into one of the other groups. Some newcomers you can expect to see soon include: the Irish Red and White Setter, the Catahoula Leopard Dog, the Thai Ridgeback, the Dogue de Bordeaux, the Bolonese, the Cesky Terrier, the Perro de Presa Canario, the Glen of Imaal Terrier, the American English Coonhound, the Azawakh, the Bluetick Coonhound, the Norwegian Lundhund, the Red Bone Treehound, the Treeing Tennessee Brindle, the Treeing Walker Coonhound, the Sloughi, and my own very special favorite–the Peruvian Inca Orchid.

Affenpinscher

Character: Obstinate, loyal, playful, game, lively, busy; needs constant companionship.

Origin: Germany or Eastern Europe; 1600

Original Purpose: Killing small vermin; lapdogs.

Physical Attributes: 9 to 12 inches; 7 to 11 pounds; balanced; alert; able to climb; a barker; cannot handle cold.

Color: Black, gray, silver, red, beige, black and tan.

Coat Type and Grooming: Harsh, dense outercoat; requires fairly high maintenance; must be brushed several times a week (even then he looks scruffy, which is part of the charm). He should be professionally shaped and trimmed every three months. Show dogs need to be stripped; pets can be clipped; slight shedding.

Lifespan: 12 to14 years.

Health Concerns: Hip dysplasia, Legg-Perthes disease, patellar luxation.

Exercise: Medium/high; likes to play, but is small enough to have its exercise needs met easily with daily walks.

Housing: Ideal for apartment life.

Interaction with Others: Must be carefully supervised with infants and toddlers; gets along fine with gentle, older children; tends to bond with one person; good with other pets if socialized early.

Trainability: Needs consistent training; probably does best with an experienced dog owner; can be difficult to housetrain.

Activities: Obedience, agility.

Remarks: The Affenpinscher is known as the monkey-faced dog, for obvious reasons.

AKC Classification: Toy Group.

Kennel Club Classification: Toy Group.

Part 2

Afghan Hound

Character: Aloof, pleasant, independent, spirited, dignified (but with a silly streak); despite independent nature, needs human companionship; should not be treated like a decoration; may bond to one person or remain aloof even to family members.

Origin: Afghanistan; however, the breed has been depicted in 4000-year-old drawings.

Original Purpose: Hunting gazelle, antelope, deer, leopards, and hares; protecting sheep.

Physical Attributes: 25 to 28 inches; 50 to 65 pounds; tall, elegant, refined, and aristocratic on the outside, but tough and agile on the inside; famous for the elegance of his movement. Can handle cold, wet, or windy weather without difficulty; are great jumpers and can easily leap over boundary fences.

Color: Any color or mixture of colors from pale cream and fawn to deep black. A pure white dog, or a dog with white markings, is not preferred.

Coat Type and Grooming: Possesses a long, thick, silky coat, which has accurately been described as a "mane;" requires very high maintenance, including several hours a week of thorough brushing to prevent mats, which form easily and daily. These dogs should not be clipped or trimmed. Older pets are sometimes shaved for their comfort. Professional grooming is highly desirable. They are known for moderate shedding; adolescent Afghans (12-18 months) who are shedding their soft puppy coat and growing in an adult coat need special care.

Lifespan: 10 to 12 years.

Health Concerns: Eye problems such as cataracts, allergic dermatitis, cardiomyopathy, hip dysplasia, hypothyroidism. Like other sighthounds, sensitive to anesthesia.

Exercise: High; needs a great amount of exercise in a fenced area; when bored, can become destructive; however, given sufficient running time, they are usually quite calm, especially as they mature.

Housing: Adaptable to apartment life if given sufficient exercise.

Interaction with Others: Gentle if well socialized; not playful; may be rather fond of the older children in the family; reserved with strangers. Good with other dogs, especially other Afghans. They have a strong prey drive, and most need to be watched around cats and other small pets.

Trainability: Low/moderate; early socialization required; can be obstinate; however, only gentle training methods work with this dog.

Activities: Lure coursing, obedience, agility, therapy dog.

Remarks: The Afghan is famous for its "double-suspension gallop" which enables it to run down the swiftest of game.

AKC Classification: Hound Group.

Kennel Club Classification: Hound Group.

Part 2

Airedale Terrier

Character: Protective, good-natured, loyal, independent, brave, people-oriented; fine guard dog; some individuals can be dominant; requires a lot of owner interaction.

Origin: Yorkshire, England (specifically the river valley of Aire); 1800; Welsh Terrier, Border Collie, and Otterhound possibly in the background.

Original Purpose: Badger, fox, and otter hunting; messenger and ambulance dogs during World War I (despite his vaunted loyalty, the Airedale served both the British and the Germans).

Physical Attributes: 22 to 24 inches; 43 to 60 pounds; stylish, rather square shaped. The tallest and newest of the terrier breeds; is often called the "King of Terriers." Great swimmers and good trackers, probably due to an early infusion of Otterhound; tail often docked.

Color: Black and tan or reddish tan with a black or grizzle saddle.

Coat Type and Grooming: The Airedale possesses a thick, hard, wiry double coat; requires medium/high maintenance. Professional grooming is necessary, especially for a show coat. Most pet owners just clip the coat. Slight shedding.

Lifespan: 10 to 14 years.

Health Concerns: Skin allergies (like many terriers); hip dysplasia, von Willebrand's disease and other bleeding disorders; gastritis; retinal dysplasia; low thyroid function.

Exercise: Moderately high, but can adapt to both city and suburban life. Sufficient leash walking is enough, but if not given enough exercise, becomes extremely restless.

Housing: Apartment life is not ideal, but adaptable if given sufficient exercise.

Interaction with Others: Tolerant with kids; good family dog, but needs to be supervised with small children because of his enthusiasm. Will try to dominate other pets; however, with early exposure and socialization, he can learn to get along.

Trainability: Average; needs consistent strong training; not for a timid owner.

Activities: Hunting; obedience (perhaps the very best in the whole Terrier Group); agility; therapy dog; search and rescue; guard dog, tracking; herding.

Remarks: Barbara Curtiss, Airedale Club of America Rescue Committee Chairperson, says, "Airedales are not hyper but they have an intense curiosity about everything, so there's never a dull moment, plus a lovable and deliberate sense of humor that captures their owners' attention, and hearts, like no other breed we know." Theodore Roosevelt, Calvin Coolidge, and Warren G. Harding were all Airedale fans.

AKC Classification: Terrier Group.

Kennel Club Classification: Terrier Group.

Akita

Character: Loyal, stubborn, bold, affectionate, courageous, fearless; fiercely protective. Territorial; a superb watchdog that barks only when it suspects something is really wrong.

Origin: The largest Japanese breed originated in Japan in the 1600s. It was rendered almost extinct during World War II and survived because defiant owners, instead of selling them for meat as was ordered, released them into the mountains, where enough of this tough, hardy breed survived.

Original Purpose: Hunting large game, including wild boar; dog fighting.

Physical Attributes: Females, at least 23 inches, usually 24; males at least 25 inches, up to 28 inches; 75 to 115 pounds; powerful, large, graceful.

Color: Any color including white, brindle, gray, red, and pinto; usually white underneath.

Coat Type and Grooming: Double coat, a soft inner and coarse, harsh outer coat; high maintenance, daily brushing with a pin brush; no trimming. Professional grooming is optional. They shed profusely twice a year.

Lifespan: 10 to 12 and more years.

Health Problems: Eye problems (PRA, retinal dysplasia), hip dysplasia, OCD, patellar luxation, autoimmune problems.

Exercise: Moderate.

Housing: Can withstand bitter cold, but has a very low heat tolerance; needs to be an indoor dog; needs a high fenced-in yard; usually quiet in the house.

Interaction with Others: Very tolerant of the family, but can be intolerant of other children; can show aggression by overprotecting "his" children. Aloof and standoffish with strangers; aggressive around strange dogs and often aggressive to small animals.

Trainability: Average to quick learners with minds of their own, Akitas must be carefully socialized and do not, as a rule, make obedience dogs. The Akita should be owned only by a very experienced person; definitely not for first-time dog owners, as the Akita may try to challenge them for dominance and win.

Activities: Guard dog, tracking.

Remarks: In 1931, the government of Japan recognized the Akita as one of seven breeds designated "national treasures." When a child is born in that country, the family typically receives a small statute of this dog, which represents health and longevity, and the Japanese government will subsidize the feeding of a champion dog, if its owner can no longer do so.

AKC Classification: Working Group.

Kennel Club Classification: Utility Group.

Alaskan Malamute

Character: Affectionate, social, loyal, dominant, tenacious, strong-willed; may be territorial with other animals.

Origin: One of the most ancient breeds believed to originate in Alaska.

Original Purpose: Sled dog, hunter of polar bear.

Physical Attributes: The Malamute is typically 23 to 25 inches and 75 to 85 pounds, with a definite wolf-like appearance. He is the largest of the sled dogs and really enjoys pulling. He is very powerful, with good sense of smell and can withstand an immense amount of cold, but has very little heat tolerance. Like many northern breeds, they have a wonderful smile.

Color: Shades of gray, cinnamon, black with white markings, more rarely pure white.

Coat Type and Grooming: Medium-long, harsh, dense outercoat; one- or two-inch soft, oily undercoat. Some come in a "wooly" variety, which, while unacceptable for show dogs, has a certain charm. High maintenance; needs daily brushing, especially when shedding, which is seasonally very heavy. Professional grooming is optional.

Lifespan: 11 to 14 years.

Health Concerns: Glaucoma, hip dysplasia, zinc-deficiency skin disorders, chondrodysplasia (dwarfism).

Exercise: Generally well-mannered in the home, but must have vigorous daily exercise; without exercise, can be hyperactive or destructive or become overweight. Lack of exercise can contribute to problem behaviors like digging and barking.

Housing: Not suited for apartment life; needs a fenced-in yard.

Interaction with Others: Good with older kids, but should be supervised; not good with young children. Very friendly to people, and does not make a good watchdog. This is not a one-person dog. Can be quite aggressive toward other dogs, at least until the hierarchy is established; will not like your cat or other small pets.

Trainability: Rather difficult to average; does best with a strong, experienced, patient owner. Will try to dominate its owner unless trained well and early; does not make a good obedience dog; a roamer that should not be let off a leash in an unfenced area.

Activities: Sledding, skijoring, weight-pulling.

Remarks: This breed was named after the native Inuit tribe called Mahlemuts, who settled in the upper western part of Alaska.

AKC Classification: Working Group.

Kennel Club Classification: Working Group.

Part 2

American Eskimo Dog

Character: Loyal, independent, alert, loving, protective, lively.

Origin: United States, early 1900s; a member of the Northern spitz family of dogs.

Original Purpose: Companion, watch dog, and performing artist.

Physical Attributes: The breed comes in three accepted sizes: 9 to 12 inches, 6 to 10 pounds for Toys; 12 to 15 inches, 11 to 20 pounds for Miniatures; and 15 to 19 inches, 20 to 40 pounds inches for Standards. However, there is no official weight standard. They are good in cold weather but have no heat tolerance. Many are extremely vocal, which means they are barkers.

Color: Snowy white preferred; cream or biscuit with white acceptable.

Coat Type and Grooming: Undercoat soft, thick, fairly soft; outercoat mostly longer guard hairs. High maintenance; requires two or three thorough brushings a week. Shed profusely once a year when they "blow their coat." Professional grooming is optional.

Lifespan: 14 to 15 years

Health Concerns: Fleabite dermatitis; urinary tract stones; PRA; seizures; hip dysplasia.

Exercise: If he does not get sufficient exercise, this breed can be destructive in the home.

Housing: Adaptable to almost any living situation.

Interactions with Others: This dog is very reserved around strangers but is devoted to his family and generally good with kids. Some individuals can be timid; usually good with other pets.

Trainability: High—the American Eskimo Dog is easily trained and is a good dog for a first-time owner.

Activities: Obedience, agility.

Remarks: The American Eskimo Dog has nothing whatsoever to do with Eskimos. It was recognized as a separate breed in England in 1913, but it was not accepted by the AKC until 1995. This breed gained renown as a circus dog; in fact, it is one of the few breeds that can walk a tight rope. (Do not try this at home.)

AKC Classification: Non-Sporting Group.

Part 2

American Foxhound

Character: This breed is independent, free-spirited, tough, kind, and gentle. Although reserved with strangers, these are not protective dogs. They are well behaved in the house, even though they were traditionally kept outside in a kennel with other Foxhounds. This breed makes an excellent watchdog.

Origin: United States, 1600s. (Of course, there was no United States in the 1600s, so let's just say "the colonies.")

Original Purpose: Of course, the American Foxhound is bred for hunting, like his English cousin. However, the American version is more streamlined and faster, because hunters in the Kentucky and Tennessee mountains were looking for a fast dog who could work alone if necessary and start, chase, and even kill a deer.

Physical Attributes: 21 to 25 inches; 60 to 70 pounds; possesses a great sense of smell; fast; has a beautiful voice and uses it.

Color: Any hound color, which in this case almost always means a tricolor: black, brown and white. The black is often confined to "saddle" over the back, and the legs and tail tip are usually white.

Coat Type and Grooming: Hard and short; minimal care; average shedding; professional grooming not necessary.

Lifespan: 10 to 12 years.

Health Concerns: Hip dysplasia; deafness.

Exercise: Needs enormous amounts of exercise in a safe, fenced area.

Housing: This very active dog does not adapt to city life; is not suitable for apartment life.

Interaction with Others: The Foxhound is tolerant and loving with children and reserved with strangers. Like most pack dogs, he is superb around other dogs, as well as most other pets.

Trainability: Easily trained for what it was bred to do, more difficult for obedience work; in this, it resembles most hounds.

Activities: Fox hunting, field trials, tracking.

Remarks: The breed is descended from the English variety, but is more lightly built, rangier, and somewhat taller, since it was adapted to a different terrain. George Washington owned American Foxhounds and kept meticulous records on his pack.

AKC Classification: Hound Group.

American Staffordshire Terrier

Character: Tenacious, stubborn, happy, affectionate, docile in the family setting; protective and territorial, but friendly to strangers if introduced by the owner; excellent watch and guard dog; can be protective.

Origin: United States, 1800s; ancestors, along with the Bulldog, Bull Terrier, and Staffordshire Bull Terrier, came from England.

Original Purpose: Dog fighting; bullbaiting.

Physical Attributes: 17 to 19 inches; 40 to 75 pounds; stocky and heavy-boned, with immensely powerful jaws. Some individuals are able to climb almost as well as a cat. Less noisy that many other terriers; ears are sometimes cropped, but uncropped ears are preferred according to the standard.

Color: This breed comes in an amazing assortment of colors, including solid, parti, and brindled. More than 80-percent white on body is discouraged.

Coat Type and Grooming: Short, glossy, stiff; minimal care, a quick brush up with a currycomb will do it. Light to moderate shedding; professional grooming is not necessary.

Lifespan: 12 to 15 years.

Health Concerns: Cataracts, CMO, hypothyroidism, hip dysplasia, thyroid and heart problems.

Exercise: Moderately high; will become restless if not given sufficient exercise.

Housing: Enjoys long walks but can live equally well in town or country.

Interaction with Others: Tends to bond with one person; usually good with family children, despite its fearsome reputation, if socialized properly. If aroused, however, this breed can be dangerous, and should not be around strange children. Will fight with other dogs; not good with other pets in general.

Trainability: Low—If carefully bred and correctly trained, this loyal dog is a wonderful pet; however, socializing must begin very early. This breed may challenge his owner for dominance. Not for novice or timid owners, this dog needs very firm training beginning from the instant you bring him home.

Activities: Tracking, agility, search and rescue.

Remarks: This is a breed sometimes considered to be a "pit bull," an animal not recognized by the AKC. It has been banned in some localities and is the source of much heated debate. Careful breeding has softened this dog's disposition, but you must be careful to purchase or adopt your pet from a reliable source. There is no getting around the fact that this breed can be extremely dangerous, even though the vast majority of its members are kind and loyal.

AKC Classification: Terrier Group.

American Water Spaniel

Character: Tractable, friendly, sensitive; some can be shy; makes a good watchdog and guard dog.

Origin: United States, 1800s; some say the dog's ancestors came to the United States with the Pilgrims.

Original Purpose: An all-purpose hunting dog that can retrieve from both land and water. This is one of the only two sporting breeds developed in the United States.

Physical Attributes: 15 to 18 inches; 25 to 50 pounds.

Color: Solid brown, chocolate, or liver.

Coat Type and Grooming: Close curls; the almost-waterproof coat needs regular care; its tight curls respond better to combing than brushing; some dogs seem to have a strong odor. Professional grooming is preferable; some trimming required; some shedding.

Lifespan: 10 to 15 years.

Health Concerns: Patellar luxation, PRA, detached retina.

Exercise: Needs a moderate amount of outdoor exercise, much more when young; must be able to swim to be completely happy.

Housing: Adaptable to apartment life only with plenty of exercise.

Interaction with Others: Excellent as a rule, although some individuals are not child-friendly; early socialization is important. Usually okay with other pets, although some can be aggressive with strange animals.

Trainability: Benefits from basic obedience training; this breed is probably not the best choice for a novice owner.

Activities: Hunting, tracking, obedience.

Remarks: The American Water Spaniel is the state dog of Wisconsin.

AKC Classification: Sporting Group.

Part 2

Anatolian Shepherd

Character: Serious, laid-back, alert, bold, independent; an excellent watchdog and guard dog; highly territorial.

Origin: Turkey.

Original Purpose: Flock guarding, wolf-hunting, combat dog.

Physical Attributes: 27 inches minimum for females; 29 minimum for males; 110-150 pounds.

Color: Fawn and black; also cream, off-white, brindle, and pinto.

Coat Type and Grooming: Outercoat variable from short and straight to long and wavy; undercoat dense and short. Needs brushing once a week; professional grooming not necessary. Average shedding.

Lifespan: 13 to 14 years.

Health Concerns: Hip and elbow dysplasia, thyroid disease.

Exercise: Rather low energy level, but needs daily exercise.

Housing: Adaptable to most living situations.

Interaction with Others: Good with children; patient, but not playful; extremely suspicious of strangers. Good but dominant with family pets; not always good with strange animals.

Trainability: Because of its propensity to guard, this dog needs early, consistent training. A strong, highly experienced owner is essential for this breed.

Activities: Shepherd's dog, guard dog.

Remarks: This is one of the few breeds said to be able to hold its own with a wolf, referring to his toughness.

AKC Classification: Working Group.

Kennel Club Classification: Pastoral Group.

Australian Cattle Dog

Character: Hard-working, independent, energetic, alert, courageous.

Origin: Australia, 1800s. Ancestry may include blue-merle collies, black and tan kelpies, dingoes, and perhaps Dalmatians.

Original Purpose: Cattle herding.

Physical Attributes: 17 to 20 inches, 35 to 45 pounds;

Color: Red speckled, blue or blue-mottled; puppies are born white.

Coat Type and Grooming: Straight outercoat, short dense undercoat. Minimal care needed; a good brushing once a week is sufficient. Average shedding.

Lifespan: 10 to 13 years.

Health Concerns: Eye problems (PRA, cataracts), deafness, hip dysplasia.

Exercise: Very high.

Housing: A tireless working dog; needs lots of space to meets his high exercise needs; would not do well in an apartment.

Interaction with Others: Playful, but can be nippy, a quality needed to herd cattle. Needs to be supervised with children; suspicious of strangers; suspicious of and dominant to other dogs; will chase cats.

Trainability: Extremely high; positive reinforcement works best with this energetic breed. He is happiest when working or training.

Activities: Cattle herding, herding trials.

Remarks: This breed is also called the Australian Heeler. An experienced owner essential for this dominant, energetic breed.

AKC Classification: Herding Group.

Kennel Club Classification: Pastoral Group.

Part 2

Australian Shepherd

Character: Very active, enthusiastic, good-natured, loving, hard-working, even-tempered; bonds to whole family.

Origin: United States, 1800s. Despite the name, these are American dogs. Their origin actually lies in Spain and France.

Original Purpose: Herding livestock.

Physical Attributes: 18 to 23 inches, 40 to 65 pounds; tail docked; active, agile.

Color: Comes in a wide array of exciting colors, including an overall coloration of black, red, blue or red merle; may have a white blaze and white markings on the chest, neck, and legs. In addition, copper markings on face and legs are permitted.

Coat Type and Grooming: Medium-length double coat; can be straight or wavy. Needs daily grooming; professional grooming is desirable. Heavy shedding.

Lifespan: 12 to 14 years.

Health Concerns: Hip dysplasia, eye problems (cataracts, PRA, collie eye anomaly), deafness, von Willebrand's, thyroid disease.

Exercise: Very high (they were bred to handle an entire herd of sheep, after all); can be hyperactive in the house.

Housing: Needs lots of space to meets his high exercise needs; would not do well in an apartment.

Interaction with Others: Good with children, although some dogs may try to herd them by nipping; aloof with strangers. Good with other dogs; needs socialization with smaller pets.

Trainability: High; experienced owner recommended for this breed; happiest when working or training.

Activities: Herding, agility, obedience.

Remarks: Heidi Mobley, of Second Time Around Aussie Rescue, writes, "The Australian Shepherd is an active, loyal, intelligent dog that needs a job to do." The genetics in breeding an Australian Shepherd are complex, so be careful to deal with an experienced breeder.

AKC Classification: Herding Group.

Kennel Club Classification: Pastoral Group.

Australian Terrier

Character: Plucky, extroverted, alert, brave, sensible, adaptable; good watchdog, although it is not a protective breed; tends to bond to one person. This terrier is more dependent than some others.

Origin: Australia, 1900s. Background includes Dandie Dinmont, Irish, and Yorkshire Terrier.

Original Function: Hunting mice and rats; tending sheep.

Physical Attributes: 10 to 11 inches; 12 to 18 pounds; tail is docked; energetic, active. One of the smallest terriers; has a spotted tongue.

Color: Blue saddle and tan body, blue black, or silver black with tan markings, sand, or red.

Coat Type and Grooming: Harsh, long double; soft top-knot. Medium to high maintenance; needs brushing two or three times a week; hair in eyes may need to be plucked; frequent bathing is recommended. Professional grooming is recommended, including monthly trimming and stripping for show dogs. Slight shedding.

Lifespan: 13 to 14 years.

Health Concerns: Legg-Perthes.

Exercise: Moderate to high; quiet (for a terrier) but has a loud bark; likes to dig.

Housing: Adapts well to apartment life if given enough exercise.

Interaction with Others: Good with children if socialized with them; however, can be snappy when irritated. Reserved with strangers; does well with other pets if raised with them; may be same-sex aggressive.

Trainability: Average to high; needs firm obedience training.

Activities: Earthdog trials, agility.

Remarks: One of the smallest of the working terriers, it is also one the few bred outside Great Britain. Like its English cousins, this dog is a digger.

AKC Classification: Terrier Group.

Kennel Club Classification: Toy Group.

Basenji

Character: Cheerful, self-reliant, affectionate, playful, curious, obedient. Alert; makes a very good watchdog, although it is not protective; some poorly bred individuals are aggressive.

Origin: Central Africa (Congo). Some maintain the dog hails originally from the Middle East.

Original Purpose: Vermin hunter, driving game into a net.

Physical Attributes: 16 to 20 inches, 22 to 25 pounds; showy, proud. Has no cold tolerance; considered both a sighthound and a scenthound, making it unique among dogs. Noted for its unique ringtail. Expression looks either worried or quizzical, depending on your viewpoint.

Color: Chestnut red is by far the most common, but can also come in black, black and tan, and brindle. All colors should have white feet, chest, and tail-tip. White legs, face blaze, and collar are permissible.

Coat Type and Grooming: Short, silky. Minimal care needed; a quick brushing once a week will suffice. These dogs are very clean, often grooming themselves like a cat. Very little shedding.

Lifespan: 10 to 13 years.

Health Concerns: Eye problems (PRA), hernias, Basenji enteropathy, anemia, kidney problems (Fanconi syndrome, peculiar to Basenjis and people).

Exercise: Medium to high; can be hyperactive in the house, and can be destructive if not given sufficient exercise. Needs to stay on a lead when not in a secure fenced area.

Housing: Most are not suited for apartment living, unless given frequent long walks.

Interaction with Others: Loves kids; not always good with very young children, and should be supervised, only because it can be almost too playful. May try to dominate other pets.

Trainability: High.

Activities: Lure coursing, obedience, agility.

Remarks: The name Basenji means "bush or wild thing." Unlike most dogs, the Basenji comes into heat only once a year. It is famous for being a "barkless" dog, but it makes several weird noises all its own, including wailing, chortling, ululating, and yodeling.

AKC Classification: Hound Group.

Kennel Club Classification: Hound Group.

Basset Hound

Character: Friendly, calm, placid, devoted, stubborn, mild. A fine watchdog, but not protective.

Origin: France, mid-1500s. Bred down from the Bloodhound.

Original Purpose: Hunting hares and rabbits. Bred to accompany pedestrian, as opposed to mounted, hunters.

Physical Attributes: 13 to 15 inches; 40 to 80 pounds; sturdy, with ears extending beyond tip of nose. Basset Hounds are second only to their ancestor the Bloodhound in their ability to scent. Despite or because of this trait, they enjoy rolling in foul-smelling messes. They drool a lot and howl delightfully.

Colors: Any hound color: red and white, tricolor, lemon and white. Liver not accepted.

Coat Type and Grooming: Medium-short, but very dense. Weekly brushing important. Eyes and ears need extra care; can develop a hound smell, and people who don't like it should bathe their Bassets regularly. No professional grooming needed (unless you want someone else to give the dog a bath). Average shedding.

Lifespan: 12 to 13 years, but some much longer.

Health Concerns: Eye ailments (glaucoma, PRA), bleeding disorders (thrombopathia, von Willebrand's), thyroid problems, allergies, orthopedic problems (elbow dysplasia, herniated disk, OCD, panosteitis), obesity.

Exercise: Low energy and moderate exercise needs, but if not given enough, the Basset gains weight rapidly; has more endurance than you might think.

Housing: They are quiet in the house and can adapt to apartment life, but need regular walks to stay fit.

Interaction with Others: Excellent with children, although not very playful—this dog loves everyone. Good with all other pets.

Trainability: Difficult to train; responds best to food rewards. Like many other hounds, bassets can be stubborn and slow to housetrain, so it is important to begin housetraining early. Also, Bassets cannot be trusted off lead.

Activities: Tracking, field trials, rabbit hunting.

Remarks: The best description of a Basset Hound was written by one William Shakespeare in his *Midsummer Night's Dream:* "I never heard so musical a discord, such sweet thunder," says Hippolytus. Theseus agrees. "Their heads are hung with ears that sweep away the morning dew/ Crook-knee'd, and dew-lapped like Thessalian bulls;/ slow in pursuit, but matched in mouth like bells/each under each...Judge when you hear." Alisa Garbrick, long-time Basset owner and activist with Basset Rescue of Old Dominion, writes, "These loving dogs have been described as the Clowns of Hounds. But they are also stubborn and opinionated as well. They are well suited to a family with a sense of humor."

AKC Classification: Hound Group.

Kennel Club Classification: Hound Group.

Part 2

Beagle

Character: Independent, merry, gentle, willful, energetic, stubborn. Some individuals are excessively shy. They are not territorial, and while they bark at everything, they are just acting as the welcoming committee.

Origin: England, 1000-1300s. Some people trace the Beagle's ancestry to Egypt; others hark to Greece. More commonly it is believed that Beagle ancestors came to England with William the Conqueror and were probably bred down from the Foxhound.

Original Purpose: Rabbit trailing.

Physical Attributes: The smallest of the scent hounds, Beagles come in two sizes for show purposes: 13 inch and 15 inch, 17-35 pounds. This two-inch division has been in place since 1890. They are sturdy, athletic, and highly energetic. They are barkers and can escape yards by digging under fences.

Color: Any true hound color allowed, such as black and tan, red and white, or lemon and white; white tip on tail preferred.

Coat Type and Grooming: Short and hard; needs minimal care. Ears need special attention. Year round shedding, with extra in spring.

Lifespan: 12 to 16 years.

Health Concerns: Eye problems (glaucoma, PRA, cataracts, ectropion), heart disease (pulmonic stenosis), allergies, ear infections, disc problems, cancer, gastritis, epilepsy, deafness, anemia, obesity.

Exercise: Average to high, depending partly on whether or not they come from show stock. Field trial and conformation Beagles are much more laid back than hunting stock. Beagles who don't get their exercise needs met become hyperactive in the house. If given company and exercise, they are quiet in the house.

Housing: They are not really suitable for apartment living, but it is possible if the dog is given generous amounts of exercise.

Interaction with Others: The Beagle is sociable to everyone, and one of the best dogs with children, especially if exposed when young. However, this is not a good breed to leave home alone all day. Beagles are pack (both human and animal) dogs and can suffer severe separation anxiety if left alone. They are excellent with other pets; in fact, they do much better with other dogs as companions.

Trainability: They can be difficult to train and are strongly food-motivated. They do best with obedience training. They take a long time to housetrain and can never be let off lead outside a fenced area—they will just follow their excellent noses and run off. Beagles are also fine howlers.

Activities: Hunting (rabbits, pheasant), tracking, flyball, agility, field trials.

Remarks: The US Department of Agriculture uses Beagles to sniff out contraband drugs, known as the famous Beagle Brigade.

AKC Classification: Hound Group.

Kennel Club Classification: Hound Group.

Bearded Collie

Character: Friendly, has sense of humor, lively, sweet-natured, cheerful, joyful; needs close human companionship.

Origin: Scotland, 1800s. Closely related to the Old English Sheepdog and Border Collie.

Original Purpose: Shepherder.

Physical Attributes: 20 to 22 inches; 45 to 55 pounds; exuberant; they seem to bounce when they run. One source I consulted claimed that one of the Beardie's most attractive features was his keen, observant eyes—this may be so; unfortunately, they are usually covered up by hair.

Color: Any shade of gray or chocolate; may have white chest, blaze, and tail tip. Some individuals have tan markings.

Coat Type and Grooming: Thick double coat with flat, harsh, shaggy outercoat and a soft furry undercoat. High maintenance; needs very thorough brushing twice a week to keep coat from matting. Professional grooming is recommended, but pet dogs can be clipped down. Profuse shedding.

Lifespan: 12 to 15 years.

Health Concerns: This is a healthy breed on the whole; some problems with CHD, epilepsy, intestinal disease.

Exercise: High to moderate; tend to slow down as they mature.

Housing: Especially when young, they do best with a lot of running room.

Interaction with Others: Good with children, but may try to herd them; may be a bit rambunctious for toddlers; friendly to strangers. Good with other pets, especially with their own breed. They may try to chase small animals.

Trainability: Moderate.

Activities: Herding, agility.

Remarks: Slow to mature. This breed was almost extinct until 1944 when it was redeveloped from one breeding pair.

AKC Classification: Herding Group.

Kennel Club Classification: Pastoral Group.

Part 2

Bedlington Terrier

Character: Companionable, mild, stubborn; much more mellow than other terriers. It makes a good watchdog, but is not protective.

Origin: Northumbria, 1800s. The breed takes its name from its English town of origin.

Original Purpose: Created by miners to help kill rabbits, foxes, and weasels.

Physical Attributes: 15 to 17 inches; 17 to 23 pounds; graceful, energetic, with a whippet-like arched topline. Some are barky.

Color: Blue, liver or sandy—although Bedlingtons look basically off-white. Born black or dark brown.

Coat Type and Grooming: Short, "linty," and curly. High maintenance; requires daily brushing. Professional grooming is required, especially for show dogs, and every couple of months to shape the coat. Almost no shedding.

Lifespan: 15 to 16 years.

Health Concerns: Copper toxicosis, PRA, cataracts.

Exercise: Moderate; able to self-exercise; calm in the house,

Housing: Suited to urban life but is adaptable to any living situation.

Interaction with Others: Tends to bond with one person; fairly good with children if socialized early. May be tolerant when socialized to other pets but aggressive to strange dogs.

Trainability: Low to moderate.

Activities: Earthdog trials, obedience.

Remarks: Don't be fooled; the lamblike appearance covers the heart of a lion. This is one tough terrier. Michelle Turk, a member of the Bedlington Terrier Club of America Inc., writes, "The Bedlington Terrier has all the qualities of a faithful friend; he is loyal, trusting, loving, and a protective family member."

AKC Classification: Terrier Group.

Kennel Club Classification: Terrier Group.

Belgian Malinois

Character: Protective, serious, energetic, confident, devoted, alert. Can be shy or protective around strangers.

Origin: Belgium, 1800s.

Original Purpose: Stock herding.

Physical Attributes: 22 to 26 inches; 60 to 80 pounds; hardy, active.

Color: Rich fawn to mahogany with black tips on hairs; black mask and ears.

Coat Type and Grooming: Hard, straight coat somewhat shorter than that of the German Shepherd; dense undercoat. Weekly brushing required; professional grooming is not needed. Shedding is heavy once a year.

Lifespan: 10 to 12 years.

Health Concerns: Cancer, skin diseases, hip and elbow dysplasia, PRA, epilepsy.

Exercise: High.

Housing: Not suited to apartment life, needs room to exercise.

Interaction with Others: Good with gentle children, usually friendly to strangers, although some are shy or reserved. Not always good with other pets; the Malinois has a strong prey drive and should be socialized early with cats.

Trainability: Extremely high.

Activities: Police work, herding, search and rescue, tracking, protection, service dog, obedience, jogging companion, Schutzhund.

Remarks: All three Belgian Sheepdogs are very similar in characteristics except for coat type. The breed needs careful training and a strong owner to avoid becoming aggressive.

AKC Classification: Herding Group.

Kennel Club Classification: Belgian Shepherd (Malinois), Pastoral Group.

Part 2

Belgian Sheepdog

Character: Protective, devoted, playful, biddable, reserved, versatile.

Origin: Belgium, 1800s.

Original Purpose: Herding.

Physical Attributes: 22 to 26 inches; 60 to 65 pounds; active.

Color: Black with or without white markings.

Coat Type and Grooming: Long, dense, with an extremely dense undercoat. Brushing required at least three times a week. Professional grooming is optional; heavy shedding once a year.

Lifespan: 10 to 12 years.

Health Concerns: Seizures, eye problems.

Exercise: High. This dog needs plenty of attention and a lot to do.

Housing: Not suited to apartment life, needs room to exercise.

Interaction with Others: Very good with gentle children; aloof with strangers; may not be good with small pets.

Trainability: Extremely high.

Activities: Herding, guard dog, obedience, sledding, agility, tracking, Schutzhund.

Remarks: Carol Morris, corresponding secretary of the Belgian Sheepdog Club of America writes, "The Belgian Sheepdog's elegant beauty, high intelligence, versatility, and sensitivity make it an awesome competition and companion dog if its owner understands the breed and trains accordingly." This breed is not for beginners. All three Belgian Sheepdogs are very similar in characteristics except for coat type.

AKC Classification: Herding Group.

Belgian Tervuren

Character: Alert, energetic; a one-person dog. Requires a lot to do and a lot of companionship.

Origin: Belgium, 1800s.

Original Purpose: Stock herding.

Physical Attributes: 22 to 26 inches; 60 to 65 pounds.

Color: Shades of red, mahogany, fawn, gray with black overlay (tip of each hair black), and a black mask.

Coat Type and Grooming: Dense double coat longer than that of the Malinois. Professional grooming is optional; heavy shedding once a year.

Lifespan: 10 to 12 years.

Health Concerns: Epilepsy.

Exercise: High.

Housing: Not suited to apartment life, needs room to exercise.

Interaction with Others: Playful with children but may try to herd them. Tends to be suspicious of strangers.

Trainability: These dogs need firm (but not harsh) handling, as well as early socialization.

Activities: Police dog, search and rescue, herding trials, Schutzhund.

Remarks: These dogs become obese easily and need to have their food intake watched. All three Belgian Sheepdogs are very similar in characteristics except for coat type.

AKC Classification: Herding Group.

Kennel Club Classification: Belgan Shepherd (Tervuren), Pastoral Group.

Bernese Mountain Dog

Character: Good-natured, cheerful, easy-going, kind, sweet, devoted. Some individuals are shy and reserved with strangers; excellent watchdog, but not protective.

Origin: The Bern canton of Switzerland. This is still the most popular dog in Switzerland – you see them everywhere, wearing their famous "cow" collars.

Original Purpose: Cart pulling, guard dog, cattle and sheep drover.

Physical Attributes: 23 to 27 inches; 75 to 120 pounds. This is a slow-maturing breed. They are exceptionally tolerant of cold and suffer in hot weather; not well suited to a warm climate.

Color: Tricolor; white on chest, paws, and tail.

Coat Type and Grooming: Soft, silky, wavy; medium long; daily grooming required. Ears and nails need special care. Professional grooming is optional; average shedding; the Bernie "blows his coat" twice a year.

Lifespan: 8 to 10 years.

Health Concerns: Orthopedic problems (hip and elbow dysplasia, OCD), histiocytosis, cancer, aortic stenosis.

Exercise: Low to moderate.

Housing: Adaptable to apartment living with adequate exercise.

Interaction with Others: Very good with people; excellent with children, but can topple a toddler, so must be supervised. Enjoys the whole family, but often forms a special attachment to just one. Generally very good with other dogs and pets.

Trainability: Very high; this is a sensitive, quick-to-learn breed.

Activities: Therapy dog, drafting.

Remarks: Although it seems hard to believe, this gentle dog's roots (as well as those of other Swiss breeds like the Saint Bernard) go back to the fierce Roman Molosser mastiff.

AKC Classification: Working Group.

Kennel Club Classification: Working Group.

Bichon Frise

Character: Playful, perky, friendly, cheerful, happy-go-lucky, affectionate; requires attention.

Origin: France or Tennarife (Canary Islands of Spain); 1300s.

Original Purpose: The word *bichon* is French for "lap dog." They were also used as performing dogs and as companions to royalty.

Physical Attributes: 9 to 11 inches; 7 to 12 pounds; active, sturdy.

Color: Adult Bichons are always white, but puppies up to 18 months old can have traces of buff, cream, or apricot.

Coat Type and Grooming: Fluffy, fine, and somewhat silkier than a Poodle's, although it has poodle-like curls that are best groomed with a slicker brush; outer coat coarser and curlier. Very high maintenance and requires grooming every day, even for a pet coat. Frequent bathing is important, and eyes need special care. Professional grooming is recommended every month for a show coat. Does not shed, but dead hair from undercoat must be combed out to prevent mats and hot spots.

Lifespan: 13 to 15 years.

Health Concerns: Skin problems (allergies), ear infections, eye problems, bladder stones, patellar luxation. The breed also benefits from a different vaccination protocol than is common for most breeds.

Exercise: Gets along on only a little exercise but can be active in the house.

Housing: Ideal in any situation; especially suited for apartment life.

Interaction with Others: Excellent with older kids, but a few are too sensitive for toddlers; friendly to strangers. Craves human companionship and should not spend long hours alone; very good with all other pets.

Trainability: High; this breed is excellent at picking up tricks. Some have housetraining problems.

Activities: Obedience, agility, therapy dog.

Remarks: In its earlier years, the breed spent much of its time accompanying peddlers and organ grinders around France.

AKC Classification: Non-Sporting Group.

Kennel Club Classification: Toy Group.

Black and Tan Coonhound

Character: Amiable, stubborn, fearless, gentle, eager, loyal. Reserved or suspicious with strangers; some are protective.

Origin: United States, 1700s.

Original Purpose: Hunting raccoon, opossum, and other climbing game, as well as deer.

Physical Attributes: 23 to 27 inches; 50 to 80 pounds; powerful hunting instinct; strong, alert, agile. Tendency to bay or howl.

Color: Black with tan markings above the eyes, muzzle, chest, and legs.

Coat Type and Grooming: Short and dense; minimal care, but need their ears cleaned regularly. Average shedding.

Lifespan: 10 to 12 years.

Health Concerns: Hip dysplasia, eye problems (PRA, juvenile cataracts, entropion).

Exercise: Moderate to high; quiet in the house if well-exercised.

Housing: Not suited for apartment life; enjoys the outdoors.

Interaction with Others: Very gentle, but basically not interactive with children. Good with other dogs; some can be testy especially with cats.

Trainability: Low to medium, depending on what you are trying to train him to do. If it's hunting raccoons, it's easy; if it's obedience work, it's not. Like other hounds, this breed is not reliable off lead, and will leave you to go hunting if left off leash outside a fenced area.

Activities: Hunting, coonhound trials.

Remarks: This determined breed hunts by treeing its prey and has even been known to tree cougars. He announces his victory by barking, which can become a problem.

AKC Classification: Hound Group.

Part 2

Bloodhound

Character: Gentle, solemn, sensitive, dignified, affectionate, kind. Deep, frightening bark may scare away strangers; in certain circumstances, can be protective, although it must be exceedingly provoked; some are shy.

Origin: Belgium, 700s, and later the rest of Europe and England, although this breed's ancestors can be traced back over 2000 years. Once called St. Hubert's Hound, it was a favorite of French royalty.

Original Purpose: Hunting and trailing.

Physical Attributes: 23 to 27 inches; 80 to 110 pounds; lots of drool, lots of slobber. This largest and strongest of all scent hounds is tireless. Has the best sense of smell of any dog and has been documented to follow a trail more than 100 hours old—one tracked his quarry for 138 miles.

Color: Black and tan, red and tan, tawny.

Coat Type and Grooming: Short, thin, and smooth. Requires minimal care; however, they need their faces and ears cleaned regularly. Average shedding, mostly seasonal.

Lifespan: 7 to 10 years.

Health Concerns: Bloat, hip and elbow dysplasia, OCD, eyelid problems, ear infections, skin infections.

Exercise: These active dogs need plenty of outdoor exercise, but are quiet, even lazy, in the house. Older dogs especially are quite calm.

Housing: Not suited for apartment life; enjoys the outdoors.

Interaction with Others: Bloodhounds are very sociable in the family and quite tolerant of children but are not playful; they may be too big for toddlers. They enjoy meeting new people but are not always demonstrative. They are very good with other pets, although a few may chase small animals.

Trainability: Low to moderate; Bloodhounds can never be let off a lead outside a secure fenced area. Once on a trail, they can't be called off. These dogs take naturally to their ancestral task of man-trailing, but are difficult to train in obedience work. They need careful training and should be the possession only of the most savvy of dog owners. Their character (let alone the drool) is not right for everyone.

Activities: Police work, tracking, search and rescue.

Remarks: The Bloodhound has traditionally been the only dog whose "testimony" is acceptable in court of law.

AKC Classification: Hound Group.

Kennel Club Classification: Hound Group.

Part 2

Border Collie

Character: Workaholic, excitable, quick-thinking, dependable, alert, intuitive.

Origin: Great Britain.

Original Purpose: Shepherding.

Physical Attributes: 19 to 22 inches; 32 to 50 pounds; hardy, extremely agile. While I promised not to evaluate the intelligence of dogs, no one denies that the Border Collie is one of the most brilliant of all breeds. (That's one reason I don't own one. I make it a firm policy not own a dog smarter than I am.)

Color: Black and white, brown, sable, and merle; most have a white blaze; many have tan markings. Solid white is not permitted; predominant white not preferred.

Coat Type and Grooming: Two types, both double and dense. One type has moderately long outercoat and the other has shorter hair. Fairly high maintenance; needs frequent hard brushing to remove dead hair. Professional grooming is optional. Average shedding.

Lifespan: 11 to 14 years.

Health Concerns: Eye problems (PRA, collie eye), seizures, deafness, hip dysplasia.

Exercise: Extraordinary; requires an athletic, motivated owner. Don't even consider this breed unless you are training for the Olympics, are an obedience or agility aficionado, or have a large herd of sheep that need regular rounding up, otherwise, you will end up with a neurotic dog. It is not enough for the Border Collie to just move around; he has to think and solve problems in order to be happy.

Housing: Under no circumstances should this breed be kept in an apartment—it really needs to live where there is plenty of room to run.

Interaction with Others: Good with children, but may try to herd small ones, and nip them in the process. Very reserved toward strangers; gets along with other dogs but may try to herd small animals.

Trainability: Highly trainable, but needs strong early socialization to prevent dominance or shyness. This dog requires a very experienced owner.

Activities: Herding trials, agility, obedience, tracking, flying disc, flyball.

Remarks: The famous Border Collie eye can hypnotize cattle, supposedly derived from the dominance glare of the wolf.

AKC Classification: Herding Group.

Kennel Club Classification: Pastoral Group.

Border Terrier

Character: Loyal, alert, affectionate, inquisitive, friendly, assertive. Not protective, but a good watchdog; some individuals are timid.

Origin: Border region (Cheviot Hills) between England and Scotland, 1700s; related to the Dandie Dinmont.

Original Purpose: Catching foxes, and later other small game.

Physical Attributes: 11 to15 inches; 11 to16 pounds; rugged, racy, very active. Many are barky and many dig.

Color: Red, tan, wheaten, grizzle and tan, blue and tan; dark muzzle.

Coat Type and Grooming: Wiry flat outercoat, short dense undercoat. Requires fairly high maintenance (once a week brushing, some trimming on the head, legs, neck, and tip of tail). Show dogs need to be handstripping every 6 months; clipping is acceptable for pets. Slight to moderate shedding.

Lifespan: 12 to15 years.

Health Concerns: Legg-Perthes, patellar luxation, eye problems (cataracts, progressive retinal atrophy), hip dysplasia.

Exercise: Moderately high.

Housing: Adaptable to apartment life, but prefers the country.

Interaction with Others: Very attached to his owner and excellent with children if well socialized. Good all-around family dog; enjoys being around people. Usually good with other dogs of the opposite sex, also good with family cats if conditioned early; may chase small or unknown animals.

Trainability: High; obedience classes are very important for this breed. They are easy to housetrain.

Activities: Earthdog trials, hunting, tracking, agility.

Remarks: This is one of the few terriers bred to run with the pack.

AKC Classification: Terrier Group.

Kennel Club Classification: Terrier Group.

Part 2

Borzoi

Character: Docile, calm, gentle, aloof, independent, courageous. Some are reserved or timid with strangers, and there is a rare but definite propensity to fierceness against enemies.

Origin: Russia, Middle Ages.

Original Purpose: Hunting of wolves and hares; often hunted in packs.

Physical Attributes: 26 to 34 inches; 60 to 110 pounds; elegant, graceful, quiet. Males are considerably larger than females. You will notice that the topline curves upward; this is to provide for the double suspension gallop characteristic of Borzois and other sighthounds; it's what makes them so fast. They handle cold very well.

Color: All colors and patterns, but white with spots is most common.

Coat Type and Grooming: Silky, shiny with feathering; either flat or wavy. Fairly high maintenance (twice a week brushing to prevent mats). The male has a longer, thicker coat than the female and needs more attention. Professional grooming is optional; some trimming is required. Periodic shedding; females may shed more than males.

Lifespan: 8 to 13 years.

Health Concerns: Bloat, bone cancer, dental problems, allergic dermatitis, PRA, cataracts, retinopathy, heart disease. This dog is sensitive to anesthesia, like most sighthounds.

Exercise: High; quiet in the house, but loves the outdoors and needs room to run.

Housing: Surprisingly good in apartments with frequent exercise. This breed is an escape artist so needs a fenced-in yard.

Interaction with Others: The Borzoi is tolerant of gentle older children, but not playful; may be too big for toddlers. He is very good with other dogs, and prefers other sighthounds most of all. In fact, it is recommended that Borzois not be the home's only dog. However, Borzois are distinctly not good with small, fluffy dogs or cats that may remind them of game.

Trainability: The Borzoi requires an experienced handler, and obedience classes are a must with this dog; they require gentle, consistent training. They are easily bored. This is a dog best purchased from a responsible and serious breeder and not ideal for a first-time owner.

Activities: Therapy dog, lure coursing.

Remarks: The Borzoi used to be called the Russian Wolfhound, in honor of his natural function. The Czars never sold these prized royal possessions, but on occasion gave them away to honored visitors.

AKC Classification: Hound Group.

Kennel Club Classification: Hound Group.

Boston Terrier

Character: Affectionate, playful, lively, devoted, friendly, strong-willed. Makes a good watchdog.

Origin: Boston, 1870s. English Bulldog and English White Terriers are in the background. The first Boston Terriers were larger than the ones seen today.

Original Purpose: Companion, although it did not object to chasing the occasional rat or two.

Physical Attributes: 12 to 17 inches; 11 to 25 pounds; short snout and muzzle; cannot handle extremes of heat or cold.

Color: Black, brindle, or seal with white markings including a muzzle band, blaze, and forechest. A white collar and white markings on the legs are also desirable.

Coat Type and Grooming: Short, shiny; easy to maintain (once a week brushing). Minimal shedding.

Lifespan: 10 to 15 or more years.

Health Concerns: Bloat, respiratory problems, tumors, Cushings disease, thyroid disease, deafness, heart problems, skin problems (allergies), cataracts, cancer.

Exercise: Low to medium; generally well-mannered; adult dogs are especially laid-back.

Housing: Ideal for apartment life.

Interaction with Others: Very good with most kids; a few not tolerant of young children. Generally good with other pets; some males can be somewhat aggressive to other male dogs.

Trainability: High, although the breed can be stubborn.

Activities: Obedience, agility.

Remarks: Despite the name "terrier," the Boston Terrier was not bred to chase vermin, but to be a companion animal.

AKC Classification: Terrier Group.

Kennel Club Classification: Utility Group.

Bouvier des Flandres

Character: Stable, protective, steady, loyal, fearless, calm. Bonds to one person. An excellent watch-dog.

Origin: Belgium and France, 1600s.

Original Purpose: Herding cows, police work, farm work, cart-pulling.

Physical Attributes: 23 to 27 inches; 90 to 110 pounds; powerful, compact, big, strong; slow to mature.

Color: Fawn to black, salt and pepper, brindle, gray.

Coat Type and Grooming: Rough, thick, wiry, medium length outercoat; soft dense undercoat. Requires a thorough brushing every day. Professional grooming is highly desirable. Average to high shedding.

Lifespan: 10 to 12 years.

Health Concerns: Hip dysplasia, OCD.

Exercise: Needs plenty of exercise.

Housing: Likes the outdoors; best living in the country or with plenty of room to run.

Interactions with Others: The Bouvier is particularly fond of children; however, it may try to dominate owners. Good with other pets if socialized very early; can be bad with cats.

Trainability: Not a good dog for novice owners, they can be domineering. Obedience classes are a must.

Activities: Herding trials, security, agility, therapy dog, police and guide dog, cattle drover.

Remarks: British writer Ouida (1839-1908) wrote a famous book, *A Dog of Flanders*, about this breed, which was almost wiped out during World War I. Nicole Martin, a Bouvier owner for 18 years, writes, "They are courageous, consistent (by this I mean I have not seen moodiness or erratic behavior), affectionate without being cloyingly so, and stubborn. It helps to have two at a time so that they can play with and chase each other to channel some of that herding energy. They are wonderful creatures to hug and nuzzle with that soft coat. However, that pleasure comes at a price; plan on spending about 20 minutes 3 or 4 times a week just grooming and managing it."

AKC Classification: Herding Group.

Kennel Club Classification: Working Group.

Part 2

Boxer

Character: Exuberant, courageous, alert, playful, affectionate, biddable; an excellent watch and guard dog.

Origin: Germany, 1800s; a German descendant of the Mastiff.

Original Purpose: Police work, pit fighting, bull and bear baiting, boar hunting.

Physical Attributes: 21 to 25 inches; 55 to 80 pounds; sturdy, agile, athletic, strong. This dog has very little tolerance for heat and snores, due to their shortened muzzles. Tails are docked. Show dogs have cropped ears in the United States, but the trend is going toward a more natural look.

Color: Fawn and brindle, usually with white markings. The brindle must show clearly defined black stripes; white markings may not exceed one-third of the coat.

Coat Type and Grooming: Smooth, short; a quick once-a-week brushing will suffice; a seasonal shedder.

Lifespan: 8 to 12 years.

Health Concerns: Various cancers (osteosarcoma), PRA, orthopedic problems (arthritis, hip dysplasia), heart disease (cardiomyopathy, SAS), dental problems, allergies, bloat, digestive difficulties (soy intolerance), obesity, enteritis, corneal ulcer. White Boxers are often blind or deaf.

Exercise: Moderate to high, especially when young.

Housing: Can manage in a large apartment if given a chance to run every day. Some are hyperactive. They can be escape artists.

Interaction with Others: Excellent with the whole family, including children, although they can be too rambunctious for very small children. They like friendly strangers also, if properly introduced, but are suspicious of unannounced visitors. They need a lot of human interaction. Males may be aggressive with dogs they do not know.

Trainability: These dogs can be stubborn and need early obedience training.

Activities: Obedience, agility, therapy dog, police work

Remarks: The Boxer's name comes from the posture he adopts when fighting—rising on his hind legs and striking out with the front paws.

AKC Classification: Working Group.

Kennel Club Classification: Working Group.

Briard

Character: Happy, dominant, devoted, self-assured, lively, strong-willed. This dog makes a superb watchdog and guard dog.

Origin: France, 1300s; probably the most ancient of the French sheepdogs.

Original Purpose: Shepherding.

Physical Attributes: 22 to 27 inches, 75 to100 pounds; strong; has double dewclaws on the hind leg; ears are cropped.

Color: Any solid color except white; mostly commonly black, tawny, fawn, or gray. A small amount of white permitted in the chest. Nose must be black.

Coat Type and Grooming: Long (up to a foot in show dogs, commonly 4 to 6 inches long in pets), slightly wavy, very dry, double; undercoat fine and tight; traditionally likened to a "goat's coat." Very high maintenance, requires lots of brushing; coat continues to grow throughout the life of the dog; some trimming needed. Professional grooming is very desirable. Average shedding.

Lifespan: 12 to14 years.

Health Concerns: Hip dysplasia, eye problems (congenital night blindness, cataracts), bloat, von Willebrand's, hypothyroidism.

Exercise: Moderate to high.

Housing: These dogs need a great deal of space.

Interaction with Others: Very suspicious of strangers, but excellent with children if socialized early; may attempt to herd them. Suspicious of other pets; aggressive with other dogs.

Trainability: High, but they need early socialization. This is not a dog for beginners. These powerful dogs can easily take over the house if permitted.

Activities: Search and rescue, police work, herding, agility, herding trials, Schutzhund.

Remarks: If you get a Briard, choose a breeder who understands that you are looking for pet, not a guard or herding dog, and who breeds for pet temperament.

AKC Classification: Herding Group.

Kennel Club Classification: Pastoral Group.

Part 2

Brittany

Character: Brave, happy, stubborn, alert, energetic, independent; tends to bond to one person; some individuals are timid. This breed requires close human companionship.

Origin: Brittany, France, mid-1800s.

Original Purpose: Hunting upland game birds.

Physical Attributes: 17 to 20 inches; 30 to 40 pounds; fast, compact, lots of stamina, weather resistant. Tails may be docked if not naturally short.

Color: White and orange, liver and white; roan patterns and with some ticking permitted. Color should be deep and clear.

Coat Type and Grooming: Dense, medium-short, lightly feathered and silky; may be flat or wavy. Requires brushing twice a week. Professional grooming is optional; some trimming required. Moderate shedding.

Lifespan: 11 to 13 years.

Health Concerns: Hip dysplasia, glaucoma, seizures, VSD.

Exercise: Very high; without exercise several times a day, they can become destructive.

Housing: Not well suited to apartment life; needs a large yard at the very least. This dog does much better in the country than in the city.

Interaction with Others: Good with children, very playful, but needs gentle treatment. Usually extremely friendly to strangers but sometimes suspicious. Generally very good with other pets, although some males dislike other males.

Trainability: High; this dog is easily bored and likes a challenge; not very reliable off lead.

Activities: Field trial, hunting (birds), hunting tests, obedience, agility.

Remarks: This all-round gun dog breed used to be known as the Brittany spaniel, but it was decided in 1982 that the dog has insufficient spaniel characteristics to be given that name. In the field, he acts more like a pointer or setter than a spaniel; thus, the Brittany became the smallest of the pointing breeds.

AKC Classification: Sporting Group.

Kennel Club Classification: Gundog Group.

Part 2

Brussels Griffon

Character: Cheeky, self-confident, bold, sensitive, lively; a one-person dog.

Origin: Belgium, 1800s. Possible ancestors include Affenpinschers, Pugs, and unknown collaborators.

Original Purpose: Vermin exterminators.

Physical Attributes: 7 to 8 inches; 8 to 11 pounds; active. Comes in two types: rough (Griffon Bruxellois) and smooth (Petit Brabaçon). Due to shortened muzzle, some snore or wheeze; docked tail.

Color: Red, beige, black, black and tan.

Coat Type and Grooming: Two coat types: rough and smooth. Both require minimal care (brush once a week). Rough-coated dogs' coats should be hard and wiry and require combing several times a week and stripping a couple of times a year. Professional grooming is recommended for the rough coat; stripping for show dogs, clipping for pets. Low to moderate shedding.

Lifespan: 12 to 15 years.

Health Concerns: Patellar luxation, PRA.

Exercise: Fairly low, but loves to play.

Housing: Ideal for apartment life.

Interaction with Others: Not very good with young children, good with older kids and other pets.

Trainability: High; good problem solvers; many, however, are hard to housetrain.

Activities: Obedience.

Remarks: Famous Dog: Memorably featured with Jack Nicholson in the movie *As Good as it Gets*.

AKC Classification: Toy Group.

Kennel Club Classification: Griffon Bruxellois, Toy Group.

Bulldog

Character: Jovial, obstinate, friendly, obstinate, amiable, obstinate, stable, obstinate, lovable, obstinate (see any patterns?). Can be given to sulking; makes a good watchdog but is not usually protective. An example of a breed that used to be ferocious, but whose character has been modified by careful breeding.

Origin: England, 1200s.

Original Purpose: Bull and bear-baiting (a cruel practice that was outlawed in England in 1835), fighting. The whole idea behind the pushed-in muzzle was that the dog could grab the opponent and still breathe, a clever anatomical trick for an absurd purpose.

Physical Attributes: 10 to15 inches; 40 to 55 pounds, with females smaller than males; does not do well in heat or cold.

Color: Brindle, solid white, fawn, red, fallow or any of these on a white background.

Coat Type and Grooming: Short; very little maintenance (once-a-week brushing); but the facial wrinkles require cleaning to avoid dermatitis. High shedding.

Lifespan: 8 to 10 years.

Health Concerns: Eyelid abnormalities (entropion, distichiasis), orthopedic problems (hip dysplasia, OCD), deafness, heart disease (pulmonic stenosis, VSD), obesity, skin problems (allergies), respiratory difficulties, especially in the heat.

Exercise: Very low; can get along with little exercise.

Housing: Can adapt to almost any environment, as long as there are no huge stairs to climb. Needs air conditioning or a cooler climate.

Interaction with Others: Wonderful with children, and usually quite tolerant of strangers. Extremely slow to become aroused, but could be dangerous if it does. Can be aggressive to other dogs but usually ignores them; usually fine with other pets.

Trainability: Low; early socialization important.

Activities: Companion.

Remarks: Debbie Paxton, of Recycled Bulldogs Rescue and Referral, states that a Bulldog "requires an educated owner with unlimited time, patience, a sense of humor, and a desire for love and laughter." George Cromer of the Detroit Bulldog Club, adds, "The Bulldog is a kindly disposed, fun-loving companion (couch potato) that is not suited for guard duty despite its fearsome appearance." Still, my favorite comment, grounded in the realities of Bulldog ownership, comes from Dot Snowden, of the Dallas Bulldog club: "Bulldog – snorting, snoring, gas passing, drooling couch potato, rather like a husband." Bulldogs are the mascot of Yale University and the Marines, as well as many other sporting teams in the US.

AKC Classification: Non-Sporting Group.

Kennel Club Classification: Utility Group.

Bullmastiff

Character: Independent, fearless, dependable, level-headed, protective, reserved; not playful. Suspicious of strangers.

Origin: England, 1800s, but not officially recognized in Britain until 1924. It is said that the Bullmastiff is about 60-percent Mastiff and 40-percent Bulldog.

Original Purpose: It was known as the "gamekeeper's night dog," a guard dog to keep away poachers; also a dog of war.

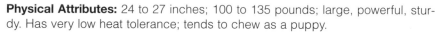

Physical Attributes: 24 to 27 inches; 100 to 135 pounds; large, powerful, sturdy. Has very low heat tolerance; tends to chew as a puppy.

Color: Red, fawn, brindle; muzzle is black.

Coat Type and Grooming: Short; requires easy care; no trimming. Light seasonal shedding.

Lifespan: 10 years.

Health Concerns: Orthopedic problems (hip dysplasia, OCD), obesity.

Exercise: Moderate; generally considered a low-energy dog, especially indoors.

Housing: Adaptable to any living situation.

Interaction with Others: Usually excellent with children, but not playful; very loving in its family. Needs proper socialization so it will not become overprotective of "his" children. Enjoys a lot of interaction. Mostly good with other pets, especially when well-socialized, but can be aggressive with same-sex dogs or with small dogs; does not approve of strange dogs.

Trainability: Needs early obedience training. This dog is difficult to train, and some try to dominate the family children. He does best with a strong, experienced owner.

Activities: Agility, obedience, police and military work.

Remarks: For an interesting inside look at the world of dog showing, try reading *Dog Eat Dog,* which features a Bullmastiff.

AKC Classification: Working Group.

Kennel Club Classification: Working Group.

Bull Terrier

Character: Sweet, obstinate, charming, playful, loyal, even-tempered; highly territorial and a good watchdog.

Origin: England, 1800s. May have Dalmatian and Bulldog in its background.

Original Purpose: Dog fighting, bull-baiting

Physical Attributes: 20 to 22 inches; 35 to 60 pounds; strong, muscular, solid, symmetrical; egg-shaped head and very small eyes.

Color: The first bull terriers were colored, then all-white ones gained popularity, until that was practically the only color seen. In the 1920s, it was recognized that the white was associated with a gene for deafness, so color (white with red or brindle) has been gradually re-introduced. Today, white and colored Bull Terriers are shown separately, although they are one breed.

Coat Type and Grooming: Smooth; requires minimal care; once a week brushing with a natural bristle brush or hound mitt. Slight shedding.

Lifespan: 11 to 14 years.

Health Concerns: Patellar luxation, allergic dermatitis, deafness in white varieties, kidney problems.

Exercise: Moderate to high; needs long walks and exercise; will become destructive if given insufficient exercise.

Housing: Can adapt to almost any living situation with adequate exercise.

Interaction with Others: Good with children, especially if socialized early; may be aloof with strangers; enjoys being center of interest. Good with other pets, although often aggressive; usually needs to be raised with other dogs and socialized early.

Trainability: Needs firm training; tends to be disobedient—this dog is nicknamed the "gladiator of the terriers."

Activities: Flyball, agility.

Remarks: Because these dogs are expected to refrain from seeking or provoking a conflict, they are sometimes called the White Cavalier. Famous Dog: Spuds MacKenzie, of beer commercial fame, is a Bull Terrier.

AKC Classification: Terrier Group.

Kennel Club Classification: Terrier Group.

Cairn Terrier

Character: Plucky, courageous, spirited, cheerful, independent, inquisitive; superior watchdog, although his bark is bigger than his bite.

Origin: Scottish Highlands and islands, Middle Ages. It is related to the West Highland White Terrier, and the two breeds were freely crossed until 1916. In fact, early Cairns, West Highland White Terriers, and Scottish Terriers often came from the same litter and were separated only by color.

Original Purpose: Hunting foxes, rats, otter, and badgers.

Physical Attributes: 9 to 12 inches; 13-15 pounds; agile, strong, tireless. Cairns are diggers and barkers.

Color: Cream, wheaten, red, gray, nearly black or brindle; solid black, white, or black and tan not permitted; ears, muzzle, and tail usually dark.

Coat Type and Grooming: Harsh, shaggy weatherproof outercoat; undercoat soft and dense. Medium care required; one or twice weekly grooming with a steel comb. Eyes need special care. Professional grooming is recommended; dead hair should be stripped a couple times a year, even for pets. Slight seasonal shedding.

Lifespan: 14 to 15 years.

Health Concerns: Portal systemic shunt (liver problem), blood disorders (von Willebrand's, globoid cell leukodystrophy); CMO, eye problems (PRA, ocular melanosis), allergies.

Exercise: Moderate; does well in an urban environment, but needs regular outdoor exercise. Can be restless in the house, but given enough room, it will self-exercise.

Housing: Adaptable to almost any living situation.

Interaction with Others: This breed is not always reliable with toddlers, but likes to play with older kids, although tends to be bossy. Enjoys the company of human beings but is not much of a snuggler. Gets along with other dogs if socialized early but not fond of sharing his household with other pets.

Trainability: Low to moderate, but responsive to his owner, and a good problem solver. Some try to dominate their owners.

Activities: Earthdog trials.

Remarks: Betty Marcum, of the Cairn Terrier Club of America, says a Cairn Terrier is a "big dog in a little dog's body with love enough for the entire household." Famous Dog: Toto, the dog in *The Wizard of Oz,* was a Cairn Terrier.

AKC Classification: Terrier Group.

Kennel Club Classification: Terrier Group.

Canaan Dog

Character: Protective, alert, inquisitive, devoted, independent; this is a dog that does not suffer separation anxiety and can be left alone for longer periods than many other dogs.

Origin: Israel.

Original Purpose: Herding and guard dog, sentry.

Physical Attributes: 20 to 24 inches; 35 to 55 pounds; acute sense of smell and hearing. These dogs are barkers.

Color: Black and white; brown and white; or solid black, liver, sand, or brown; gray and brindle are unacceptable. Dogs that are mostly white must have a colored symmetrical mask.

Coat Type and Grooming: Medium short, harsh; weather resistant outercoat, soft undercoat. Weekly grooming required. Average shedding year round; heavier in spring and fall.

Lifespan: 12 to 14 years.

Health Concerns: Because nature has been its breeder for so many years, there are very few health problems associated with this breed.

Exercise: Moderate.

Housing: Adaptable to any living situation; a good watchdog and protection dog.

Interaction with Others: Good with children it is raised with; not fond of strange children; reserved and cautious with strangers. Good with family animals, dislikes strange cats and dogs; many are same-sex aggressive.

Trainability: High. This dog is a fast learner and is easy to housetrain.

Activities: Tracking, military service, agility, herding trials.

Remarks: This breed very nearly became extinct after the Romans suppressed the Jews in the first century and the Diaspora began. Most of these dogs became feral and were rediscovered only in the 20th century by Dr. Rudolphina Menzel, a professor of animal and comparative psychology at the University of Tel Aviv, who helped the Israeli military come up with a perfect dog for their needs, and one who could survive in the desert.

AKC Classification: Herding Group.

Kennel Club Classification: Utility Group.

Cardigan Welsh Corgi

Character: More introverted, less playful, and more serious than the Pembroke Welsh Corgi; stable, alert. Good watchdog; enjoys family activities.

Origin: Wales.

Original Purpose: Cattle dog.

Physical Attributes: 10 to 12 inches; 26 to 39 pounds; active, powerful, hardy; may bark.

Color: Red, sable, brindle, blue merle, black and tri-colored; anything except all white. Usually white around the neck, chest, legs, stomach, and tail tip.

Coat Type and Grooming: Double coat, dense, medium length; outercoat harsh, undercoat soft and thick. A thorough brushing twice a week is necessary; professional grooming is optional. Moderate to heavy shedding; sheds all year, but mostly in fall and spring.

Lifespan: 10 to 12 years.

Health Concerns: Orthopedic problems (hip dysplasia, disc problems), blindness.

Exercise: High.

Housing: Can live in urban areas if given frequent exercise.

Interaction with Others: Very devoted to children; but can be protective of "his" kids. Reserved with strangers; not always good with other pets.

Trainability: High.

Activities: Therapy dog, cattle drover, herding, agility.

Remarks: The Corgis were officially divided into two breeds in 1934—the Cardigan and the Pembroke: Cardigans are the Corgis with the tails. The Cardigan is not as commonly seen as the tailless Pembroke, but is probably the older breed. In fact, it is one of the first breeds to be developed in the British Isles. Legend says that ancient Celts of central Europe brought the dog's ancestors to south Wales, settling in Cardiganshire, hence the name of the dog. Some people believe that the Cardigan Welsh Corgi (but not the Pembroke) shares the same ancestors as the Dachshund.

AKC Classification: Herding Group.

Kennel Club Classification: Pastoral Group.

Cavalier King Charles Spaniel

Character: Companionable, trusting, friendly, gay, sweet, gentle; not a good watchdog.

Origin: England, 1600s; named for both King Charles.

Original Purpose: Flushing small birds.

Physical Attributes: 12 to 13 inches; 12 to 18 pounds; elegant

Color: Ruby or mahogany (solid red); Blenheim (red and white); black and tan; tricolor.

Coat Type and Grooming: Fairly high maintenance; needs regular grooming. Professional grooming is optional. Average shedding.

Lifespan: 10 to 14 years.

Health Concerns: Heart problems (mitral valve insufficiency), patellar luxation, cataracts.

Exercise: Moderate to high.

Housing: Adaptable to any living situation.

Interaction with Others: Very good with people, including children and older folks; needs a lot of attention and kisses from his family. Delighted to meet any strangers; usually okay with other dogs; very nice with cats.

Trainability: Average.

Activities: Flyball, tracking. (At the last tracking event I attended, a Cavalier King Charles Spaniel took top honors.)

Remarks: This dog was named after the second King Charles; the first one was beheaded.

AKC Classification: Toy Group.

Kennel Club Classification: Toy Group.

Part 2

Chesapeake Bay Retriever

Character: Hardworking, strong-willed, loyal, inquisitive, courageous, protective. This breed is an excellent watchdog and can be protective and territorial.

Origin: United States, 1800s. Ancestors may have included Newfoundlands and Labrador Retrievers.

Original Purpose: Hunting and retrieving game (ducks), especially in rough conditions.

Physical Attributes: 21 to 26 inches; 55 to 80 pounds; hardy, burly, strong, rugged. Loves water; can handle icy water with ease; very talkative.

Color: Brown shades, including a light shade delightfully called "deadgrass." Many color shades including red, brown, yellow, tan, and "sedge." It comes in chocolate too, which is considerably more appetizing. White markings are permitted on the chest, belly, toes, or back of feet. The coat tends to fade a bit in the summer. Eyes are amber-colored.

Coat Type and Grooming: Double, water-resistant coat is thick, wavy, and short (not longer than 1 inch), loaded with natural oils; undercoat is dense and woolly. Frequent bathing is unnecessary, as it may strip the coat of its oils. Medium maintenance; brush twice a week. Professional grooming is optional; no trimming required. Average shedding.

Lifespan: 10 to 13 years.

Health Concerns: Hip and elbow dysplasia, bloat, eye problems (PRA, cataracts), eczema.

Exercise: High; calm in the house, but this tireless dog needs a great deal of outside exercise, preferably in water; superb swimmer.

Housing: Not suitable for urban life; needs a lot of room to run; preferably near a body of water.

Interaction with Others: Excellent family dogs, although require a strong owner as they can be dominant. Good with gentle kids; very protective of family; reserved toward strangers. Will usually accept other dogs, although it tries to dominate them; may be aggressive on occasion.

Activities: Field trials, waterfowl retrieving, obedience.

Training: Early socialization and regular obedience training is needed to stay in charge of this dominant dog; not for the first-time dog owner. They can be stubborn. Many of these dogs do not do well with crate training.

Remarks: The Chessie is the state dog of Maryland, of course, and one of two sporting dogs developed in the United States.

AKC Classification: Sporting Group.

Kennel Club Classification: Gundog Group.

Part 2

Chihuahua

Character: Alert, curious, loyal, mischievous, temperamental, spirited. Tends to bond to one person; many are shy with or dislike strangers. Chihuahuas make great pets for elderly people; they enjoy attention.

Origin: Probably Central Mexico in the 1500s, although some experts think it may have been Malta in the Mediterranean; others suggest China. Ancestry may include the long-coated Techichi, an ancient Toltec breed, and a hairless breed from Asia. Rediscovered in the state of Chihuahua, Mexico in the 1850s.

Original Purpose: Companion.

Physical Attributes: 6 to 10 inches; 2 to 6 pounds; graceful, agile. Cannot tolerate cold. Generally considered to be the world's smallest dog; great mousers.

Color: Any color or markings permitted.

Coat Type and Grooming: Chihuahuas come in Smooth and the less common Longhaired varieties. Grooming for the smooth is minimal, longhair requires brushing a couple of times a week. Slight but constant shedding for the smooth; longhaired variety sheds seasonally.

Lifespan: 16 to 18 years

Health Concerns: Heart disease (pulmonic stenosis, mitral valve insufficiency), cancer, dental problems (gingivitis), orthopedic problems (patellar luxation, fractures), cruciate ligament ruptures, hydrocephalus, enteritis, Cushing's, dermatitis. Many have an incomplete closure in the skull; this spot is vulnerable to trauma.

Exercise: Light to moderate. Requires a lot of attention, but minimal exercise.

Housing: Ideal for urban areas or apartment life.

Interaction with Others: Not suited for homes with kids under the age of 12; good with gentle older children. Gets along with other Chihuahuas, but not good with other breeds; good with cats and other household pets.

Trainability: Variable—medium to high; needs extensive early socialization. Despite their small size, Chihuahuas can become dominant or nippy if not properly trained.

Activities: Obedience.

Remarks: Despite their reputation for being frail frou-frou dogs, a Chihuahua named Spicey fell off a boat in Wisconsin, swam three miles to an island, and survived for seven days honing her bug and mousing skills. Spicey was discovered by workers on the island and reunited with her owner, who had given her up for dead.

AKC Classification: Toy Group.

Kennel Club Classification: Toy Group.

Chinese Crested

Character: Playful, happy, devoted, gay, cheerful; can be territorial. These dogs do not do well left alone for long periods.

Origin: China, 1200s.

Original Purpose: Ratter, companion.

Physical Attributes: 9 to 13 inches; 11 to 13 pounds. This breed has no cold tolerance, and hairless dogs need to be protected from the sun.

Color: Any color or combination of colors acceptable.

Coat Type and Grooming: Two types: hairless (no coat at all), and "powderpuff," which is described in the standard as "double soft and silky" with "long, thin guard hairs over the short silky undercoat."

Although you would think the hairless brand of Chinese Crested Dogs are easy to groom, they are subject to pimples, acne, and even pustules. If they are outside in the summer, they need sunscreen. Professional grooming is not needed except for show dogs. Mild shedding.

Lifespan: 13 to 15 years.

Health Concerns: Legg-Perthes, skin allergies and infections.

Exercise: Minimal to moderate, although they are quite active.

Housing: Ideal for urban areas or apartment life.

Interaction with Others: Both varieties are good with children, although some say the Hairless is somewhat better than the Powderpuff. Excellent with other pets.

Trainability: Average to high; requires gentle handling.

Activities: Obedience.

Remarks: Although somewhat strange looking, these dogs are well known for their happy and sweet temperaments.

AKC Classification: Toy Group.

Kennel Club Classification: Toy Group.

Chinese Shar-Pei

Character: Independent, calm, self-assured, alert, regal, friendly; loving to its family but reserved with strangers.

Origin: China (Han Dynasty), 1200s.

Original Purpose: Hunting wild boar, dog fighting, herder and protector of livestock and homes.

Physical Attributes: 18 to 20 inches; 45 to 60 pounds; very wrinkled skin with short hair. The tongue is blue-black (like Chow Chows). The original Chinese description of the Shar-Pei included a head like a "melon-shaped pear," ears like clamshells, nose like a butterfly, back like a shrimp, and neck like a water buffalo.

Color: Solid colors: black, cream, fawn, or red.

Coat Type and Grooming: Easy maintenance; once a week brushing. The word "shar-pei" means "sandy coat," referring to its texture. Special care needed for folds of the skin. Needs frequent ironing (just kidding!). Average shedding.

Lifespan: 9 to 12 years.

Health Concerns: Skin allergies, orthopedic problems (OCD, elbow dysplasia), eye problems (entropion).

Exercise: Moderate.

Housing: Can adapt to any living situation.

Interaction with Others: If not socialized, not good with children; reserved toward strangers. Not good with other dogs, but usually gets along fine with other pets.

Trainability: Low to average; this independent breed needs patient training.

Activities: Companion, obedience.

Remarks: "Having a Chinese Shar-Pei is like having a three year old," comments Susan Lauer, Secretary of the Chinese Shar-Pei Club of America. "They are past the negativity of a two year old, and they want to be with you all the time. They are very eager to please, and then they go off to play or sleep." The breed almost became extinct after dogs were prohibited as pets on the Chinese mainland, but breeders in Hong Kong kept them going. The temperament of the Shar-Pei is steadily improving.

AKC Classification: Non-Sporting Group.

Kennel Club Classification: Utility Group.

Part 2

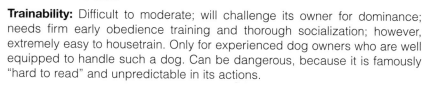

Chow Chow

Character: Self-contained, independent, dignified, strong-minded, stubborn, loyal. Some individuals are aggressive, and most are highly territorial. Very fine guard dogs.

Origin: Mongolia, maybe 4000 years ago; later introduced into China.

Original Purpose: Fighting, guarding, cart-pulling, and food.

Physical Attributes: 17 to 22 inches; 45 to 85 pounds; very powerful. Chow Chows have black/purple tongues and straight hind legs (for a dog). They can handle cold but have no tolerance for heat. The deep-set eyes of the Chow Chow give it limited vision, and the dog should be approached within those limitations.

Color: Solid red, black, cream, blue, fawn, and cinnamon. All colors equally acceptable. The baby coat will change at about three months to the color and texture of the adult dog.

Coat Type and Grooming: Two types—rough and smooth; both have thick, plush double coats, with a soft woolly undercoat. High maintenance; brushing four times a week. Professional grooming is optional; profuse shedding twice a year.

Lifespan: 9 to 12 years.

Health Concerns: Hip and elbow dysplasia, eye problems (entropion, glaucoma, cataracts), OCD, color dilution alopecia, eczema, VS.

Exercise: Low to moderate.

Housing: Can adapt to any living situation.

Interaction with Others: Aloof; not playful; not good with children outside those in its own family, to whom it is usually devoted. Generally picks one person in the family to bond to and may not always be friendly to others; dislikes or ignores strangers. Has excellent memory for those they dislike; for example, one Chow disliked any person in a UPS uniform. Most do not get along with dogs of their own sex and dislike cats.

Trainability: Difficult to moderate; will challenge its owner for dominance; needs firm early obedience training and thorough socialization; however, extremely easy to housetrain. Only for experienced dog owners who are well equipped to handle such a dog. Can be dangerous, because it is famously "hard to read" and unpredictable in its actions.

Activities: Guarding, companion.

Remarks: Some people believe the slang word "chow" for food comes from the name of this breed. Less creative people insist that the word derives from chaou meaning "strong dog" or even tchau, an important trader. Known as the Lion Dog of China.

AKC Classification: Non-Sporting Group.

Kennel Club Classification: Utility Group.

Clumber Spaniel

Character: Easygoing, friendly, calm, gentle, laid back, dependable; has very low watchdog or protection ability or interest.

Origin: England, 1700s.

Original Purpose: Bird flushing and retrieving.

Physical Attributes: 17 to 20 inches; 50 to 80 pounds; aristocratic, somewhat slow. Acute sense of smell, probably the best of all sporting dogs; enjoys retrieving from water. Some may snore or drool.

Color: Mostly white with orange or lemon markings.

Coat Type and Grooming: Soft, wavy, silky; high maintenance, needs daily thorough brushing. Professional grooming is desirable; needs trimming about twice a month. Average shedding.

Lifespan: 10 to 12 years.

Health Concerns: Autoimmune hemolytic anemia, cataracts, entropion, hip dysplasia.

Exercise: Moderate energy level, not much for vigorous exercise.

Housing: Enjoys being outside so much that he is not suitable for urban life.

Interaction with Others: Excellent with children and strangers; never aggressive. Very well adapted to family life, but may select one person for special attention.

Trainability: High.

Activities: Therapy dog, bird flushing, tracking, hunting.

Remarks: The name Clumber Spaniel comes from Clumber Park Kennels of the Duke of Newcastle who lived in Nottinghamshire. I suppose Clumber Spaniel is less of a mouthful than the Duke of Newcastle in Nottinghamshire Spaniel.

AKC Classification: Sporting Group.

Kennel Club Classification: Gundog Group.

Part 2

Cocker Spaniel

Character: Curious, upbeat, merry, affectionate, loyal, trustworthy. A few individuals can be protective. Some can be shy. Many choose one person for special attention.

Origin: United States, 1800s; although earliest ancestors hail from Spain. The breed came to the US from England between 1870 and 1880; the main split between this breed and the English Cocker took place around 1920.

Original Purpose: Hunting woodcocks and quail, flushing game.

Physical Attributes: 14 to 15 inches; 21 to 30 pounds; docked tail. The Cocker is the smallest of all the spaniels; some are barkers.

Color: Jet black (includes black-and-tan,), buff, chocolate, cream, red, particolor (any solid color broken up with a white background), tricolor.

Coat Type and Grooming: Outer coat silky; very high maintenance; two or three times weekly brushing, even for household pets; grooming for show dogs is immense. Professional grooming is necessary every few weeks; dogs that go untrimmed develop unmanageable coats. Regular bathing needed; eyes, ears, and feet need particular attention. Average shedder.

Lifespan: 10 to 15 years or more.

Health Concerns: Umbilical hernia, cancer, orthopedic problems (hip dysplasia, patellar luxation), obesity, sebaceous gland tumors, allergies, ear problems, eye problems (cataracts, PRA, distichiasis, glaucoma), autoimmune diseases, heart problems (pulmonic stenosis, mitral valve insufficiency, cardiomyopathy).

Exercise: Moderate to very high; needs regular walks; quiet in the house.

Housing: Can adapt to any living situation.

Interaction with Others: Excellent with all kinds of people, including children, if the dog was bred by a responsible breeder and properly socialized, and friendly to strangers. Some can be very unpredictable and snappish, but that is not the normal temperament for this breed. Usually good with other pets.

Trainability: High; many enjoy learning tricks.

Activities: Retrieving, agility, obedience, flyball.

Remarks: Breeders are working hard to improve the temperament of the Cocker Spaniel, which seriously degenerated during the period of the breed's wild popularity after the production of Disney's *Lady and the Tramp*. Although officially classed as a sporting dog, they have lost most of their hunting instincts.

AKC Classification: Sporting Group.

Kennel Club Classification: Gundog Group.

Collie

Character: Patient, sensitive, friendly, independent, gentle, gay. Some individuals are shy, high-strung, or stubborn. They make good watchdogs. Some (especially the smooth coat) can be quite protective, others not at all.

Origin: Scotland (Lowlands), 1800s. The word "collie" may descend from "collies" or Scottish Highlands. Others suggest it comes from Colley, a variety of sheep that the dog herded. It has been suggested that Borzoi and Deerhound may be in the background.

Original Purpose: Shepherding.

Physical Attributes: 22 to 26 inches; 45 to 75 pounds; active, lithe. The rough collie is not well suited to extreme heat but can handle bitter weather with ease. Originally, the long-haired variety may have been the herder, and the smooth hair the drover. Some are barkers.

Color: Sable and white, tricolor, blue merle, predominantly white.

Coat Type and Grooming: Two types: rough and smooth: smooth has a short, dense, straight, flat coat; rough has an abundant, long, straight, harsh outer coat; both have a dense undercoat. The rough collie is a high maintenance dog; brushing an hour a week; needs frequent bathing. Professional grooming is desirable for the rough collie; not necessary for the smooth. Sheds a lot (in clumps) twice a year.

Lifespan: 8 to 12 years.

Health Concerns: Bloat, skin problems, cancer (osteosarcoma), PDA, eye problems (collie eye anomaly, PRA), collie nose, food allergies, deafness (merle color). This breed is also very sensitive to many kinds of heartworm medication and worm pills in general.

Exercise: High exercise requirements; enjoys regular organized activities.

Housing: Not usually suited for apartment life; however, they have been known to adapt as long as they get plenty of exercise and attention.

Interaction with Others: Excellent with children, especially if raised with them. They may try to herd them, though. Collies are also quite friendly to strangers.

Trainability: High, although they have an independent streak. Collies make excellent obedience prospects.

Activities: Herding, obedience, agility.

Remarks: Lorrie Oreck, President of Minnesota Wisconsin Collie Rescue says, "The Collie is a sensitive, soft-natured dog that can be a wonderful family dog; however, take note that it is high in maintenance for coat type, very prominent for "herding" nips, and very vocal. It is also a high-maintenance dog for training [requiring] positive reinforcement. To train negatively will only break the spirit of a Collie. If you want a Collie, be prepared to accept the breed with an unconditional spirit. The collie wants to be with its master... it wants to be inside as a companion. It is a loyal breed, giving unconditional love and companionship. The collie is dignity."

AKC Classification: Herding Group.

Kennel Club Classification: Pastoral Group.

Curly-Coated Retriever

Character: Versatile, lively, calm, sensitive, faithful, adaptable. These sharp dogs make great watchdogs. Bonds to whole family; needs a lot of attention.

Origin: England, 1700s. There is obviously Poodle, probably water spaniel, and maybe some St. John's Newfoundland in the background of this breed.

Original Purpose: Hunting both quail and duck.

Physical Attributes: 22 to 27 inches; 50 to 85 pounds. The most graceful of the retrievers, this strong, active dog enjoys swimming. The Curly can handle any kind of weather. The breed is slow to mature, acting like puppies until three or four years of age.

Color: Solid black or liver.

Coat Type and Grooming: Despite the dense, waterproof, tight, crisp, poodle-like curls, this dog is easy to groom. They should be combed twice a week rather than brushed, so the curls stay intact. Some trimming is required. Unlike the Poodle, whose coat continues to grow, the Curly's coat is naturally quite short. If shampooed, extra rinsing is essential. One way to get a perfect coat is to take the dog swimming, and let the coat dry naturally. Heavy shedding once a year, then not at all.

Lifespan: 9 to 13 years.

Health Concerns: Hip and elbow dysplasia, PRA, entropion, bloat, heart murmurs, epilepsy, fleabite dermatitis. The gene pool for this breed is small, so it is essential to go to a good breeder for a puppy to ensure good health.

Exercise: This dog is calm and quiet indoors, but he does need vigorous daily outdoor exercise, preferably in the water or he will become destructive.

Housing: Not suitable for urban areas or apartment life.

Interaction with Others: Excellent; bonds very well with kids if socialized to them early; generally friendly to strangers. Excellent with other pets.

Trainability: High; this breed is easily bored and does best at high-level work. They can be stubborn and respond best to positive reinforcement.

Activities: Hunting (retrieves) over land and water, service dog, search and rescue, agility, obedience, flyball.

Remarks: While the Curly has never attained the popularity of other retrievers, this charming breed makes an equally good pet, show dog, or hunting companion.

AKC Classification: Sporting Group.

Kennel Club Classification: Gundog Group.

Dachshund

Character: Affectionate, bold, lively, alert, confident, determined; a very loyal family dog, affectionate without slavishness. The Longhaired variety is calmest, the Shorthaired the liveliest, and the Wirehaired more affectionate and clownish. Depend on the Dachshunds to give the alert at the approach of strangers—you can't sneak up on this dog; most are territorial.

Origin: Germany, 1500s. No one is sure if the Longhairs are a result of mutation and selective breeding or of crossbreeding, possibly with spaniels. The wirehair is probably the result of crosses of smooth Dachshunds with Schnauzers, and even Dandie Dinmont Terriers. The Miniatures may have a touch of Papillion in their veins.

Original Purpose: Badger hunting.

Physical Attributes. The smallest of the hounds, he comes in two sizes; Standard and Miniature; three coat types; and many colors. The Miniatures are less than 11 pounds; Standards, between 16 and 32 pounds. (Dogs in between are known as "tweenies.") There is no height standard for this breed. Doxies can also be barkers and diggers. The Smooth hair has little tolerance for cold. Known for their long backs, giving them a "hot-dog-like" appearance.

Colors: The Dachshund comes in a rainbow of colors; red, black and tan, cream, black, sable, chocolate, dapple, double dapple, piebald, and wild boar.

Coat Type and Grooming: Three types: Smooth, Longhaired, and Wirehaired. Minimal grooming for the smooth coat; longhair coat needs to be brushed daily; wirehair coat should be stripped a couple of times a year. The ears need special attention. Has no doggy odor, but longhairs benefit from frequent bathing. Professional grooming is not necessary for the shorthair, but is preferable for the long and Wirehaired; only the Wirehaired Dachshund is trimmed. Seasonal shedding.

Lifespan: 15 to 16 years; miniatures live longer—15 to 19 years.

Health Concerns: Orthopedic problems (intervertebral disk disease, patellar luxation, elbow dysplasia), epilepsy, cancer, diabetes, color dilution alopecia, PRA, dermatitis, gastritis, enteritis, von Willebrand's, deafness (in dappled coats).

Exercise: Variable; many Dachshunds are highly energetic dogs, both in and out of the house.

Housing: Can adapt well to apartments, especially if few stairs are involved.

Interaction with Others: Devoted to children in its own family but may not be crazy about other kids. Reserved toward strangers until introduced. Usually alright with other dogs; not good with rodents and other small pets.

Part 2

Dachshund

Trainability: Moderate; the Longhaired variety is more obedient than the other types. This breed needs consistent training and confident owners.

Activities: Earthdog trials (the Dachshund is the only hound that is allowed to compete in AKC Terrier go-to-ground events); field trials, tracking, obedience.

Remarks: Margo D. Mossburg, of Dachshund Rescue NW, writes, "The Miniature Dachshund is bred to be a hunting dog by flushing games out of warrens. Later they became highly prized for their exceedingly loyal personalities and protective natures. Although they can be stubborn at times, they are truly happy family members highly prized by their owners who usually have more than one at a time."

AKC Classification: Hound Group.

Kennel Club Classification: Hound Group.

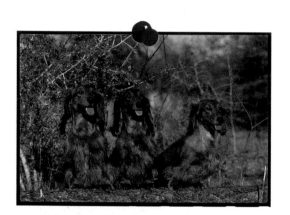

Dalmatian

Character: Lively, eager, loyal, outgoing, versatile; excellent watchdog.

Origins: Whether the breed really comes from Dalmatia or not is debatable, even if you know where Dalmatia is (it's in what used to be Yugoslavia).

Original Purpose: Almost everything—hunting dog, vermin exterminator, carriage dog, fire engine dog, guard dog, draft dog, shepherd dog, war dog, and, of course, circus dog.

Physical Attributes: 19 to 24 inches; 45 to 60 pounds; athletic, extremely active.

Color: White base coat, spotted, with round, well-defined black or liver spots (other colors not permitted) distributed evenly over its body. Spots can range from dime-size to half dollar size. Patches (as opposed to spots) are not permitted, although the spots may overlap. Dalmatian puppies are born pure white, and get their spots in two or three weeks.

Coat Type and Grooming: Short, sleek; easy maintenance; brushing three times a week. High shedding, every day year round.

Lifespan: 12 to 14 years.

Health Concerns: Epilepsy, hip dysplasia, inhalant and food allergies, bladder stones (urolithiasis), and most common, deafness and partial deafness. One-third of all Dalmatians are deaf; these dogs should not be placed in homes with children.

Exercise: Extremely high; tireless; a good jogging partner. If not given sufficient exercise, they become restless, destructive, and neurotic.

Housing: Not suitable for urban areas or apartment life.

Interaction with Others: Very loving in its family, but not suited to families with young children unless carefully socialized. Okay with introduced strangers but is protective if it senses danger to its owner. May be aggressive to strange dogs but all right with family pets, traditionally likes horses.

Trainability: Average to high; this excitable breed needs firm but kind training.

Activities: Guarding, jogging companion.

Remarks: This once stable breed was overbred several years ago (due to the Disney movie *101 Dalmatians*) and its disposition suffered as a result. Dalmatian breeders are working hard to restore the dog's natural good character, so it is especially important to select a good breeder or rescue organization when considering this dog.

AKC Classification: Non-Sporting Group.

Kennel Club Classification: Utility Group.

Dandie Dinmont Terrier

Character: Strong-minded, tenacious, "rough-and-tumble," independent, affectionate, persistent; bonds to one person.

Origin: The border region between England and Scotland.

Original Purpose: Hunter of mice, fox, otter, and even badger.

Physical Attributes: 8 to 11 inches; 18 to 21 pounds. The hind legs are longer than the front legs. Likes to dig and is an escape artist.

Color: Mustard (all shades of reddish brown); pepper (all shades of blue/gray); puppies tend to be darker than adults.

Coat Type and Grooming: Rough coat with a silky topknot. Frequent grooming; three times a week with a pin brush. Does best with professional care and periodic stripping or plucking, especially for the show dog. Slight shedding.

Lifespan: 13 to 15 years.

Health Concerns: Intervertebral disc disease, elbow problems.

Exercise: Moderate to high.

Housing: Can adapt to any living situation.

Interaction with Others: Fairly good with children, especially if socialized early. Some are shy or unfriendly with strangers; aggressive with other pets.

Trainability: Average; may try to dominate owner.

Activities: Earthdog trials, obedience.

Remarks: Sandra Stuart, a long time Dandie Dinmont owner and breeder says, "With large eyes showing a wise expression, silky topknot crowning the head and a happy-go-lucky nature, Dandie Dinmonts are great companions—except when their stubborn nature and terrier traits take over." Famous Dog: This is the only breed to be named after a fictional character, featured in a novel, *Guy Mannering*, by Sir Walter Scott.

AKC Classification: Terrier Group.

Kennel Club Classification: Terrier Group.

Doberman Pinscher

Character: Alert, energetic, capable, sensitive, biddable, confident, territorial. An excellent watchdog and guard dog; often a one-person dog.

Origin: Germany, 1890s. Original breeder was Louis Dobermann, a tax collector who needed a guard dog while he collected taxes.

Original Purpose: Guard dog, protection dog.

Physical Attributes: 24 to 28 inches; 60 to 80 pounds; graceful, muscular, energetic, agile, strong. In the US, Dobermans are shown with docked tails and cropped ears.

Color: Black, red, fawn (Isabella), or blue with tan or rust markings; small white patch on chest permitted. White Dobermans are disqualified from the show ring.

Coat Type and Grooming: Smooth, short, glossy hard coat; requires minimal care. Minimal to average shedding seasonally.

Lifespan: 10 to 12 years.

Health Concerns: Orthopedic problems (hip dysplasia, OCD, Wobblers), heart disease (cardiomyopathy, arrhythmia), bloat, color dilution alopecia, von Willebrand's, eye problems, skin disorders (acral lick dermatitis), osteosarcoma.

Exercise: This breed needs a good amount of exercise, although less than you might think for his size. If not given sufficient exercise, this dog can become neurotic, hyperactive, and destructive.

Housing: Adaptable to urban areas, if exercised sufficiently.

Interaction with Others: Usually good with children if raised with them, but should be supervised; may become overprotective of the family kids. Some individuals may try to dominate family members; reserved and quite suspicious of strangers. Not good with dogs it does not know; may try to dominate them. Protective of family pets, so long as it is the "boss."

Trainability: Most are highly trainable, but all need firm handling and very careful training. Some individuals make superior obedience prospects.

Activities: Tracking, police dog, obedience.

Remarks: This breed makes an excellent guard dog and a sweet family dog if socialized properly.

AKC Classification: Working Group.

Kennel Club Classification: Working Group.

Part 2

English Cocker Spaniel

Character: Obedient, exuberant, cheerful, joyful, gentle, loving; a good watchdog.

Origin: England, 1800s. Ancestors may have come from Spain (hence "spaniel").

Original Purpose: Flushing woodcock.

Physical Attributes: 15 to 17 inches; 25 to 35 pounds; elegant. Bigger and more houndlike than the American Cocker Spaniel; tail docked.

Color: Solid black, red (gold), liver, black and tan, buff, liver and tan; any of the foregoing on a white background, either parti-colored, ticked, or roan.

Coat Type and Grooming: Silky, flat, or wavy. High maintenance, though with less coat than the American Cocker Spaniel. Unless carefully groomed, this dog looks messy. Ears and feet need special care. Professional grooming is recommended; some trimming required. Moderate shedding year round.

Lifespan: 12 to 15 years.

Health Concerns: Eye problems (PRA, cataracts, glaucoma, distichiasis), hip dysplasia, ear problems, cardiomyopathy, obesity, deafness (particolors). Some solid colors have a history of rage syndrome.

Exercise: High; this dog needs plenty of human companionship and doesn't do well if left alone for long periods. They are very family oriented and enjoy traveling. They also need a lot of exercise, much more than the American Cocker. This breed calms down as it matures.

Housing: Can adapt to any living situation.

Interaction with Others: Excellent, very good with children and new people alike if properly bred and healthy. Gets along with most other pets, as long as they are introduced properly.

Trainability: High

Activities: Hunting, obedience, tracking, agility.

Remarks: The English Cocker was developed in England after the creation of the American version. This breed has escaped many of the problems of its more popular cousin, the American Cocker Spaniel, but if people are serious about a hunting companion, they should go to field lines rather than show lines.

AKC Classification: Sporting Group.

Kennel Club Classification: Gundog Group.

English Foxhound

Character: Amiable, friendly, calm, stubborn, lively; similar to the American Foxhound. Although he is a very fine watchdog, the English Foxhound is not protective.

Origin: Great Britain, 1600s.

Original Purpose: To hunt fox over varied terrain.

Physical Attributes: 23 to 27 inches, 60 to 90 pounds; extremely strong, symmetrical, and solid.

Color: Any hound color, usually black, tan and white (tricolor) or tan and white (bicolor).

Coat Type and Grooming: Short, glossy, dense; easy maintenance; minimal to moderate shedding.

Lifespan: 10 to 13 years.

Health Concerns: Some epilepsy, hip dysplasia, pancreatitis, kidney and heart disease; however, one of the very healthiest breeds.

Exercise: This dog is very active, although its stable character prevents hyperactivity.

Housing: Not suitable for urban areas or apartment life; needs a very large fenced area in which to run.

Interaction with Others: Gets along well with everyone, although a bit reserved with strangers. Tolerant of children; gets along with other pets supremely well. This dog is a true pack animal and is happiest with other dogs.

Trainability: Low—unless it's for foxhunting. Any training should start early.

Activities: Hunting.

Remarks: In Merrie Old England, foxes were considered vermin that needed to be wiped out. English Foxhound pedigrees are the oldest in dogdom. Many can trace their ancestry back well over 200 years. The English Foxhound has a wonderful bay, if you like that sort of thing.

AKC Classification: Hound Group.

Kennel Club Classification: Hound Group.

Part 2

English Setter

Character: Quiet, gentle, friendly, patient, well-mannered, mild.

Origin: England, 1300s; fully developed in England and Wales in the 1800s. Ancestors may have included the Spanish pointer.

Original Purpose: Hunting pheasant, grouse, and partridge.

Physical Attributes: 24 to 27 inches; 50 to 70 pounds; active, aristocratic, graceful, rugged; the smallest of the setters, and comparatively slight in build to others. English Setters come in two basic types: Lavarack (show style) and Llewellin (field model). Show dogs are larger and have a more luxuriant coat. This is a slow maturing breed.

Color: Tricolor, orange, blue, lemon, or silver belton (white with flecks or shading of the stated color; the word comes from a village in England). Patches of color are acceptable on field dogs but are discouraged on show dogs.

Coat Type and Grooming: Long, silky coat requires daily brushing. Professional grooming is recommended; trimming required. Moderate shedding.

Lifespan: 10 to 14 years

Health Concerns: Deafness, hip and elbow dysplasia, some cancers, allergies, hypothyroidism.

Exercise: The English Setter requires a lot of outdoor activity every day.

Housing: Suited only to country living.

Interaction with Others: Likes everyone, including strangers; very sociable and gentle with children. Prefers to be with people; should not be left alone. Very playful and friendly with other dogs.

Trainability: Moderate.

Activities: Hunting, therapy dog, field trials.

Remarks: All English Setters need to be screened for deafness. Work with a breeder that is aware of this problem and breeds responsibly.

AKC Classification: Sporting Group.

Kennel Club Classification: Gundog Group.

English Springer Spaniel

Character: Energetic, friendly, merry, vivacious, loyal, eager to please; some individuals can be shy or aggressive.

Origin: England, 1800s.

Original Purpose: Springing birds, which is how it got its name.

Physical Attributes: 19 to 20 inches; 45 to 55 pounds; fast; can handle cold and wet with no difficulty; tails are docked. Show-stock Springers are heavier, stockier, with more dramatic coats than field dogs. Today very few Springers work in both field and show events; the last dual championship was awarded back in 1938.

Color: Black or liver with white; either the white or the color can predominate; some have ticking. Tan markings on eyebrows, cheeks, inside ears and under tail are permitted, as is a blue roan or liver roan effect caused by white hairs in the colored portions of the coat.

Coat Type and Grooming: Smooth, silky, wavy, weather-resistant, long; high maintenance, especially in dog from show lines. Needs regular brushing once a week because the coat picks up everything. The pendulous ears need special care. Professional grooming is recommended. Seasonal shedding.

Lifespan: 10 to 14 years.

Health Concerns: Obesity, gastritis, ear infections, orthopedic problems (hip dysplasia, OCD), eye problems (PRA, eyelid abnormalities), hemophilia, heart problems (PDA, VSD, cardiomyopathy), anemia.

Exercise: High; a tireless dog; field-bred dogs even more energetic than show types.

Housing: Adaptable to apartment life, if special care is given to their very considerable exercise needs, but best suited to the country.

Interaction with Others: Excellent with the whole family, and always happy to meet new friends. Some lines are not good with children; needs a great deal of attention. This breed may on occasion be aggressive to other dogs, although it usually well-behaved with other pets.

Trainability: Very high; this breed learns quickly; does well with professional training.

Activities: Flushing upland game birds, field trials, hunting tests, obedience, agility, tracking, flyball, therapy dog. Hunts further and faster than other spaniels.

Remarks: Judy Manley, President of English Springer Spaniel Club of America, says, "The English Springer Spaniel is a friendly, lively, outgoing, medium-sized breed requiring regular exercise and daily grooming. The Springer is typically eager to please, quick to learn, and willing to obey. His intelligence and agility, paired with his beauty, loyalty, and trustworthiness make this breed one of the most desired."

AKC Classification: Sporting Group.

Kennel Club Classification: Gundog Group.

English Toy Spaniel

Character: Sweet, haughty, gentle, stubborn, quiet, affectionate.

Origin: England, 1600s.

Original Purpose: Lapdogs, flushing small birds.

Physical Attributes: 10 to 11 inches; 8 to 14 pounds. Because of short muzzle, they are not well suited to heat; some snore.

Color: Red or burgundy (ruby), black and tan (King Charles), red and white (Blenheim), tricolor (Prince Charles).

Coat Type and Grooming: Long, soft, silky, flowing. Requires grooming two or three times a week. Professional grooming is optional; feet and whiskers need trimming. Average to low shedding.

Lifespan: 10 to 13 years.

Health Concerns: Patellar luxation, juvenile cataracts, hernia, PDA, sensitivity to anesthesia. Heart murmurs, which can escalate into a serious difficulty, are a special problem for this breed. Because the gene pool is very small, the propensity for this problem is hard to eliminate.

Exercise: Low; this dog is rather inactive.

Housing: Ideal for urban areas or apartment life.

Interaction with Others: Devoted to his family and reserved with strangers. May not be good with very young children, fine with older ones. Excellent with other pets.

Trainability: Average.

Activities: Companion, obedience.

Remarks: Thomas F. O'Neal, President of the English Toy Spaniel Club of America, writes, "The English Toy Spaniel is a small compact dog, very devoted to its family and requires minimal exercise and grooming. This dog is known as the King Charles Spaniel in Europe. The soft, gentle expression and domed head along with a merry and affectionate demeanor, make the English Toy Spaniel very special." Only in the United States is this breed called the English Toy Spaniel; in England, it is called the King Charles Spaniel.

AKC Classification: Toy Group.

Kennel Club Classification: Gundog Group.

Field Spaniel

Character: Diligent, friendly, even-tempered, willing, eager, noble.

Origin: England, 1800s. A close relative of the Cocker Spaniel and Springer Spaniel.

Original Purpose: Bird flushing and retrieving.

Physical Attributes: 17 to 18 inches; 35 to 48 pounds; hardy, agile, active, a keen nose.

Color: Liver most commonly but also black, roan, golden liver, mahogany red.

Coat Type and Grooming: Medium-long, slightly wavy, glossy; feathering on chest, body, and legs. Moderate to high maintenance; brushing twice a week. Frequent bathing is beneficial; ears must be carefully attended. Professional grooming is optional; some trimming on head, ears, throat, and feet. Average shedding.

Lifespan: 11 to 14 years.

Health Concerns: Orthopedic problems (hip dysplasia), eye problems (PRA, cataracts, entropion, ectropion), thyroid disease, subaortic stenosis (SAS).

Exercise: Moderate to high; needs regular exercise, preferably where it is able to run. These dogs can be very active in the house as well.

Housing: Not suitable for apartment life; needs room to run.

Interaction with Others: Excellent with nearly everyone, including children; needs much attention from its family. A few may be reserved with strangers; will announce visitors. Gets along extremely well with other dogs and other pets if socialized with them.

Trainability: High; these are highly intelligent dogs and good problem solvers. They are escape artists.

Activities: Bird flushing, spaniel field trials.

Remarks: At one time, because of some inexplicable fad, the Field Spaniel was bred to such absurd proportions as to make it unusable and ridiculous looking. Fortunately, this fault has been corrected by careful breeders. Law enforcement officials have been trying out Field Spaniels recently for use as drug scenting dogs. Their low profile is unlikely to make them look dangerous to innocent people or suspicious to wrongdoers.

AKC Classification: Sporting Group.

Kennel Club Classification: Gundog Group.

Finnish Spitz

Character: Cooperative, friendly, obedient, independent, active, lively; reserved with strangers.

Origin: Finland.

Original Purpose: Hunting waterfowl, small mammals, elk/moose, grouse.

Physical Attributes: 15 to 20 inches; 29 to 36 pounds; elegant and foxlike; very little doggy odor. Easily startled; known for his acute hearing. This is a very vocal, active dog.

Color: Orange, pale honey, golden red, or red. Puppies are born with a black overlay that disappears at about eight weeks of age.

Coat Type and Grooming: Stand-off stiff coat; easy maintenance; brushing once or twice a week. Professional grooming is optional. Average shedding.

Health Concerns: No major concerns; this is a very healthy breed.

Exercise: Moderate.

Housing: Not suited for urban areas or apartment life.

Interaction with Others: Playful with children; devoted to their families; may be shy around strangers and other pets.

Trainability: Average.

Activities: Hunting.

Remarks: The Finnish Spitz is the national dog of Finland, of course. It is sometimes, but thankfully not always, called the "Suomenpystykorva." It is affectionately known as the Finkie.

AKC Classification: Non-Sporting Group.

Kennel Club Classification: Hound Group.

Part 2

Flat-Coated Retriever

Character: Cheerful, good-natured, intuitive, steady, sweet, loving, sociable, adaptable. Needs human companionship; is among the most affectionate of all dogs; loves everyone, including strangers. Some individuals are a bit territorial.

Origin: England, 1800s.

Original Purpose: Retriever.

Physical Attributes: 22 to 24 inches; 60 to 76 pounds; graceful, active. These dogs are slow to mature.

Color: Generally black, although some individuals are liver.

Coat Type and Grooming: Dense, glossy, and flat; feathering at the legs. Grooming requirements easy to average; brushing twice a week. Some trimming required. Some seasonal shedding.

Lifespan: 9 to 13 years.

Health Concerns: Cancer; a widespread problem among Flatties—about 65 percent of all Flat-Coated Retrievers die of cancer. Other concerns include hip dysplasia, patellar luxation, bloat, eye problems (cataracts, PRA).

Exercise: High; this breed needs a great deal of exercise, preferably near water. If he gets it, he is quiet indoors; if he doesn't get it, you have a very unhappy retriever.

Housing: This dog is not suited for an urban environment.

Interaction with Others: Very good with people, and especially good with kids; however, may be too rambunctious for children under four. Likes strangers; gets along with all other animals.

Trainability: Very trainable, but sensitive; early training important.

Activities: Hunting (both land and water retrieval), search and rescue, avalanche dog, service dog, obedience, agility, flyball.

Remarks: Joan Dever, Membership Secretary of the Flat-Coated Retriever Society of America, writes, "The exuberant, optimistic, forever puppy-like Flat-Coated Retriever ideally should be part of an active family of dog people; that is, people whose dog is at the very center of their lives, and who enjoy spending lots of time with their dog, happily involving themselves in dog activities."

AKC Classification: Sporting Group.

Kennel Club Classification: Gundog Group.

French Bulldog

Character: Well-behaved, mild-mannered, playful, amiable, affectionate, cheerful; very good watchdog.

Origin: France, 1800s.

Original Purpose: Companion.

Physical Attributes: 11 to 13 inches; under 28 pounds; sturdy. Due to short muzzle, does not handle hot weather well; some wheeze and snore. Most famous for his "bat" ears and perfectly flat skull.

Color: Fawn, brindle, white, brindle and white.

Coat Type and Grooming: Short; minimal care required; no trimming. Slight shedding.

Lifespan: 9 to 11 years.

Health Concerns: Back problems, respiratory problems.

Exercise: Low to moderate.

Housing: Can adapt to any living situation.

Interaction with Others: Often a one-person dog; not always good with children; does not care for strangers.

Trainability: Average.

Activities: Companion, obedience.

Remarks: Jim Grebe, of the French Bulldog Club of America, remarks, "The traditional description of the "Frenchie" is that it is a clown in the cloak of a philosopher." According to the French Bulldog Rescue page, "They are housedogs whose niche in life is to be an adored pet."

AKC Classification: Non-Sporting Group.

Kennel Club Classification: Utility Group.

German Shepherd Dog

Character: Self-confident, loyal, versatile, hardy, intent, responsive; highly territorial; very protective of their families; good watchdog and guard dog. Some poorly bred individuals may be shy or inappropriately aggressive.

Origin: Germany, 1800s.

Original Purpose: Military and guard dog, sheep herding, farm work.

Physical Attributes: 22 to 26 inches; 70 to 95 pounds, with males usually larger than females. Excessive size is not desirable in this breed. Graceful, strong, agile, active; chiseled head, bushy tail.

Color: Black and tan, gray sable, red sable, black, black and red, black and cream, black and silver, solid black. The AKC does not recognize white German Shepherd Dogs, and such animals are banned from conformation shows—the UKC recognizes them as a separate breed.

Coat Type and Grooming: Double coat, medium length; outercoat dense, undercoat downy. Coats can go from short to long, but long coats are a fault in the show ring. Needs brushing two or three times a week. Professional grooming is optional. Sheds constantly.

Lifespan: 10 to 12 years.

Health Concerns: Orthopedic problems (hip and elbow dysplasia, panosteitis, hypertrophic osteodystrophy, OCD), eye problems (cataracts, collie eye anomaly), heart problems (SAS, PDA, cardiomyopathy), enteritis, ear infections, skin problems (nodular dermatofibrosis, food allergies, acral lick dermatitis), gastritis, epilepsy, cancer (osteosarcoma), von Willebrand's, exocrine pancreatic insufficiency, arthritis.

Exercise: High; needs lots of exercise and a lot of room. If he doesn't get enough exercise, he can become neurotic and even aggressive.

Housing: Not suited for apartment life, unless he receives an enormous amount of exercise.

Interaction with Others: Very good with children he knows; wary of strangers. Usually good with other pets, once he accepts them as part of the family.

Trainability: High; but needs early training and socialization. These dogs do best with experienced owners, because they may challenge their owners for leadership. It is extremely important to get a puppy of the right temperament from a reputable breeder.

Activities: Obedience, guide dog for the blind, herding, Schutzhund, agility, drug detection, therapy dog, search and rescue, police work.

Remarks: The first German Shepherd Dog registered with the AKC back in 1908 was named "Queen of Switzerland." Famous Dog: The original Rin Tin Tin was a homeless German Shepherd pup rescued by an American airman in France during World War I.

AKC Classification: Herding Group.

Kennel Club Classification: Pastoral Group.

German Shorthaired Pointer

Character: Gentle, friendly, even-tempered, adaptable, proud, excitable; excellent watchdog.

Origin: Germany, 1600s. Possible Spanish Pointer and Bloodhound in the background.

Original Purpose: Hunting fowl.

Physical Attributes: 21 to 25 inches; 46 to 70 pounds; hardy, versatile, powerful, active, with lots of endurance; tail is docked; enjoys the water; will bark if ignored.

Color: Solid liver, to any combination of liver and white including ticked, spotted, roan.

Coat Type and Grooming: Short, sleek, water-repellant outercoat; thick, short undercoat; very easy maintenance; twice a week quick brushing; no trimming; ears need special attention. Moderate shedding.

Lifespan: 13 to 16 years.

Health Concerns: Lymphedema, hip and elbow dysplasia, localized eczema around paws, juvenile cataracts, epilepsy, hypothyroidism.

Exercise: High; needs a lot of room and a lot of attention from its owner. Otherwise, this dog can be extremely destructive in the house.

Housing: Not suitable for urban areas or apartment life.

Interaction with Others: Very loving, although this breed needs to be supervised with smaller kids. Most like strangers, although a few may be somewhat suspicious. Very good with other dogs; some individuals may chase cats.

Trainability: Very high.

Activities: Hunting, field trials, tracking, obedience.

Remarks: According to the Eastern German Shorthaired Pointer Club, "This breed can make a great family pet and/or hunting dog if attention is given to its high energy needs."

AKC Classification: Sporting Group.

Kennel Club Classification: Gundog Group.

German Wirehaired Pointer

Character: Loyal, stubborn, friendly, goofy, energetic, aloof; one of those dogs that seems to have a sense of humor. Can be dominant if not properly trained; will warn of approaching strangers; barks in general. Bonds to one person, can be protective. Character very similar to the German Shorthaired Pointer.

Origin: Germany, 1800s.

Original Purpose: Versatile gun dog.

Physical Attributes: 21 to 26 inches; 55 to 75 pounds; rugged, energetic, sturdy; can handle cold and wet weather with no trouble. Slightly larger on the average than the German Shorthaired Pointer.

Color: Solid liver, liver and white.

Coat Type and Grooming: Short, wiry; medium maintenance; brushing twice a week. For best look, should be hand-stripped occasionally. Professional grooming is optional; some trimming is helpful. Average shedding.

Lifespan: 11 to 14 years.

Health Concerns: Hip and elbow dysplasia.

Exercise: Very high; can be hard to handle in the house.

Housing: Not suitable for urban areas or apartment life.

Interaction with Others: Not always good with kids, unless socialized early; aloof with strangers; may try to dominate other dogs.

Trainability: High, but it takes some patience.

Activities: Hunting, retrieving, field trials.

Remarks: This dog is the most popular hunting breed in Germany where it is known as the Drahthaar.

AKC Classification: Sporting Group.

Kennel Club Classification: Gundog Group.

Giant Schnauzer

Character: Confident, loyal, playful, exuberant, reliable, spirited; not overtly affectionate. This territorial breed is a good watchdog and very protective of its family.

Origin: Germany, Middle Ages.

Original Purpose: Driving cattle, carting, guarding, police work.

Physical Attributes: 23 to 27 inches; 65 to 95 pounds.

Color: Black or salt and pepper.

Coat Type and Grooming: Outercoat hard and wiry; undercoat soft; high maintenance; trimming around eyes and ears. Whiskers should be cleaned after meals. Professional grooming is recommended; coat needs to be stripped twice a year. Low to average shedding.

Lifespan: 11 to 12 years.

Health Concerns: Hip dysplasia, OCD, PRA.

Exercise: Moderate to high; this big dog needs a lot of room; dogs left alone become destructive.

Housing: Not suitable for urban areas or apartment life.

Interaction with Others: They are tolerant and protective of family kids, but may be too rough for small children; may also try to "herd" kids. This breed lives to be near people and is usually very good with them; tends to bond with only one person. They can be reserved and suspicious of strangers, including strange children. They may be all right with other pets, if socialized early, but will attempt to dominate.

Trainability: High; all Giant Schnauzers should be taken to puppy kindergarten and later to obedience classes. These dogs require firm handling and an experienced owner.

Activities: Police work, search and rescue, tracking, obedience, bomb squad, therapy dog, canine assistant, Schutzhund.

Remarks: This is a very dominant breed and will try to challenge owners to be "leader of the pack."

AKC Classification: Working Group.

Kennel Club Classification: Working Group.

Golden Retriever

Character: Eager to please, trustworthy, outgoing, versatile, self-confident; requires human attention. This breed is not protective, but it may bark to welcome strangers.

Origin: England/Scotland, 1800s. The modern breed was developed by an English nobleman with the interesting name of Lord Tweedmouth. (His estate was on the Tweed River near Inverness, Scotland.) Ancestors include setters, waters spaniels, and the Curly-Coated Retriever.

Original Purpose: Gundog, hunting and retrieving shot waterfowl.

Physical Attributes: 21 to 25 inches; 55 to 75 pounds; solid, strong, rugged, active, enjoys swimming. Working lines somewhat smaller than show lines; can handle extremes of heat and cold better than many other breeds but does best in a colder climate.

Color: Golden or "lion" color, all shades from pale to reddish; white markings are not permitted. Originally, darker, redder shades were favored, but nowadays, lighter, more "golden" shades are more common.

Coat Type and Grooming: Either flat or wavy, moderately long; undercoat dense and water-repellant. Fairly high maintenance; two or three times a week brushing. Professional grooming is desirable; some trimming. Average shedding.

Lifespan: 10 to 14 years.

Health Concerns: Bloat, orthopedic problems (hip dysplasia, OCD), epilepsy, eye problems (distichiasis, PRA, cataracts), von Willebrand's, enteritis, cancer, heart problems (cardiomyopathy, SAS) skin problems (hot spots, dermatitis, inhalant and food allergies), ear infections, diabetes, obesity.

Exercise: Needs moderate outdoor exercise, but perhaps not as much as some of the other retrievers; however, if the Golden doesn't get a sufficient amount, it can have behavior problems.

Housing: This is not a good apartment dog; needs room to run.

Interaction with Others: He is very affectionate to the entire family and excellent with children; however, may be too rambunctious for very small kids. He likes strangers, so don't expect the well-bred Golden to guard your property; very friendly with other pets.

Trainability: Extremely high; very easy to train; Goldens hang around and wait to be told to do something. Quite reliable off lead, because it is very responsive to its owner.

Activities: Guide dog, search and rescue, hunting, therapy dog, flyball, obedience, agility.

Remarks: The Golden's famously calm, kindly disposition has been sullied in recent years by poor breeding; however, this is a breed that ought to have a perfect temperament. Unspoiled Golden Retrievers are among the most affectionate of dogs. A well-bred Golden is such a superb first dog that it will spoil you for any other breed.

AKC Classification: Sporting Group.

Kennel Club Classification: Gundog Group.

Gordon Setter

Character: Good-humored, conscientious, capable, lively, devoted to family, faithful; excellent watchdog; more protective of family than other setters.

Origins: Scotland, 1600s. Daniel Webster imported the first one to the United States.

Original Purpose: Field dog.

Physical Attributes: 23 to 27 inches; 55 to 80 pounds; immense endurance, simply tireless; dramatic long wavy coat. They are slower and heavier, but more powerful, than other setters. The Gordon is a slow-maturing breed that goes thorough a gangling adolescence; however, the results are worth the wait.

Color: Black with tan, chestnut, or gold markings.

Coat Type and Grooming: Wavy, long, silky; daily grooming is necessary to prevent mats. Professional grooming is recommended; trimming required. Low to moderate seasonal shedding.

Lifespan: 10 to 12 years.

Health Concerns: Hip dysplasia, bloat, PRA.

Exercise: Needs a lot of strenuous hard exercise every day. Most become calmer as they mature, although mine is five years old, gets unlimited amounts of exercise every day, and is still a handful. Gordons are generally quiet and pleasant in the house.

Housing: Not suitable for urban areas or apartment life.

Interaction with Others: A very good dog with children; some are suspicious of strangers. Amiable for the most part with other pets, but wants to be boss; some are aggressive to other dogs.

Trainability: The Gordon is a "soft" dog that responds to gentle but firm handling; reliability off lead is low.

Activities: Hunting upland game birds, field trials, therapy dog, agility, obedience.

Remarks: The original description of the Gordon listed him as "hardest to endure," but as an owner of Gordon Setter, I can assure you that there is no more beautiful and splendid dog.

AKC Classification: Sporting Group.

Kennel Club Classification: Gundog Group.

Part 2

Great Dane

Character: Regal, stable, good-natured, affectionate, friendly, dignified; makes a fine watchdog; bonds to the entire family. Some are dominant and will not back down if threatened.

Origin: Germany, Middle Ages. Despite its name, the Great Dane has nothing to do with Denmark; it is a refined version of a mastiff.

Original Purpose: Dog of war, boarhound, guarding, drafting.

Physical Attributes: At least 28 inches for females and at least 30 inches for males; 100-180 pounds; strong, powerful, dignified, and elegant; does not fare well in extremely cold weather. Ears may be cropped or left natural.

Color: Fawn (tan) with a black mask, brindle, black, blue, harlequin (white with black patches); no other colors are permitted.

Coat Type and Grooming: Short, thick, smooth, glossy; minimal care; twice a week brushing. Average to high shedding, but there's a lot of dog.

Lifespan: 8 to 10 years.

Health Concerns: Bloat, allergies, orthopedic problems (hip dysplasia, OCD, hypertrophic osteodytrophy, Wobblers), color dilution alopecia, heart disease (cardiomyopathy, subaortic stenosis, arrhythmia), thyroid problems (hyperthyroidism), cancer (osteosarcoma), entropion, deafness (in white and harlequin), acral lick dermatitis.

Exercise: Moderate to high; lower as the dog matures. With moderate daily outdoor exercise, the breed is calm in the house.

Housing: Adaptable to any living situation, with sufficient exercise. Generally does better in the suburbs than in the city.

Interaction with Others: Very good with children, although its great size merits supervision; best if raised with them. Very friendly with other pets; may be somewhat suspicious of other dogs.

Trainability: High; because of its great size, this dog should be given obedience training early and is best with an experienced owner. Otherwise, the breed can become dominant and try to challenge the owner.

Activities: Therapy dog, obedience.

Remarks: This breed is sometimes called the King of Dogs or, if one prefers gods to kings, the Apollo of Dogs. Famous Dog: Cartoon character Scooby Doo is a Great Dane.

AKC Classification: Working Group.

Kennel Club Classification: Working Group.

Great Pyrenees

Character: Independent, sedate, affectionate, confident, serene, patient; may become a one-person or one-family dog; territorial; protective; a superior watchdog.

Origin: Pyrenees Mountains between Spain and France. Fossil remains estimated to date as far back as 1800 BC, and some estimates place the breeds origins back 11,000 years.

Original Purpose: Guarding sheep from wolves and bears, later guard dogs for people.

Physical Attributes: 26 to 32 inches; 99 to 132 pounds; imposing, elegant; double dew claws on the hind leg; one of the strongest of all dogs. Has great endurance and loves the cold but cannot handle heat. This breed drools.

Color: White or white with markings of gray, badger, reddish brown, or tan. These marking may appear on ears, head, tail, and a few body spots; however, markings should not cover more than one-third of the body.

Coat Type and Grooming: Outercoat long, thick, and coarse; undercoat downy; daily grooming and occasional trimming required. Professional grooming is desirable. Profuse shedding twice a year.

Lifespan: 10 to 12 years.

Health Concerns: Hip (although less common than in other large breeds) and elbow dysplasia, deafness, patellar luxation, Factor XI deficiency (a bleeding disorder), bloat, bone cancer, sensitivity to anesthesia.

Exercise: Needs regular walks, but moderate exercise will suit him fine; needs a lot of space and a fenced yard.

Housing: Not suitable for urban areas or apartment life. An escape artist and should be kept within a secure area

Interaction with Others: Gentle, tolerant, and protective of the family children; adapts well to family life and bonds to all; wary of strangers, can be aggressive. Often antagonistic to dogs of their own sex; may protect other pets in "their" family.

Trainability: Low; needs strong motivational training and an experienced owner. Some individuals attempt to dominate submissive members of the family.

Activities: Rescue dog, avalanche dog, drafting, carting, backpacking, guard dog.

Remarks: Louis XIV, known to his friends as the Sun King, named the Great Pyrenees the Royal Dog of France in 1675. Although he was not much of a royalist, General Lafayette brought two Great Pyrenees to the US in 1824, as a gift for a friend.

AKC Classification: Working Group.

Greater Swiss Mountain Dog

Character: Sensitive, dominant, gentle, calm, attentive, patient, affectionate; can be territorial; a superior watchdog.

Origin: Switzerland, antiquity.

Original Purpose: Guarding, drafting, herding, cattle driving.

Physical Attributes: 24 to 29 inches; 90 to 130 pounds; sturdy, powerful.

Color: The ground color is jet black; markings are rich rust and white.

Coat Type and Grooming: Dense outercoat and thick undercoat; minimal care required; weekly brushing. Sheds only a little seasonally.

Lifespan: 8 to 10 years.

Health Concerns: Hip, elbow, or shoulder dysplasia.

Exercise: Moderate to high; the country is the best home for the Greater Swiss.

Housing: This dog is not well suited to urban life, although his exercise needs are only moderate. He enjoys being outdoors.

Interaction with Others: Very gentle with children, but may be too large for toddlers. Wary of strangers until introduced, then friendly. Very good with other pets.

Trainability: Average to high.

Activities: Weight pulling, carting, herding.

Remarks: Greater than what, you ask? Greater than everything! This gentle breed is a superb family dog for those who can handle his large size.

AKC Classification: Working Group.

Part 2

Greyhound

Character: Independent, even-tempered, sensitive, lovable, strong-willed, gentle. Some are timid and reserved with strangers.

Origin: Middle East; ancestors are supposedly seen on Egyptian tomb paintings dating to 2900 BC, and the Greyhound is the only breed of dog specifically mentioned in the Bible.

Original Purpose: Coursing hares and rabbits, racing.

Physical Attributes: 23 to 30 inches; 60 to 80 pounds; the fastest of all dogs, can run up to 40 miles an hour. This breed has little tolerance for cold.

Color: Most commonly, black, brindle, fawn, but any color accepted, including red, white, and blue.

Coat Type and Grooming: Thick, short, and smooth; minimal care required; weekly brushing. Slight to average shedding.

Lifespan: 9 to 14 years.

Health Concerns: Bloat, brittle bones, PRA, hypothyroidism, deafness, allergic dermatitis, may be sensitive to anesthesia and certain flea treatments.

Exercise: Medium to high; these dogs need large fenced exercise areas, but very quiet and well-behaved in the house; older dogs are quite sedate.

Housing: Adaptable to any living situation with sufficient exercise. This dog must be kept on a leash or inside a safe fenced area.

Interaction with Others: Good, although some are not suited to small children; usually however, they are very gentle and biddable. Usually good with strangers, although some may be shy. Good, even submissive, with other dogs. May be all right with smaller pets and cats if raised with them, but need to be watched. They have a natural instinct to chase small animals.

Trainability: Low; easily distracted; early socialization required to prevent shyness.

Activities: Racing, lure coursing.

Remarks: Sue LeMieux, President of the Greyhound Club of America, writes, "Those who own Greyhounds love them for their intelligence, warm personalities, stable temperaments, and unswerving devotion." The name "Greyhound" appears to refer merely to a color, although greyhounds are by no means always gray. Some say its name comes from the word "Grecian;" others say it comes from old British grech or greg, meaning dog and hundr, meaning hunting. Many ex-racing Greyhounds are available for adoption.

AKC Classification: Hound Group.

Kennel Club Classification: Hound Group.

Harrier

Character: Amiable, mild, easy-going, alert, active; makes a fine watchdog, but is not a protection dog. These dogs have a superlative sense of smell

Origin: Great Britain; probably derived from the English Foxhound. The first pack was established by Sir Elias de Midhope in 1260: The pack existed for 500 years.

Original Purpose: Hunting rabbits and hares.

Physical Attributes: 19 to 21 inches; 45 to 60 pounds.

Color: Any hound color, usually black, tan, and white.

Coat Type and Grooming: Short; minimal care required. Little to moderate shedding.

Health Concerns: Hip dysplasia (about 16 percent in this breed); elbow dysplasia, PRA, anal fissures.

Exercise: High; Harriers need room to exercise in a large, high fenced area. This dog is very active, and may be hyperactive in the house without sufficient exercise.

Housing: Not suitable for urban areas or apartment life.

Interaction with Others: Excellent with children; more playful than his larger cousin the Foxhound, but less so than the smaller Beagle; reserved with strangers. Excellent with other pets.

Trainability: Average.

Activities: Hunting rabbits and foxes.

Remarks: The oldest known Harrier pack, the Pennine, has records going back to the 1200s. In both physical and attributes and character they combine elements of Beagle and Foxhound. Donna Smiley-Auborn, charter member of the Harrier Club of America and Harrier National Rescue Coordinator, says, "Harriers are very loving, athletic, independent scenthounds that possess a good sense of humor. They are best suited for active owners capable of meeting their exercise and training requirements."

AKC Classification: Hound Group.

Part 2

Havanese

Character: Affectionate, playful, clownish, merry, willing to please; will give a welcoming bark to strangers.

Origin: Cuba; this breed is closely related to the Maltese and Bichon Frise.

Original Purpose: Lapdog, companion.

Physical Attributes: 8 to 11 inches; 7 to 14 pounds; sturdy, agile and vocal; can handle both heat and cold.

Color: All colors and combinations of colors, including champagne and chocolate (which I think is a great combination under any circumstances).

Coat Type and Grooming: Double wavy, undulating, or curly; needs to be groomed two to four times a week. Professional grooming is optional. Does not shed, but the long hair can tangle and mat all too easily.

Lifespan: 12 to 15 years.

Health Concerns: PRA, juvenile cataracts, patellar luxation.

Exercise: Has a lot of energy, but does not need a great deal of room.

Housing: Can adapt to any living situation

Interaction with Others: Craves attention; loves everyone, including strangers and young children; good with other pets.

Trainability: High; this breed will perform on command and makes a good pet for the novice dog owner.

Activities: Obedience, agility.

Remarks: Like the Pekingese and other "royal" dogs, only the nobility were allowed to own a Havanese. They were never sold and could be presented only as gifts. They came into the United States with the Cuban exiles after the Revolution in Cuba.

AKC Classification: Toy Group.

Kennel Club Classification: Toy Group.

Ibizan Hound

Character: Energetic, gentle, loving, curious, restless, adaptable. Some individuals are shy, especially around loud noises. Not a protection dog, although they appear daunting.

Origin: Ibiza (Balearic Islands in the Mediterranean) or Egypt; probably developed from the Pharaoh Hound.

Original Purpose: Sighthound, bred to chase prey.

Physical Attributes: 23 to 27 inches; 45 to 50 pounds; graceful, tireless, strong, fast. An amazing jumper; acute sense of smell and hearing; not suited to cold weather.

Color: Red or white, chestnut, tawny, solid or in combination. One tawny-red shade is called "lion."

Coat Type and Grooming: Two types, one smooth and short, and one longer and more wiry (seen mostly in Spain). Professional grooming is not needed for the smooth, but is recommended for the wire-haired, which requires stripping. Minimal shedding.

Lifespan: 12 to 14 years.

Health Concerns: Axonal dystrophy, cardiopathy, deafness, seizures, sensitive to anesthesia.

Exercise: Moderate to high; needs a safe, fenced area.

Housing: Adaptable if given sufficient exercise. Because the Ibizan is such a good jumper, fences need to be very high.

Interaction with Others: Very good with children; gets along with the whole family. Very good with other pets; unlike many sighthounds, it gets along with small animals and cats.

Trainability: Average; however, this breed requires very careful and thorough socialization.

Activities: Therapy dog, lure coursing, search and rescue, tracking, agility.

Remarks: Cleopatra kept a pack of these dogs and King Tutankhamen wrote a poem in honor of one. In 2003, an Ibizan Hound won the Best in Group at the Westminster Kennel Club for the first time.

AKC Classification: Hound Group.

Kennel Club Classification: Hound Group.

Irish Setter

Character: Tireless, sweet, energetic, playful, gay, happy; not protective, but will bark to welcome guests. This breed needs a lot of attention; it has a wonderful zest for life.

Origin: Ireland, 1700s.

Original Purpose: Locating and retrieving birds.

Physical Attributes: 24 to 27 inches; 55 to 70 pounds; very fast, graceful, aristocratic; highly energetic, acute sense of smell. This breed is slow to mature and is quite long-living.

Color: Deep red or chestnut to mahogany, although many of the first Irish setters were white and red. By the 1870s, however, the dogs became solid red, although a very tiny patch of white is allowed on the chest.

Coat Type and Grooming: Silky, long, feathery, wavy, with heavy feathering on the legs, tail and ears. High maintenance required; brushing three times a week. Coat tends to tangle, especially behind the ears. Professional grooming is recommended; some trimming required. Average shedding.

Lifespan: 12 to 14 years.

Health Concerns: Eye problems (PRA, entropion, cataracts), bloat, osteosarcoma, epilepsy, skin problems (allergies, acral lick dermatitis), hypothyroidism, orthopedic problems (hip dysplasia, hypertrophic osteodystrohy), ear infections.

Exercise: High; a place where the dog can run freely is absolutely essential.

Housing: Cannot live happily in an apartment and really does best in the country.

Interaction with Others: Excellent, but rambunctious with people. My Irish was terribly fond of babies, but many are too joyfully wild for very small children. Excellent with other pets; my Irish Setter would chase unknown cats, but was fond of her own.

Trainability: Slow to train, but remembers its lessons well. It is extremely sensitive and responds only to positive reinforcement; needs very soft handling.

Activities: Hunting (not common nowadays, but some breeders are working on returning the breed to its original use), therapy dog, field trials, obedience.

Remarks: The dignified and elegant appearance of the setter belies a rollicking sprit and a joyful heart. The Irish Setter has been branded as being unstable and flighty, but a well-bred Irish, given sufficient exercise, is a wonderful pet and a perfect show dog.

AKC Classification: Sporting Group.

Kennel Club Classification: Gundog Group.

Irish Terrier

Character: Bold, fearless, intuitive, playful, loyal, adaptable; an excellent watchdog; will protect his family.

Origin: Southern Ireland, 1700s; one of the oldest terrier breeds.

Original Purpose: Hunting fox and otter.

Physical Attributes: 18 to 19 inches; 25 to 27 pounds; graceful; can handle any climate.

Color: Red and wheaten solid colors.

Coat Type and Grooming: Harsh, wiry, weather-resistant; moderate maintenance. Professional Grooming is recommended; hand-stripping for show dogs, clipping for pets. Slight shedding, if groomed correctly.

Lifespan: 13 to 16 years.

Health Concerns: Bladder or kidney stones.

Exercise: Daily exercise needed; quiet in the house.

Housing: Adaptable to any living situation; does well in the city; can be an escape artist.

Interaction with Others: Very good with kids; loves to play; reserved with strangers. Will probably be aggressive or dominate strange dogs; may tolerate family pets if socialized early.

Trainability: High, but may try to dominate its owner.

Activities: Vermin elimination, terrier trials.

Remarks: Some people have named this breed the "red devil." Hmm... At any rate, they require a strong owner. Terriers in general can be tough to own, but once you train one, they are excellent pets.

AKC Classification: Terrier Group.

Kennel Club Classification: Terrier Group.

Part 2

Irish Water Spaniel

Character: Playful, courageous, willing, sense of humor, gentle, loyal; suspicious of strangers; a very good watchdog.

Origin: Ireland, 1800s. Some say the breed is 6000 years old; obviously some Poodle blood (or at least curls) in the background.

Original Purpose: Water retriever.

Physical Attributes: 21 to 24 inches; 55 to 65 pounds. This is the tallest of the spaniels, and is often confused with a Poodle, although the Irish Water Spaniel has a rat tail. Active, but heat intolerant; lots of endurance; needs to be around water to be happy and has many retriever qualities. Some individuals drool.

Color: Liver.

Coat Type and Grooming: Tight curls. Medium to high maintenance; oily coat can give off a characteristic smell. Professional grooming is recommended; trimming required. Negligible shedding.

Lifespan: 10 to 12 years.

Health Concerns: Hip dysplasia, von Willebrand's, autoimmune diseases.

Exercise: High, especially as a puppy. Likes to swim and happiest around water.

Housing: Not suited to urban areas or apartment life.

Interaction with Others: Fair with children; initially rather standoffish to strangers, but gradually becomes friendly. Very good with other pets; a few unaltered males dislike other males.

Trainability: Highly trainable, but requires early socialization.

Activities: Hunting, obedience, field trials, tracking, agility, service dog.

Remarks: The Irish Water Spaniel is known as the Clown of the Spaniels.

AKC Classification: Sporting Group.

Kennel Club Classification: Gundog Group.

Irish Wolfhound

Character: Adaptable, fearless, peaceful, willing to please, calm, gentle; tends to be a one-person dog. He is known as the "gentle giant."

Origin: Ireland, antiquity.

Original Purpose: Hunting boar, Irish elk, and wolves. It was apparently so good at this that wolves are extinct in Ireland.

Physical Attributes: At least 30 inches for females, and at least 32 inches for males; 105 to 120 pounds. The Irish Wolfhound is one of the tallest of all dogs; has very little tolerance for heat.

Color: Any color, but gray, brindle, red, black, white, and fawn are most common.

Coat Type and Grooming: Rough, hard, and wiry; short to medium. Professional grooming necessary for a show dog, which needs to be stripped occasionally; not necessary for a pet; some trimming advised. Slight shedding if coat is correctly maintained.

Lifespan: 6 to 8 years.

Health Concerns: Bloat, von Willebrand's, OCD, heart problems (arrhythmia, cardiomyopathy).

Exercise: Needs daily exercise; however, he is a low-energy dog and is quiet in the house.

Housing: Not suited to small apartments but can be happy in an urban area with a lot of exercise.

Interaction with Others: Very calm, reliable, and sociable with children, but not playful, at least as an adult; puppies can overwhelm a child with good-natured exuberance. Very good with other pets; benefits from the company of other dogs.

Trainability: Very high, especially for a sighthound; needs an experienced owner.

Activities: Lure coursing.

Remarks: The Irish Wolfhound is supposed to have cleared the wolves out of Ireland.

AKC Classification: Hound Group.

Italian Greyhound

Character: Gentle, devoted, calm, sensitive, alert, vivacious; likes to be the center of attention; thrives on human companionship; however, he does not need constant attention.

Origin: Italy, Greece or Turkey, antiquity; Romans bred them for pets.

Original Purpose: Companion.

Physical Attributes: 13 to 16 inches, 7 to 13 pounds; elegant, quick-footed. This dog is so delicately built that it is considered a toy dog. Should not be allowed to play roughly, as it could be injured. This breed has no cold tolerance and is slow to mature.

Color: Usually black, fawn, red, cream blue, with or without broken white. Any color but brindle or black and tan allowed.

Coat Type and Grooming: Short, soft, and glossy; minimal grooming; once a week. This dog has no doggy odor. Very little shedding.

Lifespan: 13 to 16 years.

Health Concerns: Periodontal problems, PRA, fractures, color dilution alopecia, patellar luxation, sensitivity to anesthesia and barbiturates.

Exercise: Moderate to high; enjoys running. Sedate in the house, especially as it matures.

Housing: Suitable for any type of living environment.

Interaction with Others: Good with older, gentle children; too fragile for toddlers; reserved with strangers. Good with larger dogs; likes familiar pets, including cats. May chase very small pets or quarrel with dogs its own size.

Trainability: Average; tends to jump on people. Some are hard to housetrain.

Activities: Agility.

Remarks: Both Queen Victoria and Frederick the Great owned one of these dogs.

AKC Classification: Toy Group.

Kennel Club Classification: Hound Group.

Jack Russell Terrier/Parson Russell Terrier

Character: Cheeky, outgoing, playful, independent, spunky, bold. Some individuals are shy. Demand a lot of attention from their owners; make excellent watchdogs.

Origin: England, late 1800s. Same basic stock as the Fox Terrier.

Original Purpose: Bred to follow red fox, both over and underground.

Physical Attributes: 10 to 15 inches; 10 to 16 pounds. Most dig and bark.

Color: All colors permitted; most are white with black, tan, or brown markings.

Coat Type and Grooming: Two types: smooth and broken. Minimal grooming for the smooth, more for the broken coat. Professional grooming not necessary for smooth; optional for broken.

Lifespan: 14 to 15 years.

Health Concerns: This is a very healthy breed and has no unusual health problems.

Exercise: The JRT will get fat if not given sufficient exercise, and they need a tremendous amount of it. They will hunt, play, chase, and run around all day long.

Housing: This breed is not suitable for apartments; needs lots of exercise.

Interaction with Others: Likes to play with kids, but is not especially tolerant and will not stand teasing. If irritated, they will nip. Reserved with strangers. May show same sex aggression; prefers other Jack Russells. Not good with cats or small animals.

Trainability: High; not reliable off lead; needs an owner experienced with both terrier and hunting dogs.

Activities: Hunting, earthdog trials, agility.

Remarks: This breed was developed by a clergyman, Parson John Russell. For many years the Jack Russell Terrier Club of America fiercely opposed the breed's recognition by the AKC, believing it would result in loss of the breed's character and working ability. This dog's name changes to Parson Russell Terrier on April 1, 2003.

AKC Classification: Terrier Group.

Kennel Club Classification: Terrier Group.

Japanese Chin

Character: Playful, devoted, sensitive, alert, cheerful; enjoys human company.

Origin: China (despite its name), antiquity.

Original Purpose: Companion. Early breeds were supposedly sometimes kept in hanging birdcages.

Physical Attributes: 8 to 11 inches; 4 to 7 pounds; does not tolerate heat or cold. Some can climb; some snore.

Color: Black and white, red and white, or tricolor.

Coat Type and Grooming: Long, profuse, and silky. Moderate grooming; two or three times a week. It is a naturally clean dog. Professional grooming is optional. Moderate shedding; heavy seasonally.

Lifespan: 12 to 14 years.

Health Concerns: Respiratory problems, patellar luxation, mitral valve insuffiency, sensitive to anesthesia.

Exercise: Low.

Housing: Ideal for urban areas and apartment life.

Interaction with Others: Very good with gentle, well-behaved children; a few are reserved around strangers, others enjoy meeting new friends. Tends to bond to one person. Very good with other pets.

Trainability: Variable, often very high. This dog has been known to make up its own tricks.

Activities: Therapy dog.

Remarks: In 1853, some Japanese Chins were presented to Commodore Matthew Perry, who then presented a pair to Queen Victoria.

AKC Classification: Toy Group.

Kennel Club Classification: Toy Group.

Part 2

Keeshond

Character: Confident, bold, happy, adaptable, stubborn, friendly; one of the most delightful of the spitz-type dogs.

Origin: Holland, 1700s.

Original Purpose: Barge guard, watchdog, rat-killer.

Physical Attributes: 17 to 18 inches; 38 to 40 pounds; solidly built, good swimmer. The tail is carried over the back, and a double curl is preferred. Handles cold and damp well, but not good in the heat. Can be barky. They are also known for their Keeshond smile, a real grin.

Color: Gray with black-tipped overcoat, the undercoat colored pale gray or cream. The dark puppy coat gradually lightens as they mature.

Coat Type and Grooming: Double undercoat and lion-like mane; high maintenance; vigorous grooming three or four times a week. Professional grooming is recommended. Heavy shedding; the undercoat "blows" in big clumps twice a year. .

Lifespan: 12 to 14 years

Health Concerns: Hip dysplasia, heart problems (VSD), von Willebrand's, epilepsy.

Exercise: Moderate.

Housing: Adaptable to any living situation.

Interaction with Others: Quite good with both adults and children; usually good with other pets, but aggressive on occasion.

Trainability: Average; needs an experienced dog owner. Some have housetraining problems.

Activities: Agility, obedience, tracking.

Remarks: The "original" Keeshond was a dog named Kees, said to be short for Cornelius. They became the symbol for peasant resistance against the nobility. If you have more than one Keeshond, you have Keeshonden. Keeshonden were originally shown in England as "Overweight Pomeranians."

AKC Classification: Non-Sporting Group.

Kennel Club Classification: Utility Group.

Kerry Blue Terrier

Character: Hardworking, fun-loving, adaptable, game, intense, fearless; superior watchdog; territorial; attaches itself to the whole family.

Origin: Ireland (County Kerry, of course), 1700s. Its ancestry is a mystery. There are tales of Russian shipwrecks, and more plausible stories of breeding from Soft-Coated Wheatens and Irish Terriers.

Original Purpose: Ratting, hunting.

Physical Attributes: 17 to 19 inches; 33 to 39 pounds; elegant, powerful. Tail is usually docked.

Color: Any shade of blue-gray, including light silver and dark slate. Puppies are born almost black, but must show a color change by 18 months of age.

Coat Type and Grooming: Silkier coat than most terriers; can mat overnight. High maintenance; combing two or three times a week. Professional grooming is recommended; monthly shaping and scissoring. Low shedding.

Lifespan: 13 to 16 years

Health Concerns: Cataracts, bleeding disorders, progressive neuronal abiotrophy, sebaceous cysts, hip dysplasia.

Exercise: Fairly high, but does not need large amounts of open space.

Housing: Adaptable to any living situation.

Interaction with Others: Very good with well-behaved children, if socialized. Not friendly to strangers, but very amiable once it gets used to them. Bad with other dogs and not good with other pets either including birds, unless socialized very early.

Trainability: Moderate; needs a great deal of early, firm socialization. They are easily housetrained, and good problem solvers; however, they may try to dominate owner.

Activities: Police dog, ratting, obedience.

Remarks: A dog for an experienced owner, this is the National Dog of Ireland.

AKC Classification: Terrier Group.

Kennel Club Classification: Terrier Group.

Komondor

Character: Serious, independent, aloof, stubborn, bold, wary; excellent watchdog; strong protective instincts.

Origin: Hungary, antiquity.

Original Purpose: Flock guarding.

Physical Attributes: 21 to 31 inches; 79 to 130 pounds; powerful. Males are considerably larger than females. Loves the outdoors, but does not tolerate heat.

Color: White.

Coat Type and Grooming: Corded, long; requires high maintenance. The coat tends to get dirty very easily, and it takes about two hours to wash; furthermore, it takes about a full day to dry. Professional grooming is necessary for the show dog; pets are easiest clipped. Non-shedding, but coat tends to knot.

Lifespan: 12 years.

Health Concern: Hip dysplasia, bloat.

Exercise: Needs moderate to intense exercise for a fairly long period.

Housing: Adaptable to urban areas or apartment life with effort.

Interaction with Others: This breed is not good with children; although it may get along well with its own family, it may be too protective; reserved with strangers. Aggressive toward strange dogs; amenable with its "own" pets and will guard them.

Trainability: High; however, this dog may challenge its owner for dominance; needs a very experienced owner.

Activities: Sheep guarding, agility.

Remarks: Its original aggressive temperament is being softened by careful breeding; however, extensive early socialization and an experienced and strong owner is still required for this independent dog which can be dangerous if not handled properly. If you have more than one Komondor, you have Komondorok.

AKC Classification: Working Group.

Kennel Club Classification: Pastoral Group.

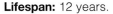

Kuvasz

Character: Gentle with its family, loyal, brave, wary, spirited; not especially demonstrative; this is a one-family dog. Very protective; suspicious of strangers; highly territorial; high watchdog and guarding ability.

Origin: Hungary, by way of Tibet.

Original Purpose: Shepherder and protector of flocks.

Physical Attributes: 26 to 30 inches; 84 to 130 pounds; strong, sturdy; likes cold weather. This breed looks soft, but it is a very tough customer.

Color: White with no markings.

Coat Type and Grooming: Thick, medium length, wavy. Moderate grooming; no trimming. Heavy shedding.

Lifespan: 10 years.

Health Concerns: Hip and elbow dysplasia, OCD, von Willebrand's.

Exercise: Moderate. Needs a lot of space. Can be restless in the house.

Housing: Not well suited for urban areas or apartment life. Kuvasok are escape artists.

Interaction with Others: Very protective of family children, but not trustworthy around strange kids. Fine, even protective, with family dogs; can be aggressive toward other pets.

Trainability: Requires strong training. Since the ancestors of this breed were sheep guarders and were bred to bond to sheep, not people, this dog must be very well socialized early. This dog frequently tries to dominate, so must have an experienced owner.

Activities: Livestock guarding.

Remarks: If you own more than own Kuvasz, you have Kuvasok.

AKC Classification: Working Group.

Labrador Retriever

Character: Loyal, outgoing, playful, confident, hardworking, easy-going. Can be a pretty good watchdog, notifying the family of strangers.

Origin: Newfoundland, Canada, 1800s. Others say the breed actually originated in Greenland. All Labradors can be traced back to a certain Tramp, owned by Lord Malmsbury, who supposedly arrived in a ship carrying salted codfish.

Original Purpose: Water retriever.

Physical Attributes: 21 to 24 inches; 55 to 75 pounds; fine sense of smell, active, strong. His tail is said to resemble that of an otter; happiest if it can swim. Some of these dogs can be barkers and diggers, and most become obese easily.

Color: Black, yellow, chocolate. The yellow can range from pale cream to a reddish hue. Chocolate Labradors have a reputation of being more active than yellow or black. Black used to be the most popular color by far, but yellow seems to have taken over these days.

Coat Type and Grooming: Short, straight dense outercoat; soft water repellant undercoat. No trimming. Weekly brushing. Sheds seasonally.

Lifespan: 11 to 13 years.

Health Concerns: Orthopedic problems (hip and elbow dysplasia, cruciate ligament injuries, arthritis, OCD), ear infections, gastritis/enteritis, obesity, cardiomyopathy, bloat, eye problems (cataracts, retinal dysplasia, PRA), skin problems (inhalant and food allergies, acral lick dermatitis), cancer (osteosarcoma).

Exercise: High; especially when young; happiest in homes where he has access to swimming. Makes an ideal family dog and is generally calm in the house. If exercise needs are not met, Labs can become destructive, chewing anything in their path.

Housing: Not suited for apartment life.

Interaction with Others: One of the best "people" dogs; very friendly to children, but young Labs may be too exuberant for toddlers. This is a great family dog that loves the rough and tumble games of children. Good with other pets.

Trainability: Exceptional; these dogs are eager to please. They are very reliable off lead. A good dog for first-time dog owners; however, early training is important.

Part 2

Labrador Retriever

Activities: Guide dog, hunting and retrieving, obedience, flyball, sniffer dog, therapy dog, search and rescue.

Remarks: The wonderful disposition of this breed is now threatened by careless and unscrupulous breeders, so be careful to choose a breeder who values temperament and health.

AKC Classification: Sporting Group.

Kennel Club Classification: Gundog Group.

Lakeland Terrier

Character: Frisky, spunky, clever, playful, self-confident, quiet for a terrier; likes to be the center of attention; superb watchdog, but too small to be really protective.

Origin: Lake District of England, 1700s.

Original Purpose: Killing vermin.

Physical Attributes: 13 to 14 inches; 16 to 20 pounds; energetic, agile, curious.

Color: Blue, red, black, wheaten, or liver; may have a saddle of black, blue, liver, or grizzle.

Coat Type and Grooming: Short, wiry; medium to high maintenance required; brushing three times a week. Professional grooming is necessary; pets need to be clipped and show dogs stripped regularly. Slight shedding.

Lifespan: 12 to 13 years.

Health Concerns: Legg-Perthes, cataracts.

Exercise: Moderate to high.

Housing: Adaptable to any living situation.

Interaction with Others: Enjoys playing with children, but bonds to one person; may be too active for toddlers; reserved with strangers. Not always good with other pets, but better than many other terriers.

Trainability: Difficult, can be stubborn.

Activities: Earthdog trials, varmint eradication.

Remarks: Lynn McCain, of the US Lakeland Terrier Club, says (with a twinkle in her eye): "Owning a Lakeland Terrier is like having Jesse James guard the bank. Charming and disarming – until you turn your back."

AKC Classification: Terrier Group.

Kennel Club Classification: Terrier Group.

Part 2

Lhasa Apso

Character: Creative, playful, bold, loyal, companionable, independent; protective of its family, sometimes too much so. Good as a family dog or companion for one person.

Origin: Tibet, antiquity.

Original Purpose: Indoor watchdog, companion.

Physical Attributes: 10 to 11 inches; 14 to 16 pounds; acute hearing; can handle cold weather.

Color: Any color; golden, dark grizzle, black, parti-color, sandy, honey, white, brown are all acceptable.

Coat Type and Grooming: Long (floor length), hard, straight, heavy; very high maintenance required; brushing every other day; lots of shampooing to bring out the shine. The hair over the eye was protective against Tibetan winds, but serves little purpose now. The coat is parted in the middle. Pet owners often have their dogs clipped and tie the hair back. Shedding slight.

Lifespan: 12 to 15 years.

Health Concerns: Allergies.

Exercise: Low; this dog needs plenty of attention and love, but it is by no means a sissy and doesn't expect to be treated like a toy dog. Small as it is, it is not in the toy group, and does not have a "toy" personality.

Housing: Adaptable to any living situation; can be noisy.

Interaction with Others: All right with older children if they are well behaved; some are snappish with toddlers; reserved or very wary with strangers. Not always good with other dogs; good with other pets.

Trainability: Difficult; responds to positive reinforcement; needs a lot of repetition. Some challenge their owners for dominance.

Activities: Companion, obedience.

Remarks: In their native Tibet, Lhasas were called *Abso sen kye* or "bark lion sentinel dog."

AKC Classification: Non-Sporting Group.

Kennel Club Classification: Utility Group.

Löwchen

Character: Willing to please, devoted, alert, affectionate, fun-loving, spunky; needs a lot of human company and attention.

Origin: France, Germany, 1500s.

Original Purpose: Companion.

Physical Attributes: 12 to 14 inches (shorter in Europe); 8 to 18 pounds (lower range in Europe); alert. Some are barkers and diggers.

Color: Any color or combination.

Coat Type and Grooming: Long, silky, soft. Professional grooming is necessary: The dog is groomed in a traditional lion clip for shows, but pet owners usually leave the dog in a puppy clip. Low to average shedding.

Lifespan: 13 to 15 years.

Health Concerns: Patellar luxation, eye problems (PRA and cataracts).

Exercise: Low.

Housing: Adaptable to any living situation.

Interaction with Others: Very good with children and strangers.

Trainability: Moderate to high.

Activities: Obedience, therapy dog.

Remarks: Although you may have never heard of this breed, they've been around for at least 600 years and are more commonly seen in Europe than in the United States.

AKC Classification: Non-Sporting Group.

Kennel Club Classification: Toy Group.

Part 2

Maltese

Character: Fearless, lively, sweet-natured, loyal, sparkly, good-natured. Becomes attached to whole family. Will alert to the presence of strangers.

Origin: Malta, or possibly Melita (Sicily), antiquity. One of the oldest breeds. (Yes, there are Egyptian tomb paintings of Maltese, or something vaguely like them.) The Maltese arrived in Britain with the Romans. It is odd to think of Roman legions carrying fluffy little Maltese around with them, but there you are.

Original Purpose: Lap dog.

Physical Attributes: 5 to 10 inches; 3 to 7 pounds; some are barkers.

Color: White.

Coat Type and Grooming: Long, silky, single; even a hint of a double coat would ruin the outline for a show dog. Very high maintenance; brushing every day. Maintenance for a show coat even more, including "wrapping" the hair in cloth to keep it from matting. Professional grooming recommended. Minimal shedding.

Lifespan: 12 to 15 years.

Health Concerns: Heart problems (PDA, mitral valve insufficiency), patellar luxation.

Exercise: Gets along with little exercise. Likes to be pampered. Cannot handle severe weather

Housing: Adaptable to any living situation.

Interaction with Others: Fine with older kids and strangers, although some individuals are reserved; most Maltese should not be placed in home with toddlers; Not good with other animals.

Trainability: Average to high; may be hard to housetrain.

Activities: Therapy dog, agility, obedience, tracking.

Remarks: The Maltese is also known as the Shock Dog, the Comforter, the Spaniel Gentle, and the Roman Lady's Dog.

AKC Classification: Toy Group.

Kennel Club Classification: Toy Group.

Manchester Terrier

Character: Independent, companionable; good watchdog.

Origin: England, 1500s.

Original Purpose: Ratting and coursing rabbits.

Physical Attributes: 16 inches; 12 to 22 pounds; sleek, quick, rather quiet; cannot handle cold.

Color: Black with mahogany or tan points

Coat Type and Grooming: Short, smooth, glossy; this breed is so clean it has been called "catlike." Low to average seasonal shedding.

Lifespan: 15 to 17 years; some have been known to live over 20 years.

Health Concerns: Legg-Perthes, PRA, von Willebrand's.

Exercise: Moderate.

Housing: Suited for apartment life and urban areas.

Interaction with Others: Good with gentle children; may be overprotective; some can be snappish. Bonds to whole family; can be shy or reserved with strangers. Good with other dogs, especially other Manchester Terriers; most chase cats and smaller pets.

Trainability: Average to high; responds better than many terriers.

Activities: Earthdog trials, obedience, agility.

Remarks: Unfortunately, many individuals in this breed have inherited shyness or aggression problems; some are also non-stop barkers. Be sure to get a dog from a reputable breeder.

AKC Classification: Terrier Group.

Kennel Club Classification: Terrier Group.

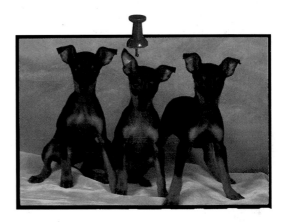

Mastiff

Character: Affectionate, even-tempered, faithful, mellow, good-natured, but not demonstrative, steady; makes a reliable watchdog. Some lines can be protective or aggressive—even Mastiffs that are not protective ward off miscreants by sheer size.

Origin: England, antiquity. Ancestors came from Asia, and there exists the typical Egyptian tomb painting of a breed resembling a Mastiff.

Original Purpose: Guard dog, fighting dog, dog of war.

Physical Attributes: At least 30 inches; 120 to 225 pounds; show Mastiffs are often a good deal bigger than the pet variety; dislikes the heat.

Color: Fawn, apricot, silver fawn, or brindle; muzzle, mask, and ears must be very dark.

Coat Type and Grooming: Short, close-lying; minimal grooming required, although there is a lot of dog here. No trimming; eyes need special care. Average shedding; tends to be constant rather than seasonal.

Lifespan: 5 to 10 years.

Health Concerns: Obesity, bloat, hip dysplasia, OCD, von Willebrand's.

Exercise: Needs frequent moderate walks and a lot of room, but is quiet in the house with a very low energy level.

Housing: Adaptable to most living situations if given enough room to move around.

Interaction with Others: Enjoys being around people; bonds to the entire family. Usually very good with children, but not playful; however, some lines not good with kids. Usually very tolerant of other dogs.

Trainability: Medium.

Activities: Therapy dog, weight-pulling.

Remarks: Mastiffs of all types (and there are many besides those in the AKC registry) are one of the major foundation stocks of many dog breeds

AKC Classification: Working Group.

Kennel Club Classification: Working Group.

Miniature Bull Terrier

Character: Comical, playful, friendly; similar to the Bull Terrier; good watch-dog.

Origins: England, 1800s.

Original Function: Ratting, dog fighting.

Physical Attributes: 11 to 14 inches; 25 to 40 pounds.

Color: Solid white and colored (any color).

Coat Type and Grooming: Short, flat, harsh; minimal care required; should be brushed once a week. No trimming. Average shedding.

Lifespan: 12 to 14 years.

Health Concerns: Eye problems (glaucoma, lens luxation), allergies, mood swings, obsessive-compulsive disorders, epilepsy, deafness in whites, patellar luxation, heart problems.

Exercise: Low to moderate.

Housing: Ideal for urban areas and apartment life.

Interaction with Others: Good with kids if well socialized; extremely play-ful; tends to bond to one person. Usually accepting of less dominant dogs; not good with cats or small pets.

Trainability: Average.

Activities: Earthdog trials, obedience.

Remarks: This dog is exactly like the Bull Terrier, except for size.

AKC Classification: Terrier Group.

Kennel Club Classification: Terrier Group.

Miniature Pinscher

Character: Self-possessed, stubborn, curious, spunky, lively, alert; a good watchdog

Origin: Germany, 1600s. Contrary to what some may think, the Miniature Pinscher is not a toy Doberman. Both the Miniature Pinscher and the Doberman come from older stock, but the "Min Pin" is not a descendant; nor is the Miniature Pinscher related to the Manchester Terrier, although there is physical resemblance between the two.

Original Purpose: Hunting small vermin.

Physical Attributes: 11 to 12 inches; 8 to 10 pounds; small and quick. Ears are usually cropped, but natural ears are permitted; tail is always docked; has little tolerance for cold. This dog is a barker, climber, and escape artist.

Color: Clear or solid red, stag, red, black and tan (or rust), black-and-rust, or chocolate-and-rust.

Coat Type and Grooming: Hard, smooth, short; minimal grooming required. Slight shedding.

Lifespan: 12 to 15 years.

Health Concerns: PRA, mitral valve insufficiency, orthopedic problems (fractures, patellar luxation, Legg-Perthes).

Exercise: Very high.

Housing: Adaptable to any living situation, perfect for apartment dwellers.

Interaction with Others: Despite its diminutive size, definitely not a lap dog. Good with gentle older children, but probably too small for rough toddlers. Tends to bond to one person; reserved with strangers. May be all right with other dogs and cats if socialized carefully; will chase smaller animals.

Trainability: Low to moderate; this is a tough, self-possessed dog that needs firm handling.

Activities: Agility.

Remarks: The breed is sometimes called the "King of Toys."

AKC Classification: Toy Group.

Kennel Club Classification: Toy Group.

Miniature Schnauzer

Character: Friendly, sweet, fearless, devoted, strong-willed, tenacious; some are high-strung, but not as dominant as bigger Schnauzers; bonds to the whole family.

Origin: Southern Germany, 1800s. The Miniature Schnauzer is not only "bred down" from the Standard size, but also has some Affenpinscher or possibly Miniature Pinscher in him.

Original Purpose: Ratting, watchdog.

Physical Attributes: 12 to 14 inches; 15 to 20 pounds; energetic, sturdy. Some are barkers.

Color: Pepper and salt, black and silver, or solid black.

Coat Type and Grooming: Harsh, wiry. High maintenance; needs brushing three times a week. Professional grooming is recommended. Slight shedding.

Lifespan: 12 to 15 years.

Health Concerns: Eye problems (juvenile cataracts, PRA, rheumy eyes), pancreatitis, pulmonic stenosis, arrhythmia, von Willebrand's, skin problems (allergies), diabetes.

Exercise: Moderate to high; needs regular exercise; well-mannered in the house.

Housing: Adaptable to any living situation; however, some are too vocal for neighbors.

Interaction with Others: Very good with people, less dominant than the bigger schnauzers. Likes children, but better with older kids; best when socialized early. Good with other dogs; okay with cats; not good with small pets.

Trainability: Very high; some may attempt to challenge their owners for dominance.

Activities: Earthdog trials, obedience.

Remarks: The Miniature Schnauzer is part of the AKC Terrier Group (the Giant and Standards are part of the Working Group). Unlike other terriers, the Miniature Schnauzer does not go to ground after its prey. The word "schnauzer" means "muzzle" in German.

AKC Classification: Terrier Group.

Kennel Club Classification: Utility Group.

Part 2

Newfoundland

Character: Benevolent, calm, adaptable, sweet, easygoing, docile; not protective, but its size is daunting; bonds to the whole family.

Origin: Canada, 1700s. Probably derived ultimately from the Mollosian Mastiffs, although a few historians give credit to the Algonquin Indians.

Original Purpose: Water dog (helped fishermen), draft, towing lines and nets. Today, they save people from drowning.

Physical Attributes: 26 to 32 inches; 100 to 150 pounds. Loves the water; to be happy, these dogs need frequent access to a lake or river. They cannot tolerate heat and need to be kept cool. They are very heavy droolers and have a deep loud bark.

Color: Solid black, brown, bronze and blue, or gray, with small white markings permissible. One variety, the Landseer, is black and white.

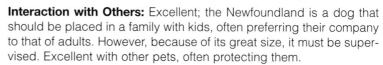

Coat Type and Grooming: Profuse, dense, flat, waterproof, slightly oily; medium long. Twice a week thorough combing desirable; no trimming. Professional grooming is optional. Major shedding, seasonally.

Lifespan: 10 to 12 years.

Health Concerns: Orthopedic problems (hip and elbow dysplasia, OCD), heart problems (SAS, cardiomyopathy, VSD) heatstroke, seizures, allergies, hypothyroidism.

Exercise: Moderate; these dogs are lazy by nature and must be encouraged to exercise; otherwise, they will become obese.

Housing: They need a lot of room and enjoy swimming.

Interaction with Others: Excellent; the Newfoundland is a dog that should be placed in a family with kids, often preferring their company to that of adults. However, because of its great size, it must be supervised. Excellent with other pets, often protecting them.

Trainability: High; of all the giant breeds, the Newfoundland makes the best obedience prospect; a fast learner.

Activities: Water search and rescue, drafting, obedience.

Remarks: The most beautiful remarks about a Newfoundland must be credited to the great English poet, Lord Byron, who wrote the epitaph for his own: "Near this spot are deposited the Remains of one who possessed Beauty without Vanity, Strength without Insolence, Courage without Ferocity, and all the Virtues of Man without his Vices. This Praise, which would be unmeaning flattery if inscribed over human ashes, is but a just tribute to the memory of Boatswain, a Dog, who was born at Newfoundland, May, 1803, and died at Newstead Abbey, Nov. 18, 1808."

AKC Classification: Working Group.

Kennel Club Classification: Working Group.

Norfolk Terrier

Character: Lively, feisty, spunky, amiable, alert, game; excellent watchdog, but not protective; requires attention; bonds to whole family.

Origin: England, 1800s.

Original Purpose: Ratting, farm dog.

Physical Attributes: 11 to 12 inches; 8 to 10 pounds; energetic, outgoing. This dog is a digger and barker.

Color: Various shades of red, wheaten, black and tan, or grizzle.

Coat Type and Grooming: Short and wiry; requires a comb out every week and stripping of dead hair a few times a year. Professional grooming is very desirable, especially for a show coat. Moderate shedding.

Lifespan: 12 to 15 years.

Health Problems: Allergic dermatitis, collapsing trachea, mitral valve insufficiency.

Exercise: Moderate.

Housing: Well suited to apartment life and urban areas.

Interaction with Others: Good with children if socialized early; very playful; not good with toddlers. Good with other pets.

Trainability: Low; not reliable off-lead.

Activities: Earthdog trials, agility.

Remarks: Originally, the Norwich and Norfolk Terriers were one breed, the main difference between the two types being the ear carriage. Because of their rarity and small litters, a good specimen of this breed can be very expensive.

AKC Classification: Terrier Group.

Kennel Club Classification: Terrier Group.

Norwegian Elkhound

Character: Independent, strong-willed, bold, loyal, energetic, friendly.

Origin: Norway; originally bred by the Vikings.

Original Purpose: Elk and moose hunting; also bear and rabbit.

Physical Attributes: 19 to 20 inches; 40 to 55 pounds; strong, solid, compact, nimble; good eyesight; a spitz-type dog. They can be barkers, but the bark is said to have a bell-like quality. The Elkhound can handle extreme cold but very little heat.

Color: Gray tipped with black.

Coat Type and Grooming: Straight, thick, coarse, abundant, long, weather resistant. Moderate maintenance. Professional grooming is optional. Major shedding.

Lifespan: 10 to 12 years.

Health Concerns: Hip dysplasia, eye problems (PRA, glaucoma).

Exercise: Needs daily moderate exercise.

Housing: Adaptable to any living situation.

Interaction with Others: He is friendly with strangers but is a fine watchdog and can be protective if he feels his owner is being threatened. He is very friendly, if rambunctious with kids, which is an unusual trait in a hound. He tends to bond with one person; not good with other pets, especially bad with cats.

Trainability: Difficult to train for obedience and is a natural puller; definitely does best with a strong, dominant owner; however, very quick to learn what they want to know.

Activities: Hunting, tracking.

Remarks: The Norwegian Elkhound is the only scenthound with erect ears.

AKC Classification: Hound Group.

Kennel Club Classification: Hound Group.

Norwich Terrier

Character: Protective, loyal, pert, game, gay, alert; a good watchdog; bonds to the whole family.

Origin: England, 1800s.

Original Purpose: Ratting.

Physical Attributes: 10 inches; 10 to 13 pounds; quick. Some may be barkers; does not do well in heat.

Color: Shades of red, wheaten black and tan, and grizzle.

Coat Type and Grooming: Short, wiry coat; requires combing two or three times a week and stripping a few times a year for show dogs. Professional grooming is very desirable. Slight shedding.

Lifespan: 12 to 15 years.

Health Concerns: Allergic dermatitis, patellar luxation, mitral valve insufficiency.

Exercise: Moderate to high; needs frequent walks or a run every day.

Housing: Adaptable to any living situation.

Interaction with Others: Good with children if exposed early. Good with other dogs; some chase smaller pets, but most are fine with cats.

Trainability: Low.

Activities: Earthdog trials, agility.

Remarks: Famous Dog: In the hysterically funny film *Best In Show,* a Norwich Terrier wins it all at the fictitious Mayflower Kennel Club show.

AKC Classification: Terrier Group.

Kennel Club Classification: Terrier Group.

Part 2

Old English Sheepdog

Character: Bold, adaptable, lovable, affectionate, friendly, home-loving; bonds to whole family. Some individuals are timid or aggressive.

Origin: England, the West Country; ancestors may include the Bearded Collie. Despite the name, the breed is not very old.

Original Purpose: Sheep and cattle drover.

Physical Attributes: 22 or more inches; 75 to 90 pounds; bear-like motion. It can handle hot weather better than you might think. The tail is usually docked. This is a fairly slow maturing breed.

Color: Any shade of gray, grizzle, or blue, often with white markings.

Coat Type and Grooming: Long, shaggy, harsh-textured, profuse; high maintenance; requires combing every other day to prevent mats. House pets are frequently clipped down to a short coat, but show

dogs must be shown in a full coat. Professional grooming is recommended; some trimming. Heavy shedding.

Lifespan: 10 to 12 years.

Health Concerns: Hip dysplasia, cataracts, deafness, cardiomyopathy.

Exercise: These dogs need plenty of room and lots of outdoor exercise, at least twice a day; well-mannered at home.

Housing: Not suited for apartment life.

Interaction with Others: Good with children; highly sociable with everyone, including strangers.

Trainability: Medium to high; this breed benefits from early obedience training.

Activities: Herding, obedience, therapy dog.

Remarks: Peggy Anderson, Secretary, New England Old English Sheepdog Club, writes: "They are big, furry, intelligent, exuberant clowns; the Peter Pans of the dog world requiring lots of coat care. In return, to the family that loves them, they offer humor, loyalty and love." Chris Lawrenz, Corresponding Secretary of the Old English Sheepdog Club of America, agrees: "The Old English Sheepdog is a very agile, friendly, and good-natured dog, and although he is an incurable clown, he may be prone to stubbornness."

AKC Classification: Herding Group.

Kennel Club Classification: Pastoral Group.

Otterhound

Character: Affectionate, persistent, laid-back, cheerful, sociable, devoted; friendly to introduced strangers, but will alert owners to newcomers. Some are territorial and have guarding ability.

Origin: England, antiquity; may have some large terriers in its ancestry; may be related to the French Wendy Hound.

Original Purpose: Otter hunting, which was outlawed in Britain in 1978.

Physical Attributes: 23 to 27 inches, 65 to 115 pounds; big, big-boned, and strong; persistent hunter; good nose; good swimmer with webbed feet. This is a slow maturing breed.

Color: All colors acceptable; black and tan, grizzle, red, liver and tan, tri-color, wheaten are common.

Coat Type and Grooming: Rough, long, crisp, shaggy outercoat; wooly water-resistant undercoat; high-maintenance required, no trimming. Professional grooming is desirable. Medium to heavy seasonal shedding.

Lifespan: 12 to 14 years.

Health Concerns: Orthopedic disorders (hip dysplasia, OCD), bloat, seizures.

Exercise: Moderate to high, especially when young.

Housing: Not well suited to urban areas or apartment life.

Interaction with Others: Excellent with people, including children and strangers; good with other dogs, sometimes object to unfamiliar cats.

Trainability: Medium, needs firm training.

Activities: Tracking, water search and rescue.

Remarks: Currently, the Otterhound has the distinction of being the least popular of the AKC-recognized breeds, although not due to disposition or care issues.

AKC Classification: Hound Group.

Kennel Club Classification: Hound Group.

Papillon

Character: Devoted, gentle, a "royal" attitude, happy, perky, lively; some individuals are timid—look for a dog who does not exhibit this trait.

Origin: Central Europe, some say France or Spain, 1500s; the breed is related to toy spaniels Some claim a Roman statue depicts one.

Original Purpose: Companion or lap dog.

Physical Attributes: 8 to 11 inches; 9 to 10 pounds; lithe, elegant; intolerant of cold. Known for "butterfly" ears, although some kinds have drop or "phalene" ears. (Phalene means "moth" in French.)

Color: Predominantly white with patches of any other color; a white blaze is preferred.

Coat Type and Grooming: Long and silky, no undercoat; easy grooming; once or twice a week. Minimal shedding.

Lifespan: 12 to 15 years or more.

Health Concerns: Patellar luxation, eye problems, fractures.

Exercise: Light to moderate; however, requires more than many toy breeds.

Housing: Adaptable to any living situation; enjoys both city and country

Interaction with Others: Likes everyone, including strangers; good with children, but because they are so small, they are not suited for families with toddlers. They demand attention and cuddling. Good with other pets.

Trainability: Extraordinarily high; one of the best of the toy breeds; a good obedience prospect. Some are hard to housetrain.

Activities: Obedience, agility, tracking.

Remarks: "Papillon" means "butterfly" in French; the name comes from the butterfly appearance of his ears. Anna Schwartz, who is a longtime owner, writes, "Papillons thrive on being an integral part of the life of the people they love. The "butterfly dog" flits through life spreading love and laughter. This smart little breed, with its infectious love of life, is a good choice for those desiring a constant companion who keeps them on their toes."

AKC Classification: Toy Group.

Kennel Club Classification: Toy Group.

Pekingese

Character: Courageous, determined, stubborn, loyal, companionable, aloof; a good watchdog. The Peke needs a lot of attention from his family.

Origin: China, antiquity.

Original Purpose: Pet, sacred dog, lap dog.

Physical Attributes: 6 to 9 inches, 8 to 13 pounds. This heavy-coated, compact breed cannot handle heat. Due to their shortened muzzle, they may snore (mine did).

Color: All colors and patterns except albino and liver.

Coat Type and Grooming: Long, profuse, thick; high maintenance; a lot of brushing at least once a week to prevent matting. Face and eyes need special attention. Professional grooming is desirable. Slight shedding.

Lifespan: 13 to 15 years.

Health Concerns: Umbilical hernia, eye problems (corneal ulcer, distichiasis, entropion, "dry eye"), breathing problems, stenotic nares (pinched nostrils), cysts, phobias, elongated soft palate, patellar luxation, skin allergies, congestive heart failure, arthritis, seizures, ear infections.

Exercise: Low.

Housing: Adaptable to any living situation; perfect for apartment life.

Interaction with Others: Not good with children; aloof with strangers; not playful.

Trainability: Low; some may be hard to housetrain.

Activities: Therapy dog, agility

Remarks: Chinese legend says that this dog is a cross between a lion and a monkey, inheriting the best features of each, of course. In imperial China, the penalty for stealing a Pekingese was death. This didn't deter British and America troops from grabbing five of them in 1860 and bringing them home, however.

AKC Classification: Toy Group.

Kennel Club Classification: Toy Group.

Part 2

Pembroke Welsh Corgi

Character: Alert, lively, devoted, bold, workmanlike, intuitive; bonds to whole family.

Origin: Pembrokeshire, Wales.

Original Purpose: Cattle herder, cattle drover.

Physical Attributes: 10 to 12 inches; 17 to 30 pounds.

Colors: Usually red but can also be fawn, sable, black and tan, sometimes with white markings.

Coat Type and Grooming: Outer coat is short to medium rather coarse and water-resistant; undercoat is thick and dense. Professional grooming is optional. Moderate shedding.

Lifespan: 12 to 14 years.

Health Concerns: Degenerative myelopathy, hot spots, eye problems (cataracts, glaucoma, PRA), PDA, epilepsy, intervertebral disc disease, von Willebrand's.

Exercise: Moderate/high; needs daily vigorous, exercise; many will self-exercise.

Housing: Adaptable to any living situation.

Interactions with Others: Excellent family dog; very playful with older children, probably less apt to "nip" than the Cardigan, which has kept more of its cattle-herding proclivities; usually accepting of strangers. Usually all right with other pets, some may fight with same-sex dogs.

Trainability: Highly trainable; early socialization needed.

Activities: Obedience, cattle drover.

Remarks: This breed is a favorite of the British royalty, and Queen Elizabeth II posed for a portrait with hers.

AKC Classification: Herding Group.

Kennel Club Classification: Pastoral Group.

Petit Basset Griffon Vendéen

Character: Affectionate, merry, inquisitive, happy, determined, busy; friendly to strangers, but might bark at a newcomer. These dogs bond to the whole family.

Origin: Vendée France, 1700s.

Original Purpose: Small game hunter.

Physical Attributes: 12 to 15 inches; 25 to 45 pounds; loudly vocal and sturdy.

Color: White with markings of lemon, orange, black, grizzle, or tricolor.

Coat Type and Grooming: Hard, rough, wiry outercoat; short dense undercoat. While the breed standard charmingly requests that the PBGV be "casual," and have a "rough, unrefined outline," owners should not interpret that request as "scruffy." These dogs require weekly grooming and a little trimming for show dogs. Professional grooming is optional. Minimal shedding.

Lifespan: 10 to 14 years.

Health Concerns: Orthopedic problems (hip dysplasia, patellar luxation), eye problems (PRA, lens luxation), aseptic meningitis, heart murmurs.

Exercise: This dog needs a good deal of exercise in a fenced area and requires a lot of attention.

Housing: Does best in the country.

Interaction with Others: Very good with children, although perhaps too exuberant for very young kids. Good, sometimes pushy, with other pets.

Trainability: Average; some say that males are more trainable than females

Activities: Hunting, tracking, agility.

Remarks: Aficionados of this breed are always arguing about whether it is more like a hound or a terrier, but it has characteristics of both groups. In any case, the PBGV is not closely related to the Basset Hound.

AKC Classification: Hound Group.

Kennel Club Classification: Hound Group.

Pharaoh Hound

Character: Alert, eager to please, friendly, playful, affectionate; not a protective dog, but a very good watchdog.

Origin: Malta, antiquity; they have come from Egypt as the name indicates; one of the oldest breeds.

Original Purpose: Rabbit hunting.

Physical Attributes: 21 to 26 inches; 40 to 60 pounds; sturdy, graceful elegant; lots of stamina. These dogs cannot handle cold weather (35 degrees or lower) for more than 20 or 30 minutes; ears and feet are especially prone to frostbite. This animal is also known to blush when agitated or happy.

Color: Tan, rich tan, or chestnut, with some white markings allowed; white tail tip preferred.

Coat Type and Grooming: Short, smooth, glossy; minimal care required; brush once a week with a hound mitt. This breed has no doggy odor. Minimal shedding.

Lifespan: 11 to 15 years.

Health Concerns: Optic nerve hypoplasia.

Exercise: Average to high; quiet in the house; needs large exercise yard and lots of playtime (30 minutes four times a day).

Housing: Does best in the country.

Interaction with Others: Very good with people, enjoys active playing with children; bonds to whole family. Good with other pets, not quarrelsome.

Trainability: Average to high; must be kept on a leash outside a fenced area. These dogs are escape artists of the highest order; they can unlock gates.

Activities: Lure coursing, obedience.

Remarks: C. Burns, of the Pharaoh Hound Club of America, writes, "The Pharaoh Hound is clean, and playful till old age. It strongly bonds with the family unit, has a strong hunting instinct, and is extremely intelligent. The Pharaoh Hound should have basic training, or this breed with its beautiful eyes will truly train you." Marie Henke, of Jomara's Pharaoh Hounds, adds, "I tell potential puppy buyers that living with a Pharaoh Hound is like living with a two-year-old child."

AKC Classification: Hound Group.

Kennel Club Classification: Hound Group.

Pointer

Character: Adaptable, obedient, willing to please, independent, gentle, congenial. The field variety is a "hard" dog and relentless (read "stubborn"); show-line dogs are softer with a more even temper. A good watchdog, but not a protective breed.

Origin: England, 1600s; ancestors probably include the foxhound and greyhound.

Original Purpose: Finding hares for Greyhound to chase.

Physical Attributes: 23 to 28 inches; 50 to 90 pounds; aristocratic, clean-cut, fluid, built for both speed and endurance; tireless, energetic, very active; excellent sense of smell and great stamina. As is usual with pointers and setters, the dogs used for hunting and field trials tend to run smaller than dogs from show lines.

Color: Lemon, liver, black, orange, usually with white. They say, "A good Pointer can never be a bad color."

Coat Type and Grooming: Short; easy to care for; clean dogs, with little odor; no trimming. Medium to high shedding.

Lifespan: 12 to 15 years.

Health Concerns: Entropion (eyelid problem), PRA, cataracts, hip and elbow dysplasia.

Exercise: Immense; this dog is happiest if it can hunt, as it was intended to do. Dogs from show lines are calmer and less energetic than field dogs. It is well-behaved in the house if it given sufficient exercise, but otherwise can be hyper and destructive.

Housing: Needs a good amount of room and is not suited to urban life.

Interaction with Others: Good, but rambunctious with people; tolerant of kids; gets along very well with other dogs.

Trainability: High; these dogs are easy to housetrain.

Activities: Hunting dog, obedience, field trials, agility, tracking, service dog.

Remarks: This breed is the mascot of the Westminster Kennel Club, and with good reason. To me, a pointer is a dog's dog, and one of my absolute favorites.

AKC Classification: Sporting Group.

Kennel Club Classification: Gundog Group.

Polish Lowland Sheepdog

Character: Stable, gentle, friendly, dominant, lively, alert.

Origin: Possibly related to the Bearded Collie and Puli.

Original Purpose: Shepherder.

Physical Attributes: 17 to 20 inches; 35 to 50 pounds; agile, hardy. The tail, if present at birth, is usually docked.

Color: Any color acceptable.

Coat Type and Grooming: Long, thick, harsh outercoat; dense, soft undercoat; high maintenance required; the coat needs to be thoroughly brushed every two or three days to prevent matting. Professional grooming is recommended. Low to average shedding.

Health Concerns: Hip dysplasia.

Exercise: High; regular exercise is needed.

Housing: Not suitable for urban areas or apartment life.

Interaction with Others: Very playful with children; reserved with strangers.

Trainability: High; however, this dog need very firm handling and an experienced owner because of its tendency to dominate.

Activities: Agility, obedience, herding.

Remarks: This dog is sometimes called the Polski Owczarek Nizinny, but many people strangely prefer the simple Lowland Sheepdog.

AKC Classification: Herding Group.

Kennel Club Classification: Pastoral Group.

Pomeranian

Character: Bouncy, loyal, curious, bold, alert, happy, extroverted; good watchdog; tends to bond to one person.

Origin: Germany (Pomerania is on the shore of the Baltic Sea), 1800s.

Original Purpose: Lap dogs and companions.

Physical Attributes: 6 to 7 inches; 4 to 6 pounds; the smallest of the spitz breeds, miniaturized from its larger cousins. They have small feet, even for their tiny size. These dogs can be very vocal.

Color: The earliest Pomeranians were all white. Today all colors and patterns are allowed, including chocolate and white.

Coat Type and Grooming: Heavy, dense, harsh, double, abundant; high maintenance required; daily grooming when shedding; twice a week the rest of the year; some trimming. Professional grooming is recommended. Heavy seasonal shedding.

Lifespan: 12 to 16 years.

Health Concerns: Patellar luxation, PDA.

Exercise: Low; well-behaved in the house; able to self exercise.

Housing: Adaptable to any living situation, but the breed can be noisy.

Interaction with Others: Okay with older well-disciplined children, but are not suited for rough play; reserved and wary of strangers; some individuals may be snappish. Often suspicious of other pets and may be aggressive

Trainability: Variable: Low to high; responds well to consistent training. This is a good breed for the first-time owner. I have a friend with a pair of them that can do anything.

Activities: Agility, flyball, obedience.

Remarks: This breed has been owned by Queen Victoria and Napoleon's Josephine, among others. Eileen Gage, who is active in Pomeranian rescue and who has owned the breed for many years, writes "These little ones are highly intelligent and if trained early in puppyhood are very well behaved. Poms will reward you with unconditional love, loyalty, and miles and miles of happiness and smiles if treated with love and patience."

AKC Classification: Toy Group.

Kennel Club Classification: Toy Group.

Part 2

Poodle

Character: Friendly, great sense of fun, proud, loyal, intuitive, sparky. Standard poodles tend to be more docile than smaller varieties; Toy Poodles may be high-strung.

Origin: Central Europe (maybe Russia) or Germany, 1500s.

Original Purpose: Water retriever, truffle finder.

Physical Attributes: Poodles come in three sizes, Standard, Miniature, and Toy, but, except for size, the standard for each is exactly the same. Toy Poodles are under 10 inches, 7 to 12 pounds; Miniatures are 11 to 15 inches, 16 pounds; and Standards are usually over 21 inches, 45 to 55 pounds. Tails are usually docked.

Color: Any solid color including black, white, silver, blue, apricot, brown.

Coat Type and Grooming: Single, harsh, curly coat; all need daily grooming and regular clipping; no doggy odor. Professional grooming is recommended; however, you are not required to have a Continental or English Saddle clip as show dogs do. Ask for a sensible, easy-care trim. Very little shedding.

Lifespan: 13 to 15 years—higher for smaller dogs.

Health Concerns: PRA (Miniature and Toy), distichiasis, Legg-Perthes (Miniature and Toy) glaucoma, patellar luxation (Toy and Miniature), cancer, epilepsy (Miniature and Toy), sebaceous adenitis (Standard), sebaceous gland tumors, ear infections, conjunctivitis, enteritis, entropion, color dilution alopeica (Standard), PDA, cardiomyopathy (Standard), mitral valve insufficiency (Toy and Miniature), hip dysplasia (Standard and Miniature), hypothyroidism, allergies.

Exercise: Medium to high.

Housing: All sizes of Poodles can accommodate themselves to apartment living; however, Toy Poodles may be too yappy for neighborly comfort.

Interactions with Others: Superior family dog, but may be reserved around strangers. Smaller Poodles, who may be timid, do better in a calm household. All are excellent with family children, with the Standard being the best. Some Toys are too excitable. Variable with other pets; they seem to enjoy the company of other Poodles most.

Trainability: Very high, very responsive; these dogs enjoy obedience work.

Activities: Agility, retrieving, obedience, hunting, therapy dog.

Remarks: The word Poodle comes from "pudeln" which means "to splash." They were originally marsh-dogs. Although Poodles come in three sizes, the AKC considers them all one breed.

AKC Classification: Standard and Minature: Non-Sporting Group; Toy: Toy Group

Kennel Club Classification: Utility Group.

Part 2

Portuguese Water Dog

Character: Bouncy, adaptable, fun-loving, spirited, calm, stubborn; can be protective.

Origin: Algarve, Portugal, Middle Ages. The Goths may have originally brought the breed to Portugal, although others trace the origin of the breed to Russia.

Original Purpose: Retrieving fish for fishermen.

Physical Attributes: 17 to 23 inches; 35 to 60 pounds; active, strong, compact. Great swimmers, so they need access to a body of water. They can catch anything in their mouths.

Color: Solid black, brown, white, particolor.

Coat Type and Grooming: Wavy or curly, profuse; very high maintenance required; brushing three times a week; professional clipping every six to eight weeks. Ears need special attention, particularly after swimming. Professional grooming is recommended. This breed does not shed (or sheds very little).

Lifespan: 9 to 15 years.

Health Concerns: Hip dysplasia, PRA, glycogen storage disease.

Exercise: High; this dog is tireless; needs a lot of exercise and attention

Housing: Not suited to apartment life, but can adapt if given an extreme amount of exercise.

Interaction with Others: Tends to bond to one person; good with children if well socialized, but tends to play very hard; may be somewhat reserved with strangers. Good with other pets; some individuals can be jealous.

Trainability: Average to very high; needs consistency.

Activities: Obedience, agility, water sports.

Remarks: One of the Portuguese Water Dog's original duties was to bark aboard ship on foggy days to prevent collisions with other vessels. Unfortunately for them, a great many were on the Spanish Armada of 1588, and the resulting shipwreck scattered them to the coasts of Cornwall and Ireland.

AKC Classification: Working Group.

Kennel Club Classification: Working Group.

Part 2

Pug

Character: Good-natured, confident, affectionate, stable, lively, willful; needs a lot of attention.

Origin: Uncertain, possibly China, others suggest a Russian origin. The breed may be more than 1000 years old.

Original Purpose: Lap dog

Physical Attributes: 11 to 13 inches; 14 to 24 pounds; compact. A double twist in the tail is especially prized. Although the skin is loose, there are no wrinkles except on the head. Not good in very hot or cold weather; snores.

Color: Red, sable, apricot, fawn, silver fawn, black and tan, silver; with or without white markings. Back moles on cheeks; black mask.

Coat Type and Grooming: Short, fine, glossy; outercoat is water-resistant; undercoat is dense and velvety soft; low maintenance required; eyes need special care. Average shedding.

Lifespan: 12 to 15 years.

Health Concerns: Obesity, breathing problems, eye and eyelid abnormalities (prolapse of the eye), dental problems, orthopedic problems (patellar luxation, hip dysplasia), Pug Dog encephalitis, seizures, allergies.

Exercise: Light; calm in the house.

Housing: Adaptable to any living situation; ideal for apartment life.

Interaction with Others: Good with older children; aloof with strangers; does equally well as family dog or a sole companion; enjoys showing off. Good with other pets, but doesn't mind being an only dog.

Trainability: Easily trained; obedience training is useful.

Activities: Obedience, therapy dog.

Remarks: The name "pug" supposedly comes from the Latin, "pugnus," or fist (from which we get the word pugnacious). The pug is not pugnacious, but his head does look like a fist.

AKC Classification: Toy Group.

Kennel Club Classification: Toy Group.

Part 2

Puli

Character: Energetic, lively, devoted, stubborn, affectionate, busy; good watch and guard dog; bonds to whole family.

Origin: Hungary, Middle Ages; ancestors possibly from Central Asia.

Original Purpose: Herding sheep, hunting in marshy areas, later used as a police dog.

Physical Attributes: 15 to 18 inches; 29 to 33 pounds. These fast, agile dogs are barkers.

Color: Rusty black, dull black, black, white, gray, apricot; specks of other colors permitted, but overall impression should be that of a solid color.

Coat Type and Grooming: Long (ground-length), corded, weather-resistant; outercoat wavy or curly, but not silky; undercoat soft, woolly, dense. Very high maintenance required; professional grooming is recommended. Beginning very early, cords must be separated out. Dog may be shown either corded or brushed out. The corded coat requires at least 45 minutes of grooming a week, including care every day. Brushed coats need grooming every other day; no trimming. A damp Puli, especially one with a correctly corded coat, is a smelly Puli. To avoid the smell, the dog must be dried as fast as possible with a dryer. Low shedding.

Lifespan: 12 to 16 years.

Health Concerns: Eye problems.

Exercise: Very high; Pulis are restless in the house if not given sufficient exercise.

Housing: Adaptable to any living situation, with a great deal exercise; best in the country.

Interaction with Others: Not good with kids; aloof and wary with strangers. Likes other Pulik, but aggressive to other breeds.

Trainability: Low to moderate for obedience work, but a clever dog in things that matter to it; easily housetrained.

Activities: Sheep guard dog, herding trials.

Remarks: The word "Puli" means "leader" in Hungarian. If you have more than one Puli, you have Pulik.

AKC Classification: Herding Group.

Rhodesian Ridgeback

Character: Loyal, proud, dignified, bold, aloof, strong-willed.

Origin: Southern Africa, 1800s. The original Ridgebacks were owned by Hottentots. Other ancestors include Great Danes, Mastiffs, Greyhounds, Salukis, and Bloodhounds.

Original Purpose: General farm dog, hunting lion and other game, guarding. (Of course, Rhodesian Ridgebacks did not kill lions. They merely found out where they were and alerted the hunters.)

Physical Attributes: 24 to 27 inches; 70 to 85 pounds; strong, active, elegant, stylish, powerful; cannot handle very cold weather. The ridged line of hair along the back is the predominant feature.

Color: Light to red wheaten; a small amount of white on the chest or toes is permitted.

Coat Type and Grooming: Short, hard, sleek, dense with a ridge along the spine. Minimal care; brushing once a week with a curry comb; no trimming. Average shedding.

Lifespan: 10 to 12 years.

Health Concerns: Hip dysplasia, hypothyroidism, dermoid sinus.

Exercise: High, especially when young; can be destructive if not given enough of it.

Housing: Not suitable for urban areas or apartment life.

Interaction with Others: It is generally fine with older family children; however, this energetic dog may be too rambunctious for toddlers. This breed tends to bond with one person. They are very reserved with strangers and make good watch and guard dogs. Not always good with dogs it does not know well; may try to dominate; not good with small pets like rabbits and cats.

Trainability: Medium; can be distracted; positive reinforcement necessary. Some individuals have a tendency to be dominant. This dog needs an experienced owner and early socialization.

Activities: Therapy dog, lure coursing, obedience, tracking. They also seem to be quite good at herding, although they don't have AKC approval for this activity yet.

Remarks: Rhodesia, named after Cecil Rhodes, is now Zimbabwe.

AKC Classification: Working Group.

Kennel Club Classification: Hound Group.

Rottweiler

Character: Bold, calm, headstrong, stern, somewhat aloof, courageous; very territorial; may be aggressive. Extremely good watchdog and guard dog, but can be overprotective.

Origin: Rottweil, Germany, Middle Ages.

Original Purpose: Boar hunting, cart-pulling, cattle driving, guardian, later police work. Early drafting dogs larger than today's version, which are descended from the shepherding type.

Physical Attributes: 22 to 27 inches; 75 to 125 pounds; rugged, strong. Tail is usually docked.

Color: Black with rust or mahogany markings.

Coat Type and Grooming: Shiny, thick, medium-short double coat; minimal grooming required, once a week brush up; no trimming. Average to heavy shedding.

Lifespan: 8 to 9 years.

Health Concerns: Orthopedic problems (hip and elbow dysplasia, panosteitis, OCD), eye problems (PRA, entropion), aortic stenosis, seizures, allergies, bone cancer, von Willebrand's.

Exercise: Moderate to high; enjoys outdoor exercise.

Housing: Surprisingly good in apartments or urban areas with adequate exercise.

Interaction with Others: Not good with young children; tends to dominate them; good with older children if well-socialized. A one-person dog; wary of strangers; may be aggressive. Will try to dominate strange dogs or dogs of the same sex.

Trainability: High; this dog needs early obedience training and strong early socialization. Not right for the first-time dog owner; will try to dominate. Everyone in the family should be dog savvy.

Activities: Guard dog, herding, weight pulling, carting, obedience, agility, search and rescue, therapy dog, Schutzhund.

Remarks: The Board of Directors of the American Rottweiler Club says, "The Rottweiler is an intelligent, focused dog who is loyal and protective of family and home; his powerful build and working temperament make him ideal for active, intelligent owners willing to train and socialize their dog."

AKC Classification: Working Group.

Kennel Club Classification: Working Group.

Part 2

Saint Bernard

Character: Faithful, quiet, obedient, easygoing, steady, gentle.

Origin: Switzerland, Middle Ages; developed further during the 17th century. Originally accompanied Roman armies to the region; ancestors include the Molossian Mastiff.

Original Purpose: Guarding, herding.

Physical Attributes: 25 to 34 inches (males must be 27 inches); 140 to 190 pounds; great sense of smell. This dog has little tolerance for heat, but can handle very cold weather. They drool and snore.

Color: White with varying shades and amounts of orange or red; never solid white or completely without white.

Coat Type and Grooming: Two types, long- and short-haired. Long-haired variety has a thick, rather wavy coat (and is really medium in length, despite the name). The short-haired coat is dense and short. The long-haired variety needs brushing three times a week. Eyes, face, and ears need special care. They drool a lot. Professional grooming is optional. Heavy seasonal shedding.

Lifespan: 8 to 10 years.

Health Concerns: Bloat, hip dysplasia, eye problems (distichiasis, entropion, ectropion), OCD, osteosarcoma, cardiomyopathy.

Exercise: Medium; adapts very well to family life; needs lots of room and regular, although not excessive, exercise.

Housing: Due to his large size and need for regular exercise, this breed does best with a fenced-in yard or room to run.

Interaction with Others: Well-bred Saints are excellent with people and very patient with children, although too big for toddlers. Excellent with other pets, especially if brought up with them.

Trainability: Average; some attempt to dominate their owners.

Activities: Search and rescue work, weight pulling, agility, obedience, draft dog.

Remarks: Famous Dog: The most famous St. Bernard was Barry, who lived at the St. Bernard hospice on Great St. Bernard Pass in Switzerland. Barry is credited with having saved more than 40 lives.[3]

AKC Classification: Working Group.

Kennel Club Classification: Working Group.

Saluki

Character: Loyal, responsive, independent, sensitive, companionable, affectionate; quite reserved with strangers (and almost everybody except the family remains a stranger—even some people in the family stay strangers). However, once it attaches itself to one person, it remains steadfast. Some individuals can be shy.

Origin: Middle East, (probably Sumer) antiquity. It is named after the Arabian city of Saluk. Migrated to Europe during the Crusades.

Original Purpose: Hunting gazelle and foxes.

Physical Attributes: 21 to 28 inches; 35 to 60 pounds; graceful, elegant, fast; naturally thinner than most dogs; sensitive to loud noises. The breed comes in two varieties: feathered and smooth-haired.

Color: White, cream, fawn, golden red, red grizzle, black and tan, grizzle and tan.

Coat Type and Grooming: Two coat types: Short, and, more commonly, short with long silky feathering. They are very clean dogs and do not have a doggy smell; easy to care for. Not much to moderate shedding.

Lifespan: 10 to 12 years.

Health Concerns: Phobias, glaucoma, like most sighthounds, sensitivity to anesthesia.

Exercise: Moderate to vigorous; needs outdoor exercise; generally quiet indoors.

Housing: Does best in the country, but can adapt to any situation if given sufficient exercise.

Interaction with Others: Good with family kids, especially if raised with them; not good with toddlers; tends to bond to one person. Okay with other dogs, not good with small pets, including cats.

Trainability: Medium; Salukis need to be kept on a leash when in an unfenced area, as they can easily leap a five-foot fence. These dogs need gentle handling and early socialization; regular obedience classes are must. They tend to be easily distracted.

Activities: Lure coursing, obedience, agility.

Remarks: Originally known as the Persian Greyhound, Salukis could only be given as gifts and were never sold. Although Islamic societies consider dogs unclean, Salukis were always an exception.

AKC Classification: Hound Group.

Kennel Club Classification: Hound Group.

Samoyed

Character: Independent, vivacious, full of fun, dominant, person-oriented, alert; bonds to the entire family; friendly to strangers, but an excellent watchdog.

Origin: Northeast Siberia, antiquity; developed by the nomadic Samoyed people.

Original Purpose: Reindeer herding, pulling sleds, guarding from bears.

Physical Attributes: 18 to 24 inches; 38 to 70 pounds; active, sturdy. Loves cold weather, but has no tolerance for heat (some liken them to small polar bears). Can be vocal and may dig. They are known for their beautiful Samoyed smile.

Color: Pure white, cream white, silver white, white and biscuit, or all biscuit. Any other colors disqualify. (Originally the dog came in dark colors, but those were gradually weeded out.)

Coat Type and Grooming: Heavy, harsh, bushy, weather resistant outercoat; undercoat is short, thick, soft. High maintenance required; brushing at least every other day. Professional grooming is recommended. Major seasonal shedding.

Lifespan: 10 to 12 years.

Health Concerns: Hip dysplasia, eye problems (PRA, glaucoma), hypothyroidism, deafness, pulmonic stenosis, VSD.

Exercise: Medium to high; calm in the house.

Housing: Adaptable to any living situation with plenty of exercise.

Interaction with Others: Very good with people; human companionship is critical to this breed. Extremely good with children; enjoys the company of strangers. Good with other pets.

Trainability: Average to low; this dog will wander off if not kept in a secure fenced area; not a great obedience prospect because of independent nature.

Activities: Herding trials, skijoring, sledding, obedience, therapy dog.

Remarks: Sheila Herrmann, Corresponding Secretary of the Samoyed Club of America, says, "Bringing home a Samoyed puppy is more like adopting a child than buying a dog. They are a vital part of the family and they will try to outthink you." Famous Dog: Roald Amundsen used a Samoyed lead dog on his 1911 trip to the South Pole. It was the first animal to cross the Pole.

AKC Classification: Non-Sporting Group.

Kennel Club Classification: Pastoral Group.

Schipperke

Character: Confident, independent, fearless, bold, headstrong, amiable; a superior watchdog.

Origin: Belgium, 1600s.

Original Purpose: Hunting, guarding, and ratting. The original dogs were larger than today's specimens.

Physical Attributes: 10 to 13 inches; 12 to 18 pounds; fast, nimble, quick-thinking; tailless, usually docked; can handle extremes of weather; very acute hearing. The silhouette is the most pronounced aspect of the breed's appearance.

Color: Black.

Coat Type and Grooming: Double coat is slightly harsh and forms a mane around the neck. Weekly grooming necessary (more when shedding). Professional grooming is optional. Medium to high shedding; gets much worse if grooming is not attended to.

Lifespan: 14 to 16 years. Some individuals live until they are 20.

Health Concerns: Eye problems, hypothyroidism.

Exercise: Low to moderate.

Housing: Adaptable to any living situation.

Interaction with Others: Mostly gentle with kids; some can be snappish; not fond of strangers. Very good with other pets; loves to play with them.

Trainability: High; may have housetraining problems; may guard possessions. Firm training needed.

Activities: Obedience, agility.

Remarks: This breed is sometimes known as "the little captain."

AKC Classification: Non-Sporting Group.

Kennel Club Classification: Utility Group.

Part 2

Scottish Deerhound

Character: Stable, courageous, companionable, dignified, alert, quiet; not a watchdog, but his size is intimidating to people who don't know what they're looking at. Some individuals are timid.

Origin: Scotland; may descend from the Greyhound or the Irish Wolfhound.

Original Purpose: Hunting red deer.

Physical Attributes: At least 27 inches for the female and 30 inches for the male (most are 32 inches); 75 to 110 pounds; strong, graceful.

Color: Dark blue gray (preferred), pastel shades of gray, dark gray. Light shades of yellow, brindle, fawn were formerly seen, but have now been practically eliminated.

Coat Type and Grooming: Hard, harsh, wiry, ragged, shaggy coat; medium length. Minimal grooming required, although there's lot of dog there; some trimming. Professional grooming is optional. Average shedding.

Lifespan: 8 to 10 years.

Health Concerns: Bloat, osteosarcoma, OCD, cardiomyopathy.

Exercise: Needs a good deal of supervised exercise; not a "self-starter." Generally a calm and quiet dog, but needs to run.

Housing: Due to their size, they are not well suited to apartment life or urban areas.

Interaction with Others: Excellent with people; very sociable with older children especially; friendly with strangers. They generally prefer children to everyone else in the family, but need proper socialization with toddlers. The one I know best likes to stand up and hug everybody. Okay with family pets if introduced carefully; may chase strange cats.

Trainability: Moderate.

Activities: Lure coursing.

Remarks: Sir Walter Scott, who owned one named Maida, called the Scottish Deerhound: "The most perfect creature of Heaven."

AKC Classification: Hound Group.

Kennel Club Classification: Hound Group.

Scottish Terrier

Character: Alert, inquisitive, fearless, assured, sophisticated, bold; superior watchdog; territorial; bonds strongly to one owner. Some members of this breed can be aggressive, an unacceptable trait that good breeders are trying successfully to eliminate.

Origin: Scottish Highlands, 1800s; closely related to the Cairn Terrier and West Highland White Terrier.

Original Purpose: Hunt rodents, foxes.

Physical Attributes: 10 inches; 18 to 22 pounds; lots of stamina, agile, active; cannot abide heat. Some individuals are barkers.

Color: This breed comes in a mix of colors, including wheaten, steel, and brindle, not just the commonly seen black; sprinklings of white and silver not to be penalized.

Coat Type and Grooming: Harsh, wiry, long, weatherproof; high maintenance required; brushing three times a week. Professional grooming is recommended at least four times a year; clipping for pets and stripping for show dogs. Slight shedding.

Lifespan: 12 to 15 years.

Health Concerns: Bladder cancer, CMO, von Willebrand's, allergies, hypothyroidism.

Exercise: Considerable.

Housing: Adaptable to any living situation.

Interaction with Others: Not good with young children, all right with respectful school-aged kids; aloof with strangers. Usually all right with dogs of opposite sex if socialized early.

Trainability: Low; needs early obedience training. This dog is difficult to train; many will challenge their owners for dominance.

Activities: Earthdog trials.

Remarks: The breed is not nicknamed Diehard for nothing, and needs an experienced owner. Famous Dog: The most famous Scottish Terrier of all was undoubtedly President Franklin Roosevelt's Fala, who was his ever-present companion, and who was buried at his side.

AKC Classification: Terrier Group.

Kennel Club Classification: Terrier Group.

Part 2

Sealyham Terrier

Character: Cheerful, stubborn, stable, alert, fearless, sociable; calmer than many other terriers; good watchdog, but not protective.

Origin: Wales (Sealyham), 1800s.

Original Purpose: Hunting badger, otter, and fox.

Physical Attributes: 10 to 12 inches; 18 to 24 pounds.

Color: All white, or with lemon, tan, or badger markings.

Coat Type and Grooming: Wiry, longer than many other terriers; moderately high maintenance, brushing several times a week. Professional grooming is recommended; clipping for pets, stripping for show. Slight shedding.

Lifespan: 11 to 14 years.

Health Concerns: Eye problems, allergies, deafness.

Exercise: Medium; quiet in the house; one of the calmest, most laid-back of the terriers.

Housing: Adaptable to urban areas, but prefers the country.

Interaction with Others: Not good with young children; good with kind older kids; bonds to one owner; somewhat reserved with strangers. Not great with other pets, but tolerant if socialized early.

Trainability: Difficult; works best with food rewards; not reliable off lead. Some will attempt to dominate their owners; requires a firm hand.

Activities: Earthdog trials.

Remarks: Despite its great abilities as a hunter, the Sealyham is today best known as a companion.

AKC Classification: Terrier Group.

Kennel Club Classification: Terrier Group.

Shetland Sheepdog

Character: Kind, watchful, loyal, obedient, sensitive, affectionate; needs affection; bonds to whole family.

Origin: Shetland Islands, 1800s.

Original Purpose: Shepherding, chicken guarding.

Physical Attributes: 13 to 16 inches; 16 to 21 pounds; agile; resembles a rough-coated collie in miniature. The lightest of the working breeds; this breed barks a lot.

Color: Sable, brown, black, tricolor, or blue merle with white markings.

Coat Type and Grooming: Double coat; outercoat long, straight, bushy; undercoat thick, soft. Extensive grooming required; at least twice a week. He is a very clean dog who tries to look after himself. Professional grooming is recommended. Sheds heavily in the spring and fall.

Lifespan: 12 to 15 years.

Health Concerns: Eye problems (PRA, collie eye anomaly), PDA, thyroid disease, dermatomyositis, deafness, von Willebrand's.

Exercise: Moderate to high.

Housing: Can adapt to urban areas (if the neighbors can handle the barking) as well as the country, but needs long walks and other strenuous exercise.

Interaction with Others: Good with children, if the children are gentle; may be shy or reserved with strangers. Good with other pets.

Trainability: Very high—excellent obedience and agility dogs.

Activities: Obedience, herding, agility, therapy dog.

Remarks: My friend Shirley Taylor, who has done therapy work with Shelties for many years, comments: "They are especially well suited to doing pet therapy and seem to learn very quickly how to behave around old or sick people, including children. One difficult behavior to control is the strong herding instinct, which tends to sends them chasing things that move."

AKC Classification: Herding Group.

Kennel Club Classification: Pastoral Group.

Shiba Inu

Character: Determined, active, courageous, loyal, alert, bold; territorial.

Origin: Honshu, Japan, antiquity.

Original Purpose: Hunting and flushing small game.

Physical Attributes: 14 to 16 inches; 18 to 22 pounds; well-balanced; good jumpers. Not barkers, but they can make weird noises; have many catlike qualities.

Color: Any color; the most common colors include red, black, sesame, red sesame, black sesame.

Coat Type and Grooming: Soft double coat. Low maintenance; naturally clean. Moderate shedding.

Lifespan: 12 to 15 years.

Health Concerns: Some patellar luxation; usually a healthy breed.

Exercise: High, but quiet in the house.

Housing: Adaptable to any living situation, but are escape artists who need a fenced yard.

Interaction with Others: Aloof; not good with children. May be aggressive with other dogs, especially those of the same sex; will chase small animals.

Trainability: Moderate to high.

Activities: Hunting, therapy dog.

Remarks: This breed nearly disappeared in its native land due to a distemper epidemic. In order to restore the breed, it was reconstituted by crossing-breeding individuals of the three types of Shiba Inu left on the islands.

AKC Classification: Non-Sporting Group.

Shih Tzu

Character: Outgoing, sweet, independent, spunky, stable, friendly; likes everyone.

Origin: Probably Tibet, 600s; later China, 1800s.

Original Purpose: Pet, sacred dog.

Physical Attributes: Up to 10 inches; 10 to 16 pounds; sturdy; cannot handle hot weather. Combines attributes of the Lhasa Apso and Pekingese.

Color: All colors permitted.

Coat Type and Grooming: Long, dense; high maintenance required; daily brushing to prevent tangles. The hair grows upward on the bridge on the nose, purportedly giving it a chrysanthemum look. Professional grooming is recommended. Slight shedding.

Lifespan: 11 to 15 years.

Health Concerns: Pinched nostrils, eye problems (distichiasis, conjunctivitis), obesity, allergies and dermatitis, ear infections, cancer, nephritis (kidney disease), congestive heart failure.

Exercise: Mild, but not good in hot weather; quiet in the house.

Housing: Can adapt well to town or country.

Interaction with Others: Very good with children; in very rare cases may be snappish. Enjoys participating in family events and does not care to be left alone all day; bonds to whole family.

Activities: Companion, therapy dog.

Remarks: The word Shih Tzu is Chinese for "lion dog." It is also beautifully known as the "chrysanthemum dog."

AKC Classification: Toy Group.

Kennel Club Classification: Utility Group.

Siberian Husky

Character: Gentle, friendly, fun-loving, loyal, eager, outgoing; likes everyone; not a guard dog; bonds to whole family. Siberians suffer separation anxiety if left alone for long periods.

Origin: Siberia, antiquity. Developed by the nomadic Chukchi people for a variety of tasks.

Original Purpose: Sled pulling, reindeer herding.

Physical Attributes: 21 to 23 inches; 35 to 60 pounds; fast, agile, hardy, great stamina; the smallest and fastest of the purebred sled dogs. Cannot tolerate heat, but can handle the worst winters with aplomb, even pleasure; wonderful howlers.

Color: White, black, sable, red, gray, "wild color." Many have a white mask. Eyes may be blue, brown, or one of each; speckled eyes are also permitted.

Coat Type and Grooming: Fairly long; needs thorough brushing three times a week. Professional grooming is recommended. Double coat sheds heavily, specially in the spring and fall.

Lifespan: 12 to 14 years.

Health Concerns: Hip dysplasia, eye problems (PRA, cataracts), VSD.

Exercise: Very high; needs a couple hours of vigorous exercise every day. The Siberian will become very destructive if not given sufficient exercise.

Housing: Not suitable for apartment life or urban areas.

Interaction with Others: Especially good with children; loves strangers. Great with the family dogs, may not be crazy about strange dogs; not good with small pets or cats.

Trainability: Low; this dog must be kept on a lead outside a fenced area. He is a roamer, a digger, and an escape artist. This breed is not easy to train to do things outside its original purpose and will complain vociferously if asked—not the best dog for a first-time dog owner.

Activities: Sled racing, backpacking.

Remarks: My pal, Paulette Jones, Secretary/Newsletter Editor of the Chesapeake Husky Club, writes, "The Siberian Husky makes a wonderful companion. He will dig holes in your yard for you to plant flowers, decorate your house with his fur, and smile as the burglars make off with the silver. I've lived with them for 25 years, and I wouldn't own any other breed." The so-called Alaskan Husky is not a breed, but can be any dog designed to sled-race; a related breed is the McKenzie River Husky, a local Canadian variety of huskies.

AKC Classification: Working Group.

Kennel Club Classification: Working Group.

Silky Terrier

Character: Outgoing, stubborn, spunky, lively, friendly; some individuals reserved or shy. Can be territorial; a super watchdog. Demands a great deal of attention.

Origin: Australia, late 1800s; ancestors include Australian and Yorkshire Terriers.

Original Purpose: Vermin (rats and snakes) extermination.

Physical Attributes: 9 to 10 inches; 8 to 11 pounds; quite barky.

Color: Blue and tan.

Coat Type and Grooming: Long, silky; moderate to high maintenance. Professional grooming is recommended. Slight shedding.

Lifespan: 11 to 14 years.

Health Concerns: No major concerns. Some individuals have orthopedic problems.

Exercise: Needs more exercise than most toy breeds.

Housing: Adaptable to any living situation; perfect for apartment life.

Interaction with Others: Most Silkies do best in a home without small children, although they are fine with older kids, and they tend to bond to one person. Some individuals can be snappish. This breed can be aggressive to other dogs and small pets.

Trainability: Average; this dog does best with obedience training; can be hard to housetrain.

Activities: Earthdog trials.

Remarks: Sally Stevens, who rescues Silkies, says: "The Silky Terrier was bred in Australia as a farm protector and ratter, and to that end is a terrier through and through, with the energy, curiosity and intelligence of a strong-willed working dog, and the loyalty and playfulness of a family pet."

AKC Classification: Terrier Group.

Kennel Club Classification: Terrier Group.

Skye Terrier

Character: Devoted, sensitive, fearless, good-tempered; a good watchdog but too small to be protective; a one-person dog.

Origin: Scotland, 1500s; from the same basic stock as the Scottish Terrier.

Original Purpose: Fox, rodent, badger, and otter hunting

Physical Attributes: 9 to 12 inches; 19 to 22 pounds; agile, elegant, dignified, stylish, strong, long, low, and level.

Color: Black, gray, blue, silver, fawn, or cream, preferably with black points. Adult color may not clear until the dog is 18 months old.

Coat Type and Grooming: Long, hard, shiny, straight; high maintenance, needing frequent (at least three times a week) grooming to avoid mats. Careful cleaning needed around the eyes and mouth. Professional grooming is recommended. Average shedding.

Lifespan: 10 to 13 years.

Health Concerns: Premature closure of ulna and radius, allergies.

Exercise: Moderate.

Housing: Ideal for apartment life; the Skye is low-key enough to live happily in the city.

Interaction with Others: Most are okay with gentle children, but this is not the best breed to have with toddlers. Wary and cautious with strangers; can be snappish. Not good with household dogs, can be unfriendly to strange dogs. Can learn to tolerate cats, but small animals are in grave danger.

Trainability: Average.

Activities: Earthdog trials, tracking.

Remarks: Kathy Kaminski, who has owned and shown Skye Terriers for years, says, "Skye Terriers are truly fun guys. Don't let their moppy appearance fool you; they are hardy, courageous, and strong. Skyes are also attentive, loving, and loyal family dogs ready to play, protect, or just sit next to you as a companion and friend."

AKC Classification: Terrier Group.

Kennel Club Classification: Terrier Group.

Part 2

Soft-Coated Wheaten Terrier

Character: Affectionate, happy, good-natured, spirited, friendly; requires lots of attention.

Origin: Ireland, 1700s

Original Purpose: Vermin extermination, hunting; general farm dog.

Physical Attributes: 17 to 19 inches; 30 to 40 pounds; powerful, athletic; low heat tolerance. These dogs may dig or jump.

Color: Wheaten (what a surprise!); ranges from reddish gold to silver. Puppies may be darker (red or brown) and have black tipping. By age two, the correct color should appear.

Coat Type and Grooming: Single coat; soft, abundant, and silky; very unterrier-like; medium long. Very high maintenance required; needs to be combed out every couple of days to prevent matting. The hair grows about an inch a month. Professional grooming is optional; they can use a bath and a trim every month. Negligible shedding; this is a single-coated dog.

Lifespan: 12 to 14 years.

Health Concerns: Kidney problems (protein losing nephropathy), PRA, renal dysplasia, protein-losing enteropathy.

Exercise: Moderate to high; active in the house.

Housing: Adaptable to any living situation if given a great deal of exercise.

Interaction with Others: Very sociable family dog; excellent with older children; can be too rambunctious and dominant for smaller children; needs supervision; likes strangers. Good with other pets, much better than other terriers; not good with cats.

Trainability: High; quick learner.

Activities: Obedience, agility, therapy dog, herding.

Remarks: This breed has a tendency to be dominant, and some individuals can be aggressive. They need an owner who can provide discipline.

AKC Classification: Terrier Group.

Kennel Club Classification: Terrier Group.

Part 2

Smooth Fox Terrier

Character: Dynamic, energetic, inquisitive, alert, friendly, gay; territorial; a super watchdog.

Origin: England, 1700s.

Original Purpose: Hunting fox and badger, ratting.

Physical Attributes: 14 to 17 inches; 16 to 20 pounds; active; show dogs tend to be smaller than pets; barks and digs.

Color: White with tan or black markings; red, brindle, or liver markings not desirable

Coat Type and Grooming: Short, flat, hard; easy grooming; brushing once a week. Slight, seasonal shedding.

Lifespan: 12 to 14 years.

Health Concerns: Legg-Perthes, pulmonic stenosis.

Exercise: High, but not demanding.

Housing: Adaptable to any living situation.

Interaction with Others: Good with playful older children; rather reserved with strangers. Not good around livestock. Usually okay around bigger dogs, may try to dominate smaller ones; okay around family cats if exposed early.

Trainability: Average; best with an experienced owner.

Activities: Earthdog trials, obedience.

Remarks: The texture of the coat is the only difference between Wire and Smooth.

AKC Classification: Terrier Group.

Kennel Club Classification: Terrier Group.

Spinone Italiano

Character: Curious, gentle, courageous, gregarious, playful, willing; must be involved in household life.

Origin: Italy, 1200s; perhaps German pointer in the background.

Original Purpose: Hunting, both in forests and swamps.

Physical Attributes: 22 to 26 inches; 60 to 85 pounds; muscular, vigorous, athletic.

Color: White, or white with yellow, light brown, liver, or chocolate, or orange patches; black not permitted. There is a preferred shade of brown, called "Capuchin Friar's Frock."

Coat Type and Grooming: Rather short, rough, hard, weatherproof; no undercoat; medium-high maintenance; brushing thoroughly once a week; mouth area needs special care. Professional grooming is optional.

Lifespan: 12 to 13 years.

Health Concerns: Cerebellar ataxia, hip dysplasia.

Exercise: High, but calm inside; calmer than many other pointing breeds.

Housing: Best on a farm but can get along with regular exercise elsewhere.

Interaction with Others: Good with people; may be too large for small children. Good with both cats and dogs, but may try to retrieve them.

Trainability: High.

Activities: Hunting, obedience, agility, flyball, tracking.

Remarks: This is a preeminent hunting dog, always working closely under the hunter's control.

AKC Classification: Sporting Group.

Kennel Club Classification: Gundog Group.

Part 2

Staffordshire Bull Terrier

Character: Stubborn, fun-loving, affectionate, companionable, fearless, loyal; an excellent watchdog.

Origin: England, 1800s.

Original Purpose: Bull-baiting, bear-baiting, dog fighting, ratting.

Physical Attributes: 14 to 18 inches; 30 to 40 pounds; strong jaws.

Color: Red, fawn, black, or blue, either solid or with white. Any shade of brindle or brindle and white.

Coat Type and Grooming: Smooth and shiny; minimal care with a curry comb. Slight to moderate shedding.

Lifespan: 12 to 14 years.

Health Concerns: Cataracts. (Note: This breed's famously high pain threshold may prevent him from showing symptoms from disease or trauma.)

Exercise: Medium to high.

Housing: Adaptable to any living situation.

Interaction with Others: Good with people, usually including children, although it can be very rambunctious. If angrily aroused, it can be aggressive, so it needs to be carefully supervised. Likes strangers, but tends to bond with one person. Dislikes other dogs, although it can sometimes adjust to other dogs in the household; should be supervised. Most are bad with cats.

Trainability: Moderate; needs firm obedience training and very careful early socializing, especially if it is to be around other animals. Also needs an experienced owner.

Activities: Obedience.

Remarks: In England, this dog is sometimes called the "nanny dog," because it likes children so much.

AKC Classification: Terrier Group.

Kennel Club Classification: Terrier Group.

Standard Schnauzer

Character: Alert, clever, reliable, devoted, adaptable, fearless; territorial; makes an excellent watchdog or protection dog; tends to bond with one person.

Origin: Germany, Middle Ages. The Standard Schnauzer is the one from which the Miniature and Giant Schnauzer were developed.

Original Purpose: Ratter.

Physical Attributes: 17 to 19 inches; 45 pounds; this is the middle-sized schnauzer.

Color: Pepper and salt, black.

Coat Type and Grooming: The Standard Schnauzer does not have the typical doggy odor. However, its coat is fairly high maintenance; show dogs require hand-stripping by a professional. Low to medium shedding.

Lifespan: 12 to 14 years.

Health Concerns: Pulmonic stenosis.

Exercise: High; needs a good bit of daily exercise.

Housing: Does best in a house with a yard for exercise, but can adopt to apartment living.

Interaction with Others: Reliable and tolerant with children; does not like strangers. Not good with other pets, unless socialized early; will try to dominate strange dogs; very aggressive with small animals. (In Germany, they hold ratting trials to see which Schnauzer can kill the most rats in the least amount of time.)

Trainability: Quick learner, but may try to dominate the owner. Needs thorough socialization.

Activities: Agility, obedience, tracking, bomb squad, service dog.

Remarks: Until 1945, the Schnauzer was shown in the Terrier Group, rather than the Working Group.

AKC Classification: Working Group.

Kennel Club Classification: Utility Group.

Part 2

Sussex Spaniel

Character: Dignified, kindly, serious, conscientious, cheerful, gentle, tractable.

Origin: Sussex, England, 1800s; ancestor of the Field Spaniel.

Original Purpose: Hunting in heavy coverts

Physical Attributes: 13 to 16 inches; 35 to 45 pounds; tail docked; slow-moving, methodical hunter. These dogs drool and slobber.

Color: Golden liver. (That's the official designation.)

Coat Type and Grooming: Medium long, wavy; some trimming required. Professional grooming is optional. Average shedding.

Lifespan: 11 to 14 years.

Health Concerns: Bloat (gastric torsion), autoimmune diseases, hypothyroidism, heart problems.

Exercise: Medium; less energetic and playful than most other spaniels; calm in the house.

Housing: Adaptable to any living situation.

Interaction with Others: Excellent with both children and strangers; may be protective of family children.

Trainability: Low to average.

Activities: Hunting, tracking.

Remarks: The unique color of the Sussex Spaniel is said to come from one female owned by a Dr. Watts in the mid-nineteenth century. Another famous owner of Field Spaniel had the interesting name of Phineas Bullock.

AKC Classification: Sporting Group.

Kennel Club Classification: Gundog Group.

Tibetan Spaniel

Character: Loving (but not cuddly), gay, independent, outgoing, enthusiastic, assertive; a good watchdog; tends to bond to one person. Some may be nervous.

Origin: Tibet, antiquity.

Original Purpose: Watchdog, companion.

Physical Attributes: 10 inches; 9 to 15 pounds; active, alert; somewhat catlike in temperament.

Color: All colors and combinations permitted but golden red is the most common; white allowed on feet.

Coat Type and Grooming: Double silky coat, moderate length; neck has a mane of longer hair. Naturally clean. Brush once a week. Professional grooming is recommended. Medium shedding.

Health Concerns: PRA, patellar luxation.

Exercise: Low.

Housing: Adaptable to any living situation; perfect for apartment life.

Interaction with Others: Good with children; reserved with strangers. Good with other pets.

Lifespan: 12 to 15 years.

Trainability: Average.

Activities: Agility, obedience, therapy dog.

Remarks: It is said that these dogs used to sit atop monastery walls to watch for intruders. Even today, this "feline" breed enjoys sitting on high places.

AKC Classification: Toy Group.

Part 2

Tibetan Terrier

Character: Very person-oriented, sensitive, happy, gentle, amiable; tends to bond to one person.

Origin: Tibet, antiquity. (Although Tibetan, it is not a terrier, despite the name.)

Original Purpose: Hunting and guarding; considered a "good luck" dog.

Physical Attributes: 15 to 16 inches; 20 to 25 pounds; agile.

Color: Any color.

Coat Type and Grooming: Long; needs combing out once or twice a week. Professional grooming is recommended. Average shedding.

Lifespan: 10 to 14 years.

Health Concerns: Lens luxation.

Exercise: Low to average

Housing: Adaptable to any living situation.

Interaction with Others: Not good with children and wary of strangers. Needs to be supervised with other pets.

Training: Average; may have housetraining problems.

Activities: Therapy dog

Remarks: In their native Tibet, the lamas considered these dogs sacred animals who would bring good luck to their owners.

AKC Classification: Non-Sporting Group.

Kennel Club Classification: Utility Group.

Toy Manchester Terrier

Character: Gentle, playful, observant, devoted; good watchdog; tends to bond to one person. Some individuals are aggressive or shy.

Origin: England, 1860s.

Original Purpose: Hunting small rodents.

Physical Attributes: 10 to 12 inches; under 12 pounds, usually about 7 pounds. Does not tolerate the cold.

Color: Black and tan.

Coat Type and Grooming: Short, hard, sleek; minimal grooming; once a week. Average shedding.

Lifespan: 14 to 16 years.

Health Concerns: von Willebrand's.

Exercise: High.

Housing: Adaptable to any living situation; with regular exercise, perfect for apartment life.

Interaction with Others: Not good with children; reserved with strangers. Usually okay with other pets.

Trainability: Medium; some are hard to housetrain.

Activities: Companion.

Remarks: While sharing most characteristics of the standard Manchester Terrier, the Toy is more closely bonded to and dependent on his human family.

AKC Classification: Toy Group.

Kennel Club Classification: Terrier Group.

Part 2

Vizsla

Character: Sensitive, fearless, stubborn, gentle, steady, lively; excellent watchdog; some are territorial. Some individuals may be timid.

Origin: Hungary, 1200s or earlier; some see Weimaraner and Pointers in the background. The breed is also known as the Hungarian Pointer.

Original Purpose: Tracking deer, quail, and hare.

Physical Attributes: 21 to 25 inches; 44 to 66 pounds; noble, aristocratic; great sense of smell, energetic; tail is usually docked.

Color: Golden rust, russet gold, dark yellow.

Coat Type and Grooming: Short, silky. Care minimal, just a quick brushing a few times a week. A major shedder year round.

Lifespan: 11 to 14 years.

Health Concerns: Hip dysplasia, PRA, entropion, sebaceous adenitis.

Exercise: High; without sufficient exercise, it can be destructive; does best with an active owner.

Housing: This dog does best in the country with lots of room to run.

Interaction with Others: Good with people; usually friendly to children. Usually good with other pets.

Trainability: High; needs a sensitive touch.

Activities: Bird hunting, field trials, tracking, obedience, agility.

Remarks: Aficionados of this breed say they're psychic. Famous Dog: A Vizsla named Countess is featured in a novel, *The Liberty Campaign*, by Jonathan Dee.

AKC Classification: Sporting Group.

Weimaraner

Character: Bold, cheerful, alert, willful, determined, friendly, obedient; this dog requires company and does not do well alone.

Origin: Germany, early 1800s; the name comes from the court of Weimar; Bloodhound and Pointers in the ancestry.

Original Purpose: Gun dog, hunting bear, later retrieving fowl.

Physical Attributes: 22 to 27 inches; 54 to 80 pounds; hardy, noble, agile, strong, Eyes are blue-gray or amber; tail docked; some can be barkers.

Color: Shades of gray, including mouse and silver; this is why he is called "the gray ghost." Blue and black are not permissible.

Coat Type and Grooming: Sleek, short, straight, and shiny; minimal care required. (There is a long-haired version which is not acceptable for showing in this country.) Average shedding.

Lifespan: 10 to 12 years.

Health Concerns: Bloat, hip and elbow dysplasia, PRA, entropion, allergic dermatitis.

Exercise: High; if not given sufficient exercise, it will become destructive.

Housing: This dog is not well-adapted to city life; needs exercise and room to run.

Interaction with Others: Likes children, but may overwhelm small ones or elderly people; can be aloof with strangers; protective of owners. Generally good with other pets, although some males dislike other males; may chase cats

Trainability: Fair; this dog does best if taken to regular obedience classes; needs a strong, thorough, experienced owner.

Activities: Hunting, field trials, obedience, agility, tracking, flyball, search and rescue.

Remarks: This was the "neurotic dog" in the hit film *Best in Show*. Most Weimies, of course, share the steady temperament of other sporting dogs and excel in obedience work. Famous Dogs: Photographer William Wegman uses his Weimaraners for his well-known photographs.

AKC Classification: Sporting Group.

Kennel Club Classification: Utility Group.

Part 2

Welsh Springer Spaniel

Character: Affectionate, kindly, good-natured, adaptable, faithful; barks to welcome guests.

Origin: Wales, 1600s; may be the original version of the Springer Spaniel; Clumber Spaniel may be an ancestor.

Original Purpose: Flushing birds.

Physical Attributes: 17 to 19 inches; 35 to 44 pounds; compact, active; tail docked. Very good water dog and has a great nose. This dog can be a barker.

Color: Dark red and white.

Coat Type and Grooming: Glossy, silky, medium-long; medium maintenance required; brushing twice a week. Ears need special attention. Professional grooming is optional; some trimming needed around the feet and ears. Average shedding.

Lifespan: 12 to 14 years.

Health Concerns: Hip dysplasia, PRA, cataracts.

Exercise: Medium to high, especially as a puppy. As an adult, the Welsh is calmer than many other spaniels.

Housing: Adaptable to any living situation, with exercise

Interaction with Others: Good with people; some are a little wary of children; likes a lot of attention. Good with other dogs; may chase cats

Trainability: High; quick learner, but does need careful training.

Activities: Hunting, obedience, agility, tracking, field trials.

Remarks: Rumor has it that during World War II, only six Welsh Springer Spaniels survived the Blitz on London—they were reportedly hidden in a cellar and fed on biscuits and gravy.

AKC Classification: Sporting Group.

Kennel Club Classification: Gundog Group.

Welsh Terrier

Character: Happy, independent, alert, fearless, calm, spirited; milder than many other terriers but a superior watchdog.

Origin: Wales, 1700s.

Original Purpose: Ratting, hunting otter, fox, badger.

Physical Attributes: 15 inches; 20 to 25 pounds; enjoys water; may dig or bark.

Color: Tan with black or grizzle jacket.

Coat Type and Grooming: Wiry, short; fairly high maintenance; grooming twice a week. Professional grooming is recommended; show dogs need stripping two or three times a year; clipping for pets. Slight shedding.

Lifespan: 12 to 14 years.

Health Concerns: Patellar luxation.

Exercise: Moderate to high

Housing: Adapts well to any living situation.

Interaction with Others: Good with children, but tends to bond to one person; not good with toddlers; wary of strangers. Good with other dogs (much better than most other terriers, but can still get into quarrels); bad with cats and smaller animals.

Trainability: Average; early obedience training a must.

Activities: Earthdog trials, ratting, agility.

Remarks: Sue Weiss, Educational Chairperson of the Welsh Terrier Club of America, writes: "The spirited Welsh Terrier is calm, intelligent, sensible, and friendly, with a desire to please. He does best with positive obedience training."

AKC Classification: Terrier Group.

Kennel Club Classification: Terrier Group.

Part 2

West Highland White Terrier

Character: Tenacious, affectionate, proud, happy, spirited, friendly, independent. A lovable family pet, the Westie needs a lot of attention from his owners and does not do well alone, becoming quite destructive.

Origin: Argyleshire, Scotland, 1800s; shares ancestry with the Cairn, Scottish, and Skye Terrier.

Original Purpose: Hunting fox, otter, and badger; vermin extermination.

Physical Attributes: 10 to 11 inches; 14 to 21 pounds; active, fine sense of hearing.

Color: White, of course; however, at one time they came in a variety of colors.

Coat Type and Grooming: Dense, hard, straight outercoat; soft undercoat; medium maintenance required; brushing twice a week to avoid mats. An all-white coat is always more difficult to keep presentable. Professional grooming is recommended; stripping for show, clipping for pets. Slight shedding when groomed correctly.

Lifespan: 12 to 14 years.

Health Concerns: CMO, globoid cell leukodystrophy, anemia, skin problems (allergies), cataracts, diabetes, orthopedic problems (patellar luxation, Legg Perthes, hip dysplasia), dilated cardiomyopathy.

Exercise: Moderate to high; these dogs can dig and become destructive if not exercised thoroughly.

Housing: Can adapt well to apartments, if given sufficient exercise, but can be barky.

Interaction with Others: Playful, but does best with older children; bonds with the whole family. Not good with toddlers unless socialized very early. Some wary of strangers, others are friendly. Some can be snappish if not respected. Can get over-excited or aggressive with other pets; not good with small animals or dogs.

Trainability: Low to average; these are very independent dogs; should stay on a leash when not in a fenced area.

Activities: Obedience, agility, earthdog trials.

Remarks: One former name of the West Highland White Terrier is the Poltalloch Terrier, from the place where it was bred for more than 100 years before appearing in dog shows.

AKC Classification: Terrier Group.

Kennel Club Classification: Terrier Group.

Whippet

Character: Pleasant, affectionate, friendly, obedient (for a sighthound), quiet, charming; many individuals make good watchdogs.

Origin: Northeast England, 1700s; ancestors may include Italian Greyhounds, terriers, or possibly Pharaoh hounds.

Original Purpose: The Whippet is the only sighthound developed mainly for racing as opposed to hunting.

Physical Attributes: 18 to 22 inches; 21 to 35 pounds; fast—a Greyhound in miniature; suffers in cold weather. This elegant dog is considered the smallest, but one of the fastest, sighthounds, outrunning a Greyhound in a sprint. They say that if your Whippet has the correct topline, you should be able to put a drop of water on the back of his skull and watch it run down the neck, along the back, and off the tip of the tail.

Color: Any color.

Coat Type and Grooming: Short and dense; minimal care required; once a week with a hound mitt. The Whippet is practically odor-free and naturally clean. Very little shedding.

Lifespan: 13 years.

Health Concerns: Phobias, eye problems (PRA, cataracts, lens luxation), color dilution alopecia, gastritis, mitral valve insufficiency, sensitivity to anesthesia.

Exercise: Moderate to high; quiet, well-behaved, and calm in the house.

Housing: Adaptable to any living situation with sufficient exercise.

Interaction with Others: Excellent with gentle children; most cannot handle rough play. May be aloof with strangers. Very friendly with other dogs, but may chase rabbits.

Trainability: Average to high; this is a good breed for the first-time owner.

Activities: Therapy dog, lure coursing.

Remarks: The breed standard calls the Whippet the "poor man's racehorse," but you don't have to be either poor or a man to own one. Lori Nelson, of Wildfire Whippets, says: "They see, they chase, they go from zero on the couch to 35 mph through an open door or gate after something and run with reckless disregard for their own safety after whatever it is. I have owned this breed for more than 25 years and it still amazes me how much trouble their speed and intelligence can lead them into. But I wouldn't have it any other way."

AKC Classification: Hound Group.

Kennel Club Classification: Hound Group.

Wire Fox Terrier

Character: Adventuresome, playful, mischievous, friendly, fearless, bold; superlative watchdog, but not protective.

Origin: England, 1800s.

Original Purpose: Exterminating rats and mice.

Physical Attributes: 14 to 17 inches; 20 to 25 pounds; show dogs tend to be smaller than pets. Solid, handsome, elegant, energetic, and dynamic; may dig and bark.

Color: Basically white, with black and brown markings.

Coat Type and Grooming: Wiry, as the name indicates. Some professional care and hand stripping for show dogs advised. Pets can be clipped. Light shedding.

Lifespan: 12 to 14 years.

Health Concerns: Legg-Perthes, allergies.

Exercise: High.

Housing: Adaptable to any living environment.

Interaction with Others: Good with older children; wary of strangers. Not good with small pets; okay with opposite-sex dogs.

Trainability: This dog requires firm handling.

Activities: Therapy dog, earthdog trials, obedience.

Remarks: Winifred Stout, of the American Fox Terrier Club, writes, "Fox Terriers are lively, playful, intelligent, outgoing; affectionate but somewhat independent."

AKC Classification: Terrier Group.

Wirehaired Pointing Griffon

Character: Independent, devoted, sensitive, gentle; makes a good watchdog; can be protective if aroused.

Origin: Originated in Holland but developed in France, 1800s.

Original Purpose:

Physical Attributes: 20 to 23 inches; 50 to 60 pounds; strong.

Color: Solid or roan chestnut, gray-chestnut, steel gray with brown

Coat Type and Grooming: Double coat; outercoat short, straight, wiry; undercoat of fine down. Medium maintenance required; some trimming. Professional grooming is recommended. Low to moderate shedding.

Lifespan: 12 to 15 years.

Health Concerns: Hip dysplasia, eye problems (ectropion, entropion), hypothyroidism. Some individuals seem to have phobias.

Exercise: High; does best in a quiet, relaxed family. Some are very hyper indoors.

Housing: This dog is happiest in the country, with room to run.

Interaction with Others: Generally good with people if well socialized; devoted to its family; not a breed to have around small children; may attempt to dominate. Generally friendly with strangers. Good with other pets, but tends to dominate; will chase cats.

Trainability: High; needs gentle handling. They are instinctive retrievers.

Activities: Upland bird and waterfowl hunting, agility, flyball.

Remarks: Although not the best in any category, they score high in versatility.

AKC Classification: Sporting Group.

Yorkshire Terrier

Character: Domineering, fiery, stubborn, alert, adventuresome, lively; makes a good watchdog. Some are inappropriately aggressive.

Origin: Yorkshire, England, 1800s; may have Maltese in its background.

Original Purpose: Rat catching.

Physical Attributes: 7 to 9 inches; under 7 pounds. Pet dogs are usually larger than show dogs. Some are barky.

Color: Dark steel blue on body; golden tan on face, chest, ears, and legs. Pet types have black markings that just don't turn blue. Yorkies are born black.

Coat Type and Grooming: Long, silky, straight hair; daily grooming needed. Professional grooming is recommended. Minimal shedding.

Lifespan: 14 to 16 years.

Health Concerns: Heart problems (mitral valve insufficiency), rheumy eyes, liver disease (portacaval shunt, hepatitis), dermatitis, ear infections, enteritis, cancer, nephritis.

Exercise: Low.

Housing: Small enough for apartment life, but some are too vocal. Can get sufficient exercise in an apartment and will self-exercise.

Interaction with Others: Good with well-behaved children; most are friendly, some are shy. Enjoy being pampered but also like a chance to act like other dogs and run and play.

Trainability: Average; can be hard to housetrain.

Activities: Companion.

Remarks: Some show dogs have actually had their coats insured. Ironically, the puppies are born naked.

AKC Classification: Toy Group.

Kennel Club Classification: Toy Group.

Glossary

Acral lick dermatitis
A skin disorder caused by their licking a localized area, usually on the legs. The original cause may be physical or psychological, but the area soon becomes traumatized.

Agility
A canine sport which tests a dog's ability to balance, climb, jump, and navigate obstacles.

Allergic dermatitis
A skin condition caused by an allergy.

Anal fissures
Also called perianal fistula, an area of inflammation, ulceration and draining sores around the anus.

Anal sacs
A pair of sacs located on either side of the anus. They contain foul-smelling liquid.

Anemia
Lower than normal number of white blood cells.

Aortic stenosis
A narrowing of the aorta in the heart.

Arrhythmia
Abnormal heart rhythms; most common in larger breeds.

Arthritis
Inflammation of a joint, characteristic of geriatric dogs.

Aseptic meningitis
Meningitis (inflammation of the meninges) but not caused by an infectious agent.

Autoimmune hemolytic anemia
Severe anemia caused by an autoimmune problem.

Axonal dystrophy
Degenerative nerve disease.

Basenji enteropathy
Digestive malaborption disease that results in protein loss, diarrhea, and consequent weight loss.

Belton
Flecked colors in the coat of English setters (named after a village in Northumbria). Typically "orange" and "blue" belton (which is black and white), but also lemon belton, liver belton, and tricolor.

Biddable
Obedient, easily taught.

Biscuit
Grayish yellow.

Bloat
Condition in which gases in the stomach are produced in great amounts, which sometimes cannot be belched and may result in torsion (twisting) of the stomach, a condition which is rapidly fatal without prompt treatment. Characteristic of deep-chested breeds like Bloodhounds and Great Danes.

Blue merle
Mottled shades of blue, black, and gray with tan shadings.

Breed standard
The ideal dog, described in writing. Some breeds also have an "illustrated standard."

Brindle
A color pattern of black stripes on a brown coat. In Great Danes, gold with black cross stripes in a chevron pattern.

Broken coat
Rough coat, said of a variety of Jack Russell Terriers.

Cancer
Any malignant, cellular tumor.

Canine Eye Registration Foundation (CERF)
International organization devoted to eliminating hereditary eye disease from purebred dogs.

Cardiomyopathy
Weakened, degenerated heart muscle; more common in large and giant breeds.

Cataract
A clouding of the lens causing blindness. Surgical correction is sometimes possible. Commonly affected breeds include Staffordshire Bull Terriers, Afghan Hounds, Cocker Spaniels, Bedlington Terriers, and Boston Terriers.

Cerebellar ataxia
Inherited fatal disease of the nervous system.

Chondrodysplasia
Abnormal growth of cartilage.

Cleft palate
Hole between the oral and nasal cavities.

CMO
See cranioiomandibular osteopathy.

Collapsing trachea
Narrowing of the trachea, the main air passage to the lungs; occurs most often in small breeds.

Collie eye anomaly
An inherited trait that while it does not cause blindness, can lead to other painful eye conditions. Commonly affected breeds include Collies, Shelties, and Border Collies.

Collie nose
A crusting, depigmenting dermatitis of the nose, and sometimes also of the lip and eyelid margins. Most commonly a result of exposure to sunshine.

Color dilution alopecia
A deformity of the hair seen in dogs with a blue or fawn coat, caused by the dilution gene at the D locus.

Coonhound trials
Events in which coonhounds are tested on their ability to tree a raccoon.

Conjunctivitis
Inflammation of the conjunctiva.

Copper toxicosis
Accumulation of copper in the liver, resulting in chronic hepatitis.

Corneal ulcer
A sore in the cornea that may be caused by trauma or infectious agents.

Coursing
Visual pursuit; the hunting style of gaze or sighthounds like Afghans and Salukis.

Corded
Coat type in which the hairs intertwine to form long mats resulting in a mop-like appearance.

Craniomandibular osteopathy
Proliferative bone disease that typically affects the lower jawbone. Affects young dogs, mostly certain terriers.

Cropping
Surgical shaping of the ears. Outlawed in England and several other European countries.

Cruciate ligament ruptures
A tear in the ligament of the knee.

Cushing's disease
Abnormality of the adrenal glands leading to mineral and water imbalances.

Dapple
Mottled or variegated coat pattern.

Degenerative myelopathy
A slowly progressive condition that affects the spinal cord, causing paralysis.

Dermatitis
Skin inflammation.

Dermatomyositis
Inflammation of skin and muscles.

Dermoid sinus
An abnormal and heritable opening (sinus) into the skin along the ridge on the dog's back that can get infected. Sometimes goes into the spinal cord. Seen mostly in Rhodesian Ridgebacks, occasionally in Boxers and Shih Tzus. Surgical correction is sometimes possible.

Detached retina
Separation of the inner layers of the retina from the pigment epithelium, which remains attached to the choroid. It occurs most often as a result of degenerative changes in the eye.

Dew claw
An extra claw near the knee or below the hock, often removed when the puppy is a few days old.

Diabetes
An abnormality in sugar metabolism, leading to excess sugar in the blood.

Distichiasis
Eyelashes that project in towards the surface of the eye.

Docking
Removal of the tail.

Drafting
A canine sport involving pulling.

Dry eye
A condition in which the tear gland do not function properly.

Ear infections
This common ailment can be by caused ear mites, allergies or the yeast organism mallesezia canis. Lop-eared dogs are more susceptible than are dogs with upright ears.

Elbow dysplasia
A name for several conditions of the elbow joint, found mostly in young, rapidly growing large-breed dogs; usually a laxity of the joint.

Ectropion
Inherited condition in which the lower eyelid rolls away from the eyeball; opposite of entropion.

Enteritis
Inflammation of the intestinal mucosa.

Entropion
Turning inward of the eyelid. This condition may be congenital or acquired, and causes eye irritation and other vision problems.

Epilepsy
Seizure disorder of unknown cause.

Exocrine pancreatic insufficiency
Pancreas fails to produce needed digestive enzymes leading to incomplete digestion and absorption of nutrients.

Factor IX deficiency
A clotting disorder.

Fanconi's syndrome
Kidney disease resulting from reabsorption defects.

Fawn
A brown color ranging from light tan to mahogany; sometimes called Isabella.

Feathers
Long hairs, usually on the legs, but also on the ears and beneath the tail.

Field trials
An event testing the ability of sporting dogs and scenthounds to locate game.

Fleabite dermatitis
Skin inflammation caused by an allergic reaction to flea bites.

Flyball
A canine sport in which dogs race to retrieve balls.

Flying disc competition
Canine "frisbee."

Gastric torsion
See bloat.

Gastritis
Inflammation of the lining of the stomach.

Gazehound
A sighthound, such as a Greyhound or Whippet.

Gingivitis
Inflammation of the gums.

Glaucoma
Increased fluid pressure in the eye. Commonly affected breeds include Cocker Spaniels, English Cocker Spaniels, Welsh and English Springer Spaniels, Beagles, and Basset Hounds.

Globoid cell leukodystrophy
Inherited lysosomal storage leading to paralysis.

Grizzle
White mixed with black or red.

Glycogen storage disease
An inherited disorder marked by abnormal storage of glycogen in the body tissues.

Harlequin
White with irregular black patches; usually referring to Great Danes.

Heatstroke
Elevation of body temperature to dangerous levels

Heartworm disease
Dirofilaria, a condition in which the pulmonary artery is infested with heartworms.

Hemophilia
A bleeding disorder.

Hepatitis
Infection or inflammation of the liver.

Herding
A canine sport in which sheepdogs are tested on their ability to handle sheep.

Hernia
Abnormal protrusion of part of an organ or tissue through the structures normally containing it.

Hip dysplasia
An inherited condition in which the head of the femur (hip joint) does not fit properly into the socket. It can be mild, requiring nothing more than occasional medication for pain or inflammation. On the other hand, severe cases need surgery.

Histiocytois
Rapidly progressive cancer resulting in abnormal white blood cells infiltrating many parts of the body.

Hot spots
Acute moist dermatitis.

Hounds
A hunting dog which tracks prey by scent or sight.

Hydrocephalus
Excessive accumulation of fluid in the brain.

Hypertropic osteodystrophy
Disease of young, large-breed dogs. Inflammation of bone and derangement of normal bone development.

Hypothyroidism
A malfunction of the thyroid gland resulting in underproduction of thyroxine, which controls the metabolic rate; most common in adult dogs.

Isabella
Fawn or medium brown color, used referring to Dobermans and some other breeds.

Intervertebral disc disease
Abnormality of the soft cartiagenous disks that cushion the vertebrae. Most common in Dachshunds and Corgis.

Juvenile cataracts
Cataracts developing in very young (under 6 months) dogs.

Legg-Perthes disease
Abnormal femur head, resulting from lack of adequate blood supply.

Lens luxation
Weakening of one or more of the ligaments holding the lens in place. Commonly affected breeds include Smooth and Wire Fox Terriers, Jack Russell Terriers, and Tibetan Terriers.

Linebreeding
The breeding of related individuals.

Liver
Medium to deep mahogany brown coat.

Lure coursing
A canine sport in which sighthounds chase lures.

Lymphedema
Lymph system not draining properly; can lead to swelling.

Merle
Dark irregular blotches of color on a lighter background of the same color. Usually refers to longhaired dogs. In short-haired dogs, the same pattern is often called dappled.

Mitral valve insufficiency
Degeneration of a heart valve.

Nephritis
Inflammation of the kidney.

Nodular dermatofibrosis
A syndrome primarily of German Shepherds in which fibrous nodules form in and beneath the skin.

Obedience
A canine sport which tests a dog's ability to follow commands.

OCD
See osteochondrosis.

Orthopedic Foundation for Animals (OFA)
Organization dedicated to eliminating orthopedic diseases from purebred dogs.

Osteocondrosis
A disorder of young, usually large-breed dogs. The cartilage fails to develop into mature bone.

Osteosarcoma
A kind of bone cancer.

Outcrossing
Mating of unrelated dogs of the same breed.

Pancreatitis
Inflammation of the pancreas; tends to occur in young overweight dogs, often after ingesting a fatty meal.

Panosteitis
Bone inflammation leading to uneven bone growth; self-limiting.

Patella
Kneecap.

Patellar luxation
Loose kneecaps.

Patent ductus arteiosus (PDA)
Congenital defect in which the ductus arteriosus, an embryonic blood vessel in the heart, does not close as it should, soon after birth. Limits the amount of blood circulating to the tissues and produces a murmur.

PDA
See patent ductus arteriosus.

Pedigree
A diagram of a dog's ancestry. A good breeder will provide a three-generation pedigree to customers, a longer one may be purchased from the AKC.

Phobia
A severe, irrational fear.

Piebald
A color pattern of brown and white patches.

Portacaval shunt
Failure of the embryonic liver blood vessel to close properly after birth.

PRA
See progressive retinal atrophy.

Progressive neuronal abiotrophy:
A form of familial neunonal abiotrophy, an inherited malformation of nerve cells. Also called the Chinese Beagle syndrome.

Progressive retinal atrophy (PRA)
Progressive destruction of light-sensitive tissue at the back of the eye. Most commonly affected breeds include Collies, Shelties, Cocker Spaniels.

Protein losing enteropathy
Excessive loss of plasma proteins into the intestinal lumen. Associated with a number of bowel disorders.

Protein losing nephropathy
Excretion of excessive amounts of protein in the urine.

Pug dog encephalitis
Inflammation of the brain and its covering, possibly caused by a virus, leading to symptoms such as depression, circling, head pressing, and blindness.

Pulmonic stenosis
Congenital narrowing of the opening in a heart valve due to thickening of the heart muscle. Characterized by abnormal blood flow between the right ventricle and pulmonary artery; can result in heart failure.

Puppy
A dog under 12 months of age.

Purebred
A dog whose sire and dam are of the same breed.

Rage syndrome
Sudden episode of unprovoked aggression.

Renal dysplasia
Malformed kidneys.

Retinal dysplasia
Abnormal development of the retina.

Roan
Solid color with a sprinkling of white hairs.

Sable
Black-tipped hairs on a lighter background.

SAS
See subaortic stenosis.

Scenthound
A hound that follows game by its scent.

Schutzhund
A canine sport which tests the dog's ability to guard and protect.

Seal
Coat appears black, but has a reddish cast.

Search and rescue
An activity in which dogs locate lost or missing persons.

Sebaceous adenitis
Inflammation of the sebaceous glands.

Sebaceous cysts
A benign condition in which fluid collects in a sac under the skin.

Sebaceous gland tumors
A wart-like growth, usually benign, that can appear anywhere on the body.

Seizure
A fit or convulsion.

Service dog
A dog used to guide the blind or in other ways help the disabled.

Sighthound
A hound that locates and chases game by sight.

Sledding
A canine sport in which dogs pull sleds.

Skijoring
A canine sport in which dogs pull humans on skis.

Smooth coat
Close lying, short coat.

Spitz dogs
Members of a number of (usually) arctic breeds characterized by a short-bodied, stocky builds and heavy double coats. Examples include the Chow Chow, Alaskan Malamute, Siberian Husky, Finnish Spitz, and Norwegian Elkhound.

Stag red
Black hairs intermingling with a predominantly red coat.

Stripping
Plucking of dead hairs to maintain coat quality. A labor-intensive tasks done mostly on show dogs; pet dog are clipped instead, a much easier task, but one resulting in a softer coat.

Subaortic stenosis (SAS)
Heart condition resulting from a narrowing just below the aortic valve.

Terrier
A group of dogs used originally for hunting vermin.

Therapy dog
A dog used to visit and comfort elderly, sick, or disabled persons.

Thrombopathia
A bleeding disorder.

Ticking
Small, irregular spots in an otherwise white coat.

Toy
Dogs characterized by small size.

Tracheal collapse
Loss of rigidity of the trachea.

Tracking
A canine sport in which dogs follow scent to locate an article.

Tricolor
Black with white markings and tan shadings.

Umbilical hernia
A protrusion of the navel.

Urinary tract stones
Hard accumulations of crystals usually found in the bladder.

Ventricular septal defect (VSD)
A hole in the inner wall of the heart.

Von Willebrand's disease
A congenital bleeding disorder characterized by a prolonged bleeding time and slow clotting. Caused by a deficiency in clotting factor VIII.

VSD
See ventricular septal defect.

Weight pulling
A canine event in which dogs pull weights competitively.

Wheaten
Pale yellow or fawn coat.

Whitelies
White body color with red or dark markings, used to describe the Pembroke Welsh Corgi.

Withers
Top of the shoulders.

Wobblers
Cervical vertebral instability due to spinal cord compression, resulting in neck pain and difficulty in walking.

Resources

Organizations

American Kennel Club (AKC)

5580 Centerview Drive, Suite 250

Raleigh, NC 27606-3389

Website: www.akc.org

Phone: 919-233-9796

American Mixed Breed Obedience Registration (AMBOR)

179 Niblick Road #113

Paso Robles, CA 93446

Website: www.amborusa.org

Phone: 805-226-9275

E-mail: ambor@amborusa.org

Association of Pet Dog Trainers (APDT)

Mt. Laurel, NJ 08054

Website: www.apdt.com

Phone: 1-800-PET-DOGS

Delta Society Pet Partners Program

580 Naches Avenue SW, Suite 101

Renton, WA 98055-2297

Website: www.deltasociety.org

Phone: 425-226-7357

E-mail: info@deltasociety.org

North American Dog Agility Council (NADAC)

11550 South Hwy 3

Cataldo, Idaho 83810

Website: www.nadac.com

Phone: 208-689-3803

E-mail: Nadack9@aol.com

North American Flyball Association

P.O. Box 512

1400 West Devon Ave.

Chicago, IL 60660

Website: www.flyball.org

Phone: 309-688-9840

E-mail: flyball@flyball.org

Therapy Dogs Incorporated

P.O. Box 5868

Cheyenne, WY 82003

Website: www.therapydogs.com

Phone: 877-843-7364

E-mail: therdog@sisna.com

Therapy Dogs International

88 Bartley Square

Flanders, NJ 07836

Phone: 973-252-9800

E-mail: tdi@gti.net

United Kennel Club (UKC)

100 East Kilgore Road

Kalamazoo, Michigan 49001-5593

Website: www.ukcdogs.com

Phone: 616-343-9020

United States Dog Agility Association (USDAA)

P.O. Box 850995

Richardson, Texas 75085-0955

Website: www.usdaa.com

Phone: 972-231-9700

E-mail: info@usdaa.com

World Canine Freestyle Organization (WCFO)

P.O. Box 350122

Brooklyn, NY 11235-2525

Website: www.worldcaninefreestyle.org

E-mail: wcfodogs@aol.com

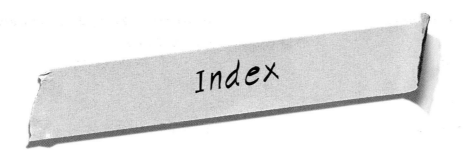

Index

Photo Credits

Paulette Braun: p.100, bottom; p.105, top; p.107, bottom; p.121; p.152, bottom; p.187, top; p.192; p.205, top.

Tara Darling: p.107, top; p.139, top; p.151, top; p.184, top.

Robert Pearcy: p.136, bottom; p. 162, bottom; p.195.

Lara Stern: p.132, top; p.167, bottom.

Judith Strom: p.69.

All other photos by Isabelle Francais.

Cartoons by Michael Pifer.